AF552762

INTERNATIONAL TOURISM AND SUSTAINABLE DEVELOPMENT

INTERNATIONAL TOURISM AND SUSTAINABLE DEVELOPMENT

Vikas Choudhary

CENTRUM PRESS
NEW DELHI-110002 (INDIA)

CENTRUM PRESS

H.O.: 4360/4, Ansari Road, Daryaganj,
New Delhi-110002 (India)
Tel: 23278000, 23261597, 23255577, 23286875

B.O.: No. 1015, Ist Main Road, BSK IIIrd Stage,
IIIrd Phase, IIIrd Block, Bangalore-560085 (INDIA)
Tel: 080-41723429

Email: centrumpress@gmail.com
Visit us at: www.centrumpress.com

International Tourism and Sustainable Development

First Edition, 2010

ISBN 978-93-80540-96-2

PRINTED IN INDIA

Printed at Balaji Offset, Delhi.

Contents

Preface

Travel & Tourism takes many different forms - from a trip only a few hours away from home to long distance travel overseas. A common belief is that most Travel & Tourism involves large numbers of visitors from developed countries travelling by air to destinations in emerging countries. In fact, in most countries, the domestic tourism market is larger than the inbound market. Of course, the social and cultural impact of inbound visitors is often greater than that of domestic tourists. Whether tourism is domestic or international, it involves visiting a destination away from the area in which one lives and using the services available in that destination. Therefore, tourists' requirements are for travel services to reach their destinations and once there, for services such as shelter, water, food, sanitation and entertainment. What makes tourism special is that, many of these different products and services are often supplied by different operators: usually small or medium sized businesses in local ownership.

This makes tourism a highly fragmented and diverse industry and so coordinated, industry-wide action is difficult to achieve. The influence of Travel & Tourism's demand also extends far beyond traditional tourism companies, into upstream suppliers like aircraft manufacturers or food producers and into the downstream service providers for travellers, like retail shops. The public sectors, particularly national and local government, have an important role to play by setting the agenda and providing the framework in which action should take place. The regulatory environment also plays an important role in creating the conditions suitable for sustainable tourism.

Self-regulation involving the agreement and cooperation of industry is always likely to be the most effective solution. Therefore, the role of trade associations and industry organisations in distributing information among their members and encouraging participation is essential. There is a downward trend in the public's willingness to pay extra for environmental protection and environmentally friendly products, including "green" Travel & Tourism. Awareness of companies making environmental commitments is only marginally up. Therefore, the challenge is to persuade the consumer that it is in their interests to adopt and promote a sustainable approach in their activities and purchasing decisions. Education programs and the development and widespread acceptance of codes of conduct are useful tools in achieving this step.

The subject matter dealt with in the book includes planning and development of sustainable tourism products, tourism personnel, ecotourism and adverse effects of tourism.

—Vikas Choudhary

1

Introduction

Creating Jobs and Wealth

Travel & Tourism is the world's largest industry and creator of jobs across national and regional economies. WTTC/WEFA research show that in 2000, Travel & Tourism will generate, directly and indirectly, 11.7% of GDP and nearly 200 million jobs in the worldwide economy.

Jobs generated by Travel & Tourism are spread across the economy-in retail, construction, manufacturing and telecommunications, as well as directly in Travel & Tourism companies. These jobs employ a large proportion of women, minorities and young people; are predominantly in small and medium sized companies; and offer good training and transferability. Tourism can also be one of the most effective drivers for the development of regional economies. These patterns apply to both developed and emerging economies.

Contributing to Sustainable Development

The 1992 United Nations Conference on Environment and Development (UNCED), the Rio Earth Summit, identified Travel & Tourism as one of the key sectors of the economy which could make a positive contribution to achieving sustainable development. The Earth Summit lead to the adoption of Agenda 21, a comprehensive program of action adopted by 182 governments to provide a global blueprint for achieving sustainable development. Travel & Tourism is the first industry sector to have launched an industry-specific action plan based on Agenda 21.

Travel & Tourism is able to contribute to development which is economically, ecologically and socially sustainable, because it:

- has less impact on natural resources and the environment than most other industries;
- is based on enjoyment and appreciation of local culture, built heritage, and natural environment, as such that the industry has a direct and powerful motivation to protect these assets;
- can play a positive part in increasing consumer commitment to sustainable development principles through its unparalleled consumer distribution channels; and
- provides an economic incentive to conserve natural environments and habitats which might otherwise be allocated to more environmentally damaging land uses, thereby, helping to maintain biodiversity.

There are numerous good examples of where Travel & Tourism is acting as a catalyst for conservation and improvement of the environment and maintenance of local diversity and culture.

Of course, there are also examples where development has not been sustainable.

Providing Infrastructure

To a greater degree than most activities, Travel & Tourism depends on a wide range of infrastructure services-airports, air navigation, roads, railheads and ports, as well as basic infrastructure services required by hotels, restaurants, shops, and recreation facilities (e.g. telecommunications and utilities).

It is the combination of tourism and good infrastructure that underpins the economic, environmental and social benefits. It is important to balance any decision to develop an area for tourism against the need to preserve fragile or threatened environments and cultures. However, once a decision has been taken where an area is appropriate for new tourism development, or that an existing tourist site should be developed further, then good infrastructure will be essential to sustain the quality, economic viability and growth of Travel & Tourism. Good infrastructure will also be a key factor in the industry's ability to manage visitor flows in ways that do not affect the natural or built heritage, nor counteract against local interests.

Challenge for the Future

Travel & Tourism creates jobs and wealth and has tremendous potential to contribute to economically, environmentally and socially sustainable development in both developed countries and emerging nations. It has a comparative advantage in that its start up and running costs can be low compared to many other forms of industry development. It is also often one of the few realistic options for development in many areas. Therefore, there is a strong likelihood that the Travel & Tourism industry will continue to grow globally over the short to medium term.

Of course, if Travel & Tourism is managed badly, it can have a detrimental effect-it can damage fragile environments and destroy local cultures. The challenge is to manage the future growth of the industry so as to minimise its negative impacts on the environment and host communities whilst maximising the benefits it brings in terms of jobs, wealth and support for local culture and industry, and protection of the built and natural environment.

Industry Initiatives for Sustainable Tourism Problems

Travel & Tourism takes many different forms-from a trip only a few hours away from home to long distance travel overseas. A common belief is that most Travel & Tourism involves large numbers of visitors from developed countries travelling by air to destinations in emerging countries. In fact, in most countries, the domestic tourism market is larger than the inbound market. Of course, the social and cultural impact of inbound visitors is often greater than that of domestic tourists. Whether tourism is domestic or international, it involves visiting a destination away from the area in which one lives and using the services available in that destination. Therefore, tourists' requirements are for travel services to reach their destinations and once there, for services such as shelter, water, food, sanitation and entertainment.

What makes tourism special is that, many of these different products and services are often supplied by different operators: usually small or medium sized businesses in local ownership. This makes tourism a highly fragmented and diverse industry and so coordinated, industry-wide action is difficult to achieve. The influence of Travel & Tourism's demand also extends far beyond traditional tourism companies, into upstream suppliers like aircraft manufacturers or food producers and into the downstream service providers for travellers, like retail shops. Despite the difficulties caused by fragmentation and lengthy supply chains, there has been a steady growth in environmental good practice across the industry in recent years. There are examples of-airlines and airports reducing pollution and noise impacts; cruise liners practising marine conservation; hotels implementing energy consumption and waste disposal programs; car rental companies investing in increasingly fuel efficient fleets and railways sound proofing to dampen noise. The result is that there are a number of excellent initiatives in place designed to improve the environmental management of Travel & Tourism businesses. Of course, more needs to be done.

Solutions

Providing Leadership

WTTC with 105 members is the global business leaders' forum for the Travel & Tourism industry.

The WTTC have set in place an extensive strategy to promote a culture of sustainable development and have put in place a three-tiered structure for its achievement. This involves:

Policy

In 1996 the WTTC, the World Tourism Organization and the Earth Council, joined together to launch an action plan entitled "Agenda 21 for the Travel & Tourism Industry: Towards Environmentally Sustainable Development"-a sectional sustainable development program based on the results of the Rio Earth Summit in 1992. Since the launch of the document, the three organisations have begun a series of regional seminars to increase awareness of the conclusions, and to adapt the program for local implementation. The program has held regional seminars in London and Jakarta in 1997 and Victoria Falls and Dominica in 1998.

WTTC has recently introduced a major addition to the program – the "Alliance for Sustainable Tourism", which invites public and private sector Travel & Tourism organisations to record their Agenda 21 based activities on a central web site and commit to cooperation with all other partners. In order to develop the program from global principles to community based action, WTTC is also discussing with the International Council for Local Environment Initiatives (ICLEI) on how the principles of "Agenda 21 for Travel

& Tourism" can be built into Local Agenda 21 programs. Furthermore, WTTC is considering pilot projects in 5 cities around the world to serve as models for other destinations.

Practice

In 1994, WTTC initiated the *"Green Globe"*, an Agenda 21 based industry improvement program, which provides guidance material and a certification process linked to both ISO standards and Agenda 21 principles. There are now 500 *"Green Globe"* members in 100 countries dedicated to improving environmental practice. The first certification has commenced with hotels groups in Jamaica and Manchester (UK). *"Green Globe"* has also developed a specific Destination Program, which provides a methodology for Travel & Tourism destinations to implement sustainable development.

The ultimate aim is that *"Green Globe"* will become the primary global standard of environmental commitment by the global Travel & Tourism industry and will be recognised by the public as such. Currently, *"Green Globe"* has the support of over 20 international industry organisations representing thousands of businesses worldwide and the support of the World Tourism Organization, the United Nations Environment Program and the Earth Council.

Information

WTTC have also developed "ECoNETT", a website containing advice and data on good practice and sources of help and advice. "ECoNETT" is increasingly recognised as a focal point for environmental information, good practice, new techniques and technologies.

The International Hotel & Restaurant Association (IH&RA), based in Paris, represents over 700,000 establishments in more than 150 countries. Its membership comprises some 50 national and international hotel and restaurant chains, over 110 national hotel and restaurant associations, independent hotel operators and restaurateurs, industry suppliers and 130 hotel schools. The IH&RA has offices in Asia-Pacific and Latin America. It is also the voice of the world's hotels and restaurants and plays a global role in representing, protecting, promoting and informing the industry to enable its members to achieve their business objectives.

The IH&RA has:

- raised environmental awareness and developed programs through joint workshops with national hotel associations and regularly encourages them to develop their own environmental awareness programs;
- established an annual Environmental Award sponsored by American Express and judged by the United Nations Environment Program (UNEP) that recognises efforts by independent and chain hotels to "green" the industry;
- published advice including practical publications such as the "Environmental Action Pack for Hotels" with the International Hotel Environment Initiative and UNEP and "Environmental Good Practice in Hotels" with UNEP;
- supported regional initiatives such as the Caribbean Action for Sustainable Tourism; and
- joined forces with UNEP and the International Hotel School Directors' Association to develop an "Environmental Teaching Resource Package for Hospitality Educational Institutes".

Corporate Initiatives

The International Hotel Environment Initiative (IHEI), based in London, England, is a program of The Prince of Wales Business Leaders Forum. Founded in 1992 by a consortium of chief executives from 10 multinational hotel groups, IHEI is an educational charity designed to encourage continuous improvement in the environmental performance of the global hotel industry. It does this through:

- raising environmental awareness in the hotel industry by promoting good practice internationally;
- developing hotel-specific guidance, enabling hotels of all sizes to implement environmental programs; and
- multiplying the reach and impact of IHEI by working with partners, including hotel associations, governments, NGOs, tourism bodies and businesses.

IHEI is a catalyst and conduit for hotels to pool their resources and to share experience via a noncompetitive platform. In 5 years it has evolved into an organisation with global impact. IHEI has worked in 111 countries, stimulating and assisting with the establishment of local initiatives such as New Zealand's "Environmental Hotels of Auckland, the Asia Pacific Hotel Environment Initiative" and the Caribbean Action for Sustainable Tourism. Member hotels now represent over 1 million guest rooms and more than 8,000 hotels on 5 continents.

The Cooperative Research Centre for Sustainable Tourism, based in Australia, was established in 1997 to enhance the strategic knowledge available to the Travel & Tourism industry through:

- long-term high-quality scientific and technological research which contributes to the development of an internationally competitive tourism industry;
- trengthening the links between research and its commercial and other applications;
- promoting cooperative research; and
- stimulating education and training, particularly in graduate programs, through active involvement of researchers from outside the higher education system in educational activities, and of graduate students ir major research programs.

Company Initiatives

The Kandalama hotel in Sri Lanka has been a recipient of the "GREEN GLOBE" award, 3 years in a row, for its commitment to environmental excellence. The hotel has undertaken measures in the following areas to ensure that its operations are more sustainable:

- cultural and social-hotel employment, providing community infrastructure and development;
- natural environment-soil erosion measures and planting forests;
- pollution-sewage, solid waste and noise pollution reduction programs; and
- environmental communication-construction of an Eco Park where all waste is treated within the park, a dry debris sorting centre, a lecture room to promote environmental awareness and a sustainable development library.

Canadian Pacific Hotels, the largest hotel conglomerate in Canada, has developed an environmental program, which is recognised as the most comprehensive in the North American hotel industry. Based on the results of a survey, employee suggestions and the recommendations of a professional environmental consultant, Canadian Pacific Hotels developed a list of 16 goals to be attained by all hotels. In addition to individual projects implemented at each of the 26 hotels, the goals set for the chain as a whole were ambitious: (I) to reduce the amount of waste sent to landfill by 50% across the chain, by launching an extensive recycling program; (ii) to redesign purchasing policies to ensure that waste is reduced at source, and supplies used in the hotels are nature friendly.

Inter-regional Level

The Caribbean Action For Sustainable Tourism (CAST) is an alliance for sustainable growth developed by the Caribbean Hoteliers Association with the support of the WTTC, the IHEI and the Caribbean Tourism Organisation. CAST has developed workshops, training courses and guidance material for its members on a wide range of environmental issues, including:

- setting up environmental management systems;
- energy efficiency;
- renewable energy; and
- waste water management.

Agents and Partnerships for Change

The public sectors, particularly national and local government, have an important role to play by setting the agenda and providing the framework in which action should take place. The regulatory environment also plays an important role in creating the conditions suitable for sustainable tourism.

Self-regulation involving the agreement and cooperation of industry is always likely to be the most effective solution. Therefore, the role of trade associations and industry organisations in distributing information among their members and encouraging participation is essential.

The major partnerships to be formed are between:

- industry and the public sector-to ensure consistency with the framework;
- industry and the voluntary sector-to tap into the enormous resources of expertise and good will that this sector is able to generate; and

- industry and the public-both travellers themselves and the people who live in the places they visit to develop more sustainable forms of tourism.

Areas for Further Action

The industry is already doing much to improve its performance in terms of sustainable development. The challenge for the new millennium is to move from the existing ad hoc approach to a more systematic one.

To do this will involve a partnership between industry and national governments to deliver the following:

(i) Governments:

- Integration of travel and tourism policy into broader government policies, especially the environment;
- Incentives for the Travel & Tourism industry, backed up where necessary by effective regulation.

(ii) Public/Private partnership:

- Infrastructure planned and developed with a long-term view and within a reference framework based on Agenda 21;
- Indicators and environmental impact assessment tools to enable effective local management and appropriate development.

(iii) International bodies:

- Coordination at an international level of environmental action undertaken by all sectors of the Travel & Tourism industry;
- Review of existing voluntary initiatives to improve the quality of reporting, their transparency and credibility, and the assessment of their contribution to sustainability.

(iv) Companies:

- Commitment to place sustainable development issues at the core of the management structure;
- Innovation of process and application through new technology;
- Commitment to education and environmental training of staff.

Influencing Consumer Behaviour to Promote Sustainable Tourism Problems

At the 1998 World Travel Market, WTTC hosted, as a part of its Environmental Awareness Day, a seminar entitled "Does the Consumer Care?" At this event, MORI presented the latest findings from their Business and the Environment survey-an annual UK survey devoted to public attitudes to the environment. The survey is now in its tenth year and illustrates the challenge facing the Travel &

Tourism industry in influencing consumer behaviour to promote sustainable tourism.

According to this survey, Travel & Tourism is now more associated with environmental damage than it has been in the past. Despite this decline in perception, the industry's economic success is not

dependent on its green record-public sensitivity to environmental problems on holiday/business trips has not increased and is no more of a deterrent to repeat travel than it was previously.

There is a downward trend in the public's willingness to pay extra for environmental protection and environmentally friendly products, including "green" Travel & Tourism. Awareness of companies making environmental commitments is only marginally up. Therefore, the challenge is to persuade the consumer that it is in their interests to adopt and promote a sustainable approach in their activities and purchasing decisions. Education programs and the development and widespread acceptance of codes of conduct are useful tools in achieving this step. Once this message has been conveyed, it is then important to back this up with the necessary information to enable consumers to make informed choices. It is here that "ecolabels" and award programs have value.

Solutions

Education Programs

The Foundation for Environmental Education in Europe (FEEE) seeks to promote environmental education by carrying out campaigns and improving awareness of the importance of environmental education. It is composed of a network of international organisations. The FEEE (headquarters in Denmark) runs three major campaigns in Europe for providing safe and clean beaches and marinas.

The award itself is given annually to beaches and marinas that satisfy a number of essential criteria in three separate areas: water quality; beach management and safety; and environmental information and education.

"Green Globe"'s Dodo Campaign, is based on a cartoon character, who features in 65 Travel & Tourism videos. Dodo explains and promotes the actions that visitors can take to reduce the impacts of their travels. The videos are aimed at children and are designed to be fun, whilst conveying important messages about sustainable Travel & Tourism. The aim is to have these videos shown on inflight and in-room television channels to raise awareness and influence consumer behaviour.

Codes of Conduct

Codes of conduct are also used to try and influence consumer behaviour. For example, "Guidelines for Responsible Environmental Tourism" are prepared and distributed by the American

Society of Travel Agents to all customers who book holidays through their members' branches. The Guidelines aim to "encourage the growth of peaceful tourism and environmentally responsible travel" and include 10 recommendations to encourage tourists to act responsibly and show respect for their hosts and the environment of their destination(s).

The Pacific Asia Tourism Association (PATA) is an industrial association, which promotes the Pacific Asia area's Travel & Tourism destinations, products and services. PATA also serves as a central resource of information and research, travel industry education and training, as well as quality product development with sensitivity for culture, heritage and environment. In 1992, PATA introduced its "Code for Environmentally Responsible Tourism" to strengthen the principles of preservation in the region. Businesses, organisations and individuals wishing to affirm their support for the PATA Code are encouraged to participate in the PATA Green Leaf program.

The Africa Travel Association has produced "Responsible Traveller Guidelines"; the Japanese Association of Travel Agents has produced the "Declaration of Earth Friendly Travellers" and there are many more examples of industry codes aimed at educating and influencing their customers.

Eco Labelling

There are numerous examples of industry sponsored labelling schemes, whose aim is to recognize good industry practice and influence consumer behaviour into purchasing the labelled products. For example, the "Green Key, Denmark" certificate operated by the Hotel, Restaurant and Leisure Industry Association (HORESTA) has 56 criteria that includes environmental information, water & energy consumption and waste management. Special features also include ecological food products, outdoor areas, non-smoking rooms, and adaptations for access by disabled persons.

Awards

There are a number of industries that runs and sponsors award programs to highlight and promote examples of good practice. For example, British Airways has run the "Tourism for Tomorrow" awards since 1992 to encourage action to protect the environment. The awards are directed at tour operators, hotels, national parks and heritage sites, and other activities associated with tourism. By selecting projects showing best practice in their field as role models, others are encouraged to follow suit and consider the environment in the everyday running of their tourism business. The awards are run annually, with a winner selected from each of five regions and an overall winner. In addition, two special awards are made for mass tourism destinations. The awards are run in association with the British Tourist Authority, the Association of British Travel Agents, the Pacific Asia Travel Association and the American Society of Travel Agents. Entries to the awards have been increases every year.

American Express also sponsors a variety of environmental awards for international tourism organisations.

Agents and Partnerships for Change

A broad based approach is called for which requires Travel & Tourism to work with:

- national governments to raise the profile of environmental and social issues within the education system;

- NGOs to raise awareness of tourism issues in their work and activities and provide feedback to the Travel & Tourism industry;
- development organisations to communicate with host communities to understand their needs and requirements;
- local authorities to engage local people through the inclusion of tourism issues in Local Agenda 21 plans;
- national and international trade associations, labour representative organisations and training providers to increase awareness and training of staff in environmental and social issues;
- Travel & Tourism publications (such as travel guides);
- Travel & Tourism journalists to raise the profile of reporting environmental and social impacts of tourism among consumers and tourism businesses; and
- the Internet as a source of information for potential travellers.

Areas for Further Action

The WTTC/MORI data shows the scale of the task still remaining. The industry has developed a number of initiatives to influence consumer behaviour. However, if consumers do not understand or are not aware of the issues involved and do not demand more sustainable products then, in the long term, it will not be in the industry's interests to move in that direction. The priority for future action, therefore, should be to raise awareness among travellers of the issues associated with tourism and the impact their activities can have on local destinations and cultures.

Agents and Partnerships for Change and Areas for further Action

The challenge facing the tourism industry in moving towards a more sustainable future is set out in "Agenda 21 for the Travel & Tourism Industry". To achieve the goals set out in this document will require a partnership between government departments, national tourism authorities, international and national trade organisations and Travel & Tourism companies. Working together in close cooperation such partnerships should aim to deliver the following:

- Close cooperation between the public and private sectors to deliver a regulatory regime, which encourages voluntary action but supplement, where necessary, with regulation in areas such as land-use and waste management.

- Agreed common standards and tools to enable the measurement of progress towards achieving sustainable development.
- Certification criteria developed and more widely applied to industry initiatives.
- A commitment to the controlled expansion, where appropriate, of infrastructure.
- Environmental taxes, where applied, should be fair and nondiscriminatory. They should be carefully thought out to minimise their impact on economic development, and revenues should be allocated to Travel & Tourism associated environment improvement programs.
- International, national and local funding bodies should include sustainable development as a part of their criteria, so that in time, all funding would be dependent on sound environmental practice.
- Contemporary research into sustainable tourism needs to be funded and developed. Issues requiring attention include design, carrying capacity, tour operator activities, environmental reporting, auditing and environmental impact assessments.
- Environmental education and training should be increased, particularly in schools, for future hotel and tourism staff.
- Greater investment and commitment to the use of new technology.

Coastal Impact of Tourism Problems

Tourism provides an essential lifeline for many coastal communities. Faced with the prospect of increasing financial hardship, more and more coastal communities have turned to tourism as a means of generating income and survival. Tourism's impact on the coastal zone has, therefore, been largely positive. Of course, as in any area, if Tourism is not properly managed and developed, it can be harmful.

Impacts arise from the construction of infrastructure (hotels, marinas, transport, waste treatment facilities, groynes etc.) and from recreation (golf courses, water sports, theme parks etc.).

Coastal communities are now faced with tourism on a considerable scale, and the host to guest ratio can be very high in such areas. At the same time, coastal communities must try to maintain the resort's attraction as tourist demands change, sometimes quite rapidly.

With coastal regions being primary tourist destinations, sensitive marine and coastal environments can suffer dramatically. For example, as a result of large-scale sea-front tourist development, considerable beach and dune erosion can occur. Tourism also impacts on environmental quality in the following ways:

- ribbon development, infrastructure requirements, particularly transport links;
- the treatment and disposal of solid and/or liquid wastes, particularly during peak tourist seasons, may be inadequate or at worst non-existent; and
- water is often consumed excessively, not only for drinking but for showers, laundry, swimming pools, maintenance of golf courses etc. This can affect the quantity and quality of fresh water available to indigenous coastal populations.

Recreational activities can also have a significant impact on the coastal zone:

- golf course's impact can be considerable, with those situated directly on coastal habitats (especially sand dunes) in particular;
- erosion of reefs and coral from divers and swimmers;
- pollution from boats and jets skis; and
- noise from motor boats and jet skis, cars and buses, nightlife and other activities.

Solutions

The development of a sustainable tourism industry in the coastal zone offers numerous opportunities. Opportunities includes, those for nature conservation – which, given the increasing interest in high quality natural and cultural experiences, can help to reverse the decline in market share of many coastal destinations. Tourism also provides important opportunities for strengthening local industries. Where industries are in decline, tourism ventures can help supplement declining income. The following examples illustrate what can be done to make the most of the opportunities offered by tourism in the coastal zone: Calvia is a Municipality on the Mediterranean coast that has undertaken an Agenda 21 project to assist the sustainable development of its tourism sector, in order to counter the negative impact of short-term tourism development since the 1960s. The local council has now implemented a transferable policy aimed at modernising, improving and diversifying the local tourist industry, involving all stakeholders, including the local population. A Project Plan was enacted, and achievements so far include:

- indigenous development, based on the sustainable use of available resources;
- high quality services and an appropriate bed night capacity;
- a ban on new development on 1,700 acres;
- active participation of the residents in community life; and
- environmental management of municipality buildings, waste recycling, reduction in spending on electricity, and use of environmentally friendly materials for office use.

Quicksilver Tours, Queensland, Australia, is owned by one of the largest tourism operators to the Great Barrier Reef. Quicksilver have five large catamarans, which take about 1,000 tourists a day to dive on the reef. They have their own reef site with fixed diving platforms. They employ a team of biologists, both for environmental management and assessment as well as widespread environmental interpretation. Recent assessment of the reef, in the vicinity of the operation, shows that it is being maintained in pristine condition.

Kingfisher Bay Resort is found at Fraser Island, Queensland. It is a large five star "ecotourism" resort built in a beautiful, but fragile environment off the Queensland coast. Its concept, design, construction and management were conceived using the latest ecologically sustainable principles. It is a state-of-the-art "ecotourism" resort, which has won Australia's top tourism awards, and its economic and environmental success has influenced new coastal tourism developments.

Maho Bay's camps and studios in the US Virgin Islands have based their product on a commitment to minimise impact on the environment, conserve natural resources, engage in active and passive environmental education of their guests, and contribute to the local economy. Specific initiatives introduced at Maho Bay include the following: use of new technology; purchasing policies; waste management; environmental education; energy and water conservation; and support for local communities and culture.

These initiatives show an appreciation of the need for alternative solutions to issues such as packaging and waste disposal through landfill. These are issues, which as the industry grows, will be increasingly important for the Travel & Tourism industry as a whole to address.

Agents and Partnerships for Change and Areas for Further Action

The agents, partnerships for change and areas for further action in relation to tourism in the coastal zone are similar to the development of broad based sustainable tourism in general as set out in Section

A number of issues do, of course, have particular importance for the coastal zone. Above all, the key to success is better participation at destination level among all the stakeholders concerned (such as at Calvia). In the case of the coastal zone, there are a number of additional organisations with an interest in coastal policy, marine conservation, shipping etc., which needs to be identified and included in partnerships for the coastal zone.

Successful planning for tourism is very important for the future of the industry in coastal regions, because a significant percentage of tourism occurs within the geographical parameters of the definition of a coastal zone. Concerted support from all countries involved (and the industries within them) is vital to protect the shared natural resources that coastal zones represent.

Historically, the influence most hoteliers have on the environmental impact of their business is limited to working within existing buildings, or after a new site has been completed. In April 1998, the IHEI convened a group of hoteliers, tour operators, architectural firms and sustainable development specialists with the goal of creating a partnership to be called the "Siting and Design Programme". The new initiative's mission will be to define responsible planning and design specifications that will cause minimal environmental damage at new sites. Particular attention will be paid to sites located within ecologically sensitive areas and upon waterfronts. The "Siting and Design Programme" will strive to reach hotel owners, investors and developers to bring these issues to the attention of the entire industry. Linkages with government authorities that uphold responsible development standards would complete the partnership.

Conclusions

Travel & Tourism has a number of advantages over other industry sectors:

- it creates jobs and wealth whilst;
- at the same time, it can contribute to sustainable development;
- it tends to have low start-up costs;
- is a viable option in a wide range of areas and regions;
- is likely to continue to grow for the foreseeable future; and
- the industry is, in a large part, aware of the need to protect the resource on which it is based-local culture and built and natural environment-and it is committed to these resources' preservation and enhancement.

The industry is, therefore, making a concerted effort to build up programs for sustainable development. However, it cannot do this alone. If Travel & Tourism is to continue to flourish and to contribute to sustainable development, it needs help from national Governments. This assistance is needed in two forms:-both positive encouragement for sustainable tourism initiatives and an understanding that policy decisions in other areas can effect Travel & Tourism. In practical terms, what this means is the following:

The first point of action needed from Governments is to incorporate Agenda 21 principles into tourism policies at international and national level, and to promote their inclusion in regional and local tourism strategies.

By providing such a lead and establishing a coherent global framework based on Agenda 21, national governments will make a vital contribution to developing a more sustainable tourism industry.

Governments should also recognise that Travel & Tourism is a core service sector which should always be considered when looking at policies to expand trade, increase employment, modernize infrastructure and encourage investment-at both domestic and international level. It should also be included in national statistics with its economic impact calculated by means of a national tourism satellite account. Governments should also consider helping Travel & Tourism by seeking to minimise regulatory impediments and by offering appropriate investment incentives.

By supporting tourism and allowing it to compete in open and fair markets, tourism's benefits can be more easily secured.

Finally, governments can address some of the fundamental barriers to tourism growth by looking at how to expand and modernise infrastructure, to apply taxes fairly and to invest in human resource development.

If the program of action outlined above can be undertaken by national governments in cooperation with continued industry commitments and initiatives for sustainable tourism then we can look to a brighter future.

World Tourism Global Update

Global Tourism 2007

Total Tourism Foreign Earnings ($B)	US$ 856
As a percent of world GDP	9.7%
Tourism Value-Added ($B)	US$ 334
As a percent of world GDP	3.8%
Tourism Employment ('000 of jobs)	72,137
As a percent of world employment	2.7%
Total Tourist arrivals (Mn)	903

Developing Trends

- Worlds Largest and fastest growing industry
- International tourism arrivals increased by 6% in 2007, to 903 million international tourist arrivals.
- By region, the highest growth is forecast for the Asian region.
- International tourism in emerging & developing markets has grown at an average rate of 6-8% over the past decade. twice the rate of industrialized countries.
- Tourism is a crucial contributor to these countries' income-up to 70% for the some of the world's poorest countries.

Regional Growth

Region 2006-10	AAGR (%)
Americas	4.79
South Asia	7.78
Southeast Asia	9.47
Northeast Asia	8.21
Oceania	4.80
Grand Total	7.51

Indirect (informal) Employment in the Tourism Sector

- Suppliers of vegetable/fish/meat/dry food etc.
- Suppliers of chemicals and additives for pools and laundry equipment
- Suppliers of stationary
- Suppliers of miscellaneous food and beverage and kitchen consumables
- Suppliers of maintenance, equipment, spare parts etc.
- Bands, entertainers, magic shows etc.
- Suppliers of tourism souvenirs, such as wood crafts, silverware, batiks etc.
- Beach vendors and beach operators
- Transport providers including hire of busses, cars, vans and three wheelers.

2

Cooperatives and Tourism: An Asian Perspective

Current Scenario

Tourism in Asia is in a thriving condition. Every country is involved in promoting tourism in a big way. Tourism has become a top priority of the economic agenda of all the countries. For example, if in Malaysia tourism is the top revenue generating sector, in India tourism is slowly getting due focus taking into account the country's rich heritage and cultural tradition. However, a review of the tourism trends in Asia clearly indicates that while economic considerations have reigned supreme, the social aspects are not being given due importance as far as the strategic tourism considerations are considered. Tourism it appears is developing an elitist bias as broadening of its social base with participation from all sections of the society is clearly not visible. The important role of participatory and community based organisations like cooperatives in promoting tourism has yet to be recognised. As a result, the concepts like "sustainable tourism", "peace through tourism", "poverty reduction through tourism", 'community tourism', etc. which can best be implemented through participatory institutions have yet to be popularised in a big way.

The cooperatives in Asia in the recent years have diversified themselves into various areas of socioeconomic activities. The cooperative model in the Asian countries is considered a strong force for solving the various socioeconomic problems. The failure of the public sector and various limitations of the private sector have compelled the policy-makers to pin their faiths on the cooperative system. For certain activities/areas, the success of which is based on the ability of the grassroot institutions to tackle them with their participatory and people-based approach, the cooperatives are considered to have an advantage over other organisations. For example, in India the cooperatives are considered most effective organisations in the field of rural insurance. Similarly, because of their vast network and reach, the cooperatives are considered best promoters for rural electrification in India.

Tourism: A Neglected Field

The cooperatives in Asia have yet to recognise the importance of tourism despite the rapid growth of tourism sector in Asia. Following are the main reasons:.

- Lack of definite data base on the number of cooperatives involved in the field of tourism, inability to highlight the strengths and weaknesses of the ones which are present, etc.
- Inability to analyse the changing socioeconomic dimensions of tourism sector in Asia, and demarcate the areas in which cooperatives have a strategic advantage over other forms of organisations.
- Lack of policy research in this field which can provide definite indicators for future. For example, it is generally agreed that taking into account the growing tourism sector in India and the presence of strong network of Indian cooperatives, there is lack of policy research in this field which can show a way ahead for definite policy initiatives.
- Inability to strategically link the cooperative sector with the tourism sector in those countries in which tourism is in a boom. For example, in Malaysia and Thailand, tourism has emerged as a big force. But, the cooperative sector has yet to come up strongly in this field.
- Inability of the cooperatives to extend their areas of operations or activities in the field of tourism. For example, some of the sectoral Asian cooperatives are in a best position to incorporate tourism in their agenda, which is not being done. For example, the dairy cooperatives in Asia should think of linking tourism in their activities, or promote tourism cooperatives exclusively. The, dairy cooperatives in India have ushered in milk revolution in the country. They have empowered the masses in the rural

areas to trigger off a milk revolution. They have developed milk brands which speak of cooperative supremacy. The areas which are strong-holds of cooperative milk sector can be promoted in a big way as hot tourist spots. Similarly, the school cooperatives in Malaysia are very strong. Taking into account the buoyant condition of tourism in Malaysia and the vibrancy of school cooperative sector, how can tourism be promoted through cooperatives in a big way?

- Weak advocacy for tourism promotion is also a big hindrance. Holding of Advocacy conferences by the cooperatives in the area of cooperative tourism can set the ball rolling in a big way and create a conducive atmosphere for tourism promotion. This can also establish links, with other international tourism organisations who have to be sensitised on the cooperative agenda.

However, due to lack of awareness, this is not being done at present. Similarly, lack of development of cooperative literature in the field of cooperative tourism is also a sign of weak advocacy. There is also lack of documentation of few successful models of cooperative tourism in the Region.

Indian Case

Starting in 1904, the Indian Cooperative Movement has made rapid strides in all the areas of socioeconomic activities. The cooperative concept has worked wonders in India. Today there are more than 5 lakh cooperative societies with a membership of 23 crores and working capital of Rs. 198.542 million. The cooperative credit institutions are disbursing 46.15% of agricultural credit and cooperatives are distributing 36.22% of total fertilisers in the country. The share of cooperatives in production of sugar is 59% and they cover 55% of the handlooms. The cooperative networking and reach is so vast that the cooperatives cover 100% of total villages and 75% of the rural households. The cooperative movement is the world's largest movement, India's economic reforms have given a big push to tourism sector. Tourism is today projected as an engine of economic growth and an instrument for eliminating poverty, solving unemployment problem, opening up new fields of activity and the uplifted of women. New opportunities are being tapped to promote eco, adventure, rural, postage, wildlife and health and herbal including medical tourism. The Indian Government is now considering Rural Tourism as one of the thrust areas. Keeping into account the strength of Indian cooperatives it wants that cooperatives should come up in the field of Rural Tourism as the cooperatives cover 100% of the villages in the country. The UNDP-Ministry of Tourism Project on Tourism talks about strong community–private and public sector partnership for boosting rural tourism in the country. The Indian cooperatives due to their immense reach and wide network are strategically well positioned to take a leading role in the field of Rural Tourism.

Paradigm Shift in Tourism

An analysis of the tourism trends in Asia clearly indicate the following:

- Shift in focus towards decentralised form of tourism which can effectively tackle the problem of poverty allegation by generating jobs. It is now well understood that tourism can best fight poverty by generating jobs, both in the rural and urban areas.
- Growir.g recognition of social aspects of tcurism which can provide equal opportunities of travel for all, promote respect for culture, values, sustainable development, etc.
- Realisation that economic spin-offs from tourism sector can be used for the betterment of the society, and creating a peaceful atmosphere in which there is understanding and cooperation amongst all.

In all the above areas, the cooperatives in the future are well-positioned to formulate effective strategies so that they emerge as lead players in promoting decentralised form of tourism. The world tourism community is looking towards the cooperatives to play a strong balancing role in tourism development so as to help in creation of an equitable society. It is heartening that cooperatives are now considered an effective instrument for poverty alleviation. A rich academic debate on this subject has emerged. International organisations now view cooperatives as an important tool for bridging the divide between rich and poor. Poverty, being endemic in Asia, can the cooperatives in Asia tackle the problem of poverty by linking their agenda with tourism? This is a big challenge.

Strategic Initiatives

ICA being the apex body of the world cooperatives must play a pro-active role in promoting tourism in the Asian Region, ICA's specialised organ, TICA must align with Bureau of International Social Tourism (BITS) with which it has strong relationship, so that initiatives in the following areas may be undertaken.

- Establishing strong networks with the Asian Cooperatives, and locating areas of collaborations.
- Undertaking, a big research project so as to gauge the effectiveness of cooperative model in tourism sector in Asia. Other projects may be conceptualized after this..
- Sensitising the tourism bodies in Asia on the importance of cooperative sector in Tourism, and forging useful collaboration with them.
- Organising conferences and seminars on important thematic issues.
- Due to lack of presence of international bodies championing the cause of social tourism in an effective manner, TICA-BITS may think of setting up a Centre with the relevant support so that definitive advocacy/ promotional measures may be taken for promoting tourism in the Region.

India's Role in the World of Tourism

Tourism in India

Tourism is the largest service industry in India, with a contribution of 6.23% to the national GDP and 8.78% of the total employment in India. India witnesses more than 5 million annual foreign tourist arrivals and 562 million domestic tourism visits. The tourism industry in India generated about US$100 billion in 2008 and that is expected to increase to US$275.5 billion by 2018 at a 9.4% annual growth rate. The Ministry of Tourism is the nodal agency for the development and promotion of tourism in India and maintains the "Incredible India" campaign.

According to *World Travel and Tourism Council,* India will be a tourism hotspot from 2009-2018, having the highest 10-year growth potential. The *Travel & Tourism Competitiveness Report 2007* ranked tourism in India 6th in terms of price competitiveness and 39th in terms of safety and security. Despite short-and medium-term setbacks, such as shortage of hotel rooms, tourism revenues are expected to surge by 42% from 2007 to 2017. India has a growing medical tourism sector. The 2010 Commonwealth Games in Delhi are expected to significantly boost tourism in India.

Tourism by State

Andhra Pradesh

Andhra Pradesh has a rich cultural heritage and a variety of tourist attractions. The state of Andhra Pradesh comprises scenic hills, forests, beaches and temples. Also known as *The City of Nizams* and *The City of Pearls,* Hyderabad is today one of the most developed cities in the country and a modern hub of information technology, ITES, and biotechnology. Hyderabad is known for its rich history, culture and architecture representing its unique character as a meeting point for North and South India, and also its multilingual culture, both geographically and culturally.

Andhra Pradesh is the home of many religious pilgrim centres. Tirupati, the abode of Lord Venkateswara, is the richest and most visited religious centre (of any faith) in the world. Srisailam, the abode of Sri Mallikarjuna, is one of twelve Jyothirlingalu in India, Amaravati's Siva temple is one of the Pancharamams, and Yadagirigutta, the abode of an avatara of Vishnu, Sri Lakshmi Narasimha. The Ramappa temple and Thousand Pillars temple in Warangal are famous for some fine temple carvings. The state has numerous Buddhist centres at Amaravati, Nagarjuna Konda, Bhattiprolu, Ghantasala, Nelakondapalli, Dhulikatta, Bavikonda, Thotlakonda, Shalihundam, Pavuralakonda, Sankaram, Phanigiri and Kolanpaka.

The golden beaches at Visakhapatnam, the one-million-year old limestone caves at Borra, picturesque Araku Valley, hill resorts of Horsley Hills, river Godavari racing through a narrow gorge at Papi Kondalu, waterfalls at Ettipotala, Kuntala and rich biodiversity at Talakona, are some of the natural attractions of the state. Visakhapatnam is home to many tourist attactions such as the INS Karasura Submarine museum (The only one of its kind in India), Yarada Beach, Araku Valley, VUDA Park, Indira Gandhi Zoological Gardens. The weather in Andhra Pradesh is mostly tropical and the best time to visit is in November through to January. The monsoon season commences in June and ends in September, so travel would not be advisable during this period.

Assam

Assam is the central state in the North-East Region of India and serves as the gateway to the rest of the Seven Sister States. Assam boasts of famous wildlife preserves – the Kaziranga National

Park (*pictured*) and the Manas National Park, the largest river island Majuli, and tea-estates dating back to time of British Raj. The weather is mostly sub-tropical. Assam experiences the Indian monsoon and has one of the highest forest densities in India. The winter months (October to April) are the best time to visit.

Assam has a rich cultural heritage going back to the Ahom Kingdom which governed the region for many centuries before the British occupation. Other notable features include the Brahmaputra River, the mystery of the bird suicides in Jatinga, numerous temples including Kamakhya of Tantric sect, ruins of palaces, etc. Guwahati, the capital city of Assam, boasts many bazaars, temples, and wildlife sanctuaries.

Bihar

Bihar is one of the oldest continuously inhabited places in the world with history of 3000 years. The rich culture and heritage of Bihar is evident from the innumerable ancient monuments that are dotted all over this state in eastern India. This is the Place of Aryabhatta, Great Ashoka, Chanakya and many more.

Bihar is one of the most sacred places of various religions such as Hinduism, Buddhism, Jainism, Sikhism & Islam. Famous Attraction includes Mahabodhi Temple, a Buddhist shrine and UNESCO World Heritage Site is also situated in Bihar, Barabar Caves the oldest rockcut caves in India, Khuda Bakhsh Oriental Library the Oldest Library of India.

Delhi

Delhi is the capital city of India. A fine blend of old and new, ancient and modern, Delhi is a melting pot of cultures, religions. Delhi has been the capital of numerous empires that ruled India, making it rich in history. The rulers left behind their trademark architectural styles. Delhi currently has many renowned historic monuments and landmarks such as the Tughlaqabad fort, Qutub Minar, Purana Quila, Lodhi Gardens, Jama Masjid, Humayun's tomb, Red Fort, and Safdarjung's Tomb. Modern monuments include Jantar Mantar, India Gate, Rashtrapati Bhavan, Laxminarayan Temple, Lotus temple and Akshardham Temple.

New Delhi is famous for its British colonial architecture, wide roads, and tree-lined boulevards. Delhi is home to numerous political landmarks, national museums, Islamic shrines, Hindu temples, green parks, and trendy malls.

Goa

Goa is one of the most famous tourist destinations in India. A former colony of Portugal, Goa is famous for its excellent beaches, Portuguese churches, Hindu temples, and wildlife sanctuaries. The Basilica of Bom Jesus, Mangueshi Temple, Dudhsagar Falls, and Shantadurga are famous attractions in Goa. Recently a Wax Museum (Wax World) has also opened in Old Goa housing a number of wax personalities of Indian history, culture and heritage.

The Goa Carnival is a world famous event, with coloruful masks and floats, drums and reverberating music, and dance performances. The celebrations run three days culminating in a carnival parade on fat Tuesday.

Himachal Pradesh

Himachal Pradesh is famous for its Himalayan landscapes and popular hill-stations. Many outdoor activities such as rock climbing, mountain biking, paragliding, ice-skating, and heli-skiing are popular tourist attractions in Himachal Pradesh.

Shimla, the state capital, is very popular among tourists. The Kalka-Shimla Railway is a Mountain railway which is a UNESCO World Heritage Site. Shimla is also a famous skiing attraction in India. Other popular hill stations include Manali and Kasauli.

Dharamshala, home of the Dalai Lama, is known for its Tibetan monasteries and Buddhist temples. Many trekking expeditions also begin here.

Jammu and Kashmir

Jammu and Kashmir is the northernmost state of India. Jammu is noted for its scenic landscape, ancient temples, Hindu shrines, castles, gardens, and forts. The Hindu holy shrines of Amarnath and Vaishno Devi attract tens of thousands of Hindu devotees every year. Jammu's natural landscape has made it one of the popular destinations for adventure tourism in South Asia. Jammu's historic monuments feature a unique blend of Islamic and Hindu architecture styles.

Tourism forms an integral part of the Kashmiri economy. Often dubbed "Paradise on Earth", Kashmir's mountainous landscape has attracted tourists for centuries. Notable places are Dal Lake, Srinagar Phalagam, Gulmarg, Yeusmarg and Mughal Gardens etc. However, the tourism industry is severely affected by the insurgency. In recent years, Ladakh has emerged as a major hub for adventure tourism. This part of Greater Himalaya called "moon on earth" comprising of naked peaks and deep gorges was once known for the silk route to High Asia from the subcontinent. Leh is also a growing tourist spot.

Karnataka

Karnataka has been ranked as fourth most popular destination for tourism among states of India. It has the second highest number of protected monuments in India, at 507.

Kannada dynasties like Kadambas, Western Gangas, Chalukyas, Rashtrakutas, Hoysalas and Vijayanagaras, ruled Karnataka particularly North Karnataka. They built great monuments to Buddhism, Jainism, Shaivism. The monuments are still present at Badami, Aihole, Pattadakal, Hampi, Lakshmeshwar, Sudi, Hooli, Mahadeva Temple (Itagi), Dambal, Lakkundi, Gadag, Hangal, Halasi, Galaganatha, Chaudayyadanapura, Banavasi, Belur, Halebidu, Shravanabelagola, Sannati and many more. Notable Islamic monuments are present at Bijapur, Bidar, Gulbarga, Raichur and other part of the state. Gol Gumbaz at Bijapur, has the second largest pre-modern dome in the world after the Byzantine Hagia Sophia. Karnataka has two World heritage sites, at Hampi and Pattadakal, both are in North Karnataka.

Karnataka is famous for its waterfalls. Jog falls of Shimoga District is one of the highest waterfalls in Asia. This state has 21 wildlife sanctuaries and five National parks and is home to more than 500 species of birds. Karnataka has many beaches at Karwar, Gokarna, Murdeshwara, Surathkal. Karnataka is a rock climbers paradise. Yana in Uttara Kannada, Fort in Chitradurga, Ramnagara near Bangalore district, Shivagange in Tumkur district and tekal in Kolar district are a rock climbers heaven.

Kerala

Kerala is a state on the tropical Malabar Coast of southwestern India. Nicknamed as one of the "*paradises of the world*" by National Geographic, Kerala is famous especially for its ecotourism initiatives. Its unique culture and traditions, coupled with its varied demography, has made it one of the most popular tourist destinations in India. Growing at a rate of 13.31%, the tourism industry significantly contributes to the state's economy. Kerala, a state situated on the tropical Malabar Coast of southwestern

India, is one of the most popular tourist destinations in the country. Named as one of the *ten paradises of the world* by the National Geographic Traveller, Kerala is famous especially for its ecotourism initiatives. Its unique culture and traditions, coupled with its varied demography, has made Kerala one of the most popular tourist destinations in the world. Growing at a rate of 13.31%, the tourism industry is a major contributor to the state's economy.

Until the early 1980s, Kerala was a hitherto unknown destination, with most tourism circuits concentrated around the north of the country. Aggressive marketing campaigns launched by the Kerala Tourism Development Corporation—the government agency that oversees tourism prospects of the state—laid the foundation for the growth of the tourism industry.

In the decades that followed, Kerala Tourism was able to transform itself into one of the niche holiday destinations in India. The tag line *Kerala-God's Own Country* was adopted in its tourism promotions and became synonymous with the state. Today, Kerala Tourism is a global superbrand and regarded as one of the destinations with the highest brand recall. In 2006, Kerala attracted 8.5 million tourists–an increase of 23.68% in foreign tourist arrivals compared to the previous year, thus making it one of the fastest growing tourism destination in the world.

Popular attractions in the state include the beaches at Kovalam, Cherai and Varkala; the hill stations of Munnar, Nelliampathi, Ponmudi and Wayanad; and national parks and wildlife sanctuaries at Periyar and Eravikulam National Park. The "backwaters" region—an extensive network of interlocking rivers, lakes, and canals that centre on Alleppey, Kumarakom, and Punnamada—also see heavy tourist traffic. Heritage sites, such as the Padmanabhapuram Palace, Hill Palace, Mattancherry Palace are also visited. Cities such as Kochi and Thiruvananthapuram are popular centres for shopping and traditional theatrical performances.

The state's tourism agenda promotes ecologically sustained tourism, which focuses on the local culture, wilderness adventures, volunteering and personal growth of the local population. Efforts are taken to minimise the adverse effects of traditional tourism on the natural environment, and enhance the cultural integrity of local people.

Historical Context

Since its incorporation as a state, Kerala's economy largely operated under welfare-based democratic socialist principles. This mode of development, though resulted in a high Human Development Index and standard of living among the people, lead to an economic stagnation in the 1980s (growth rate of 2.3% annually) This apparent paradox — high human development and low economic development — lead to a large number of educated unemployed seeking jobs overseas, especially in the Gulf countries. Due to the large number of expatriates, many travel operators and agencies set shop in the state to felicitate their travel needs. However, the trends soon reciprocated with the travel agencies noticing the undermined potential of the state as a tourist destination.

By 1986, tourism had gained an industry status. Kerala Tourism subsequently adopted the tagline *God's Own Country* in its advertisement campaigns. Aggressive promotion in print and electronic media were able to invite a sizable investment in the hospitality industry. By the early 2000s, tourism had grown into a fully fledged, multi-billion dollar industry in the state. The state was able to carve a niche place for itself in the world tourism industry, thus becoming one of the places with the 'highest brand recall'. In 2003, Kerala, a hitherto unknown tourism destination, became the fastest growing tourism destination in the world.

Today, growing at a rate of 13.31%, Kerala is one of the most visited tourism destinations in India.

Major Attractions

Beaches

Kovalam beach near Thiruvananthapuram was among the first beaches in Kerala to attract tourists. Rediscovered by back-packers and tan-seekers in the sixties and followed by hordes of hippies in the seventies, Kovalam is today the most visited tourist destination in the state.

Other popularly visited beaches in the state include those at Alappuzha Beach, Nattika beach [Thrissur], Vadanappilly beach [Thrissur], Cherai Beach, Kappad, Kovalam, Marari beach, Fort Kochi and Varkala. The Muzhappilangad Beach beach at Kannur is the only drive-in beach in India.

Backwaters

The backwaters in Kerala are a chain of brackish lagoons and lakes lying parallel to the Arabian Sea coast (known as the Malabar Coast). Kettuvallam (Kerala houseboats) in the backwaters are one of the prominent tourist attractions in Kerala. Alleppey, known as the "Venice of the East" has a large network of canals that meander through the town. The Vallam Kali (the Snake Boat Race) held every year in August is a major sporting attraction.

The backwater network includes five large lakes (including Ashtamudi Kayal and Vembanad Kayal) linked by 1500 km of canals, both manmade and natural, fed by 38 rivers, and extending virtually the entire length of Kerala state. The backwaters were formed by the action of waves and shore currents creating low barrier islands across the mouths of the many rivers flowing down from the Western Ghats range.

Hill Stations

Eastern Kerala consists of land encroached upon by the Western Ghats; the region thus includes high mountains, gorges, and deep-cut valleys. The wildest lands are covered with dense forests, while other regions lie under tea and coffee plantations (established mainly in the 19th and 20th centuries) or other forms of cultivation. The Western Ghats rises on average to 1500 m elevation above sea level. Certain peaks may reach to 2500 m. Popular hill stations in the region include Devikulam, Munnar, Nelliyampathi, Peermade, Ponmudi, Vagamon, Wayanad and Kottanchery Hills.

Wildlife

Most of Kerala, whose native habitat consists of wet evergreen rainforests at lower elevations and highland deciduous and semi-evergreen forests in the east, is subject to a humid tropical climate, however, significant variations in terrain and elevation have resulted in a land whose biodiversity registers as among the world's most significant. Most of Kerala's significantly biodiverse tracts of wilderness lie in the evergreen forests of its easternmost districts. Kerala also hosts two of the world's Ramsar Convention-listed wetlands: Lake Sasthamkotta and the Vembanad-Kol wetlands are noted as being wetlands of international importance. There are also numerous protected conservation areas, including 1455.4 km^2 of the vast Nilgiri Biosphere Reserve. In turn, the forests play host to such major fauna as Asian Elephant (*Elephas maximus*), Bengal

Tiger (*Panthera tigris tigris*), Leopard (*Panthera pardus*), and Nilgiri Tahr (*Nilgiritragus hylocrius*), and Grizzled Giant Squirrel (*Ratufa macroura*). More remote preserves, including Silent Valley National Park in the Kundali Hills, harbour endangered species such as Lion-tailed Macaque (*Macaca silenus*), Indian Sloth Bear (*Melursus (Ursus) ursinus ursinus*), and Gaur (the so-called "Indian Bison" — *Bos gaurus*). More common species include Indian Porcupine (*Hystrix indica*), Chital (*Axis axis*), Sambar (*Cervus unicolor*), Gray Langur, Flying Squirrel, Swamp Lynx (*Felis chaus kutas*), Boar (*Sus scrofa*), a variety of catarrhine Old World monkey species, Gray Wolf (*Canis lupus*), Common Palm Civet (*Paradoxurus hermaphroditus*). Many reptiles, such as king cobra, viper, python, various turtles and crocodiles are to be found in Kerala — again, disproportionately in the east. Kerala's avifauna include endemics like the Sri Lanka Frogmouth (*Batrachostomus moniliger*), Oriental Bay Owl, large frugivores like the Great Hornbill (*Buceros bicornis*) and Indian Grey Hornbill, as well as the more widespread birds such as Peafowl, Indian Cormorant, Jungle and Hill Myna, Oriental Darter, Black-hooded Oriole, Greater Racket-tailed and Black Drongoes, bulbul (*Pycnonotidae*), species of Kingfisher and Woodpecker, Jungle Fowl, Alexandrine Parakeet, and assorted ducks and migratory birds. Additionally, freshwater fish such as *kadu* (stinging catfish — *Heteropneustes fossilis*) and brackishwater species such as *Choottachi* (orange chromide — *Etroplus maculatus*; valued as an aquarium specimen) also are native to Kerala's lakes and waterways.

Festivals

The major festival in Kerala is Onam. Kerala has a number of religious festivals. Thrissur Pooram and Chettikulangara Bharani are the major temple festivals in Kerala. The Thrissur Pooram is conducted at the Vadakumnathan temple, Thrissur. The Chettikulangara Bharani is another major attraction. The festival is conducted at the Chettikulangara temple near Mavelikkara. Parumala Perunnal, Manarkadu Perunnal are the major festivals of Christians. Muslims also have many important festivals.

Radiation Tourism

Karunagappally Taluk Karunagappalli, Places of Interest in Kollam District is the world's hottest spot of natural radiation. The radiation is caused by monazite sands which contain the radioactive element, thorium. The people in the area are exposed to radiation which is 10 times greater than the worldwide average. Tourist spots that offer the chance of the Radiation experience are very rare in the world.

Ayurveda

Medical tourism, promoted by traditional systems of medicine like Ayurveda and Siddha are widely popular in the state, and draws increasing numbers of tourists. A combination of many factors has led to the increase in popularity of medical tourism: high costs of healthcare in industrialised nations, ease and affordability of international travel, improving technology and standards of care.

However, rampant recent growth in this sector has made the government apprehensive. The government is now considering introduction of a grading system which would grade hospitals and clinics, thus helping tourists in selecting one for their treatments.

Culture

Kerala's culture is mainly Dravidian in origin, deriving from a greater Tamil-heritage region known as Tamilakam. Later, Kerala's culture was elaborated on through centuries of contact with overseas cultures. Native performing arts include *koodiyattom, kathakali* – from *katha* ("story") and *kali* ("play") – and its offshoot *Kerala natanam, koothu* (akin to stand-up comedy), *mohiniaattam* ("dance of the enchantress"), *thullal, padayani,* and *theyyam*. Other arts are more religion-and tribal-themed. These include *chavittu nadakom, oppana* (originally from Malabar), which combines dance, rhythmic hand clapping, and *ishal* vocalisations. However, many of these artforms largely play to tourists or at youth festivals, and are not as popular among most ordinary Keralites. These people look to more contemporary art and performance styles, including those employing mimicry and parody. Additionally, a substantial Malayalam film industry effectively competes against both Bollywood and Hollywood.

Several ancient ritualised arts are Keralite in origin; these include *kalaripayattu* (*kalari* ("place", "threshing floor", or "battlefield") and *payattu* ("exercise" or "practice")). Among the world's oldest martial arts, oral tradition attributes *kalaripayattu*'s emergence to Parasurama. Other ritual arts include *theyyam, poorakkali* and *Kuthiyottam*.

Kuthiyottam is a ritualistic symbolic representation of human bali (homicide). Folklore exponents see this art form, with enchanting well structured choreography and songs, as one among the rare Adi Dravida folklore traditions still preserved and practiced in Central Kerala in accordance to the true tradition and environment. Typical to the Adi Dravida folk dances and songs, the movements and formations of dancers (clad in white thorthu and banyan) choreographed in Kuthiyottam are quick, peaks at a particular point and ends abruptly. The traditional songs also start in a stylish slow pace, then gain momentum and ends abruptly.

Kuthiyotta Kalaris', run by Kuthiyotta Asans (Teachers or leaders), train the group to perform the dances and songs. Normally, the training starts about one to two months before the season. Young boys between 8 to 14 years are taught Kuthiyottam, a ritual dance in the house amidst a big social gathering before the portrait of the deity. Early in the morning on Bharani, after the feast and other rituals, the boys whose bodies are coiled with silver wires, one end of which is tied around his neck and an arecanut fixed on the tip of a knife held high over his head are taken in procession to the temple with the accompaniment of beating of drums, music, ornamental umbrellas, and other classical folk art forms, and richly caparisoned elephants.

All through the way to the temple tender coconut water will be continually poured on his body. After the circumambulation the boys stands at a position facing the Sreekovil (Sanctum Sanctorum) and begins to dance. This ceremony ends with dragging the coil pierced to the skin whereby a few drops of blood comes out.

On this day just after midday the residents of the locality bring huge decorated effigies of Bhima panchalia, Hanuman and extremely beautiful tall chariots in wheeled platforms, and after having darshan the parties take up their respective position in the paddy fields lying east of the temple.

During the night, the image of Devi will be carried in procession to the effigies stationed in the paddy fields. On the next day these structures will be taken back. A big bazaar is also held at Chetikulangara as part of this festival. Kuthiyottam is the main vazipadu of the Chettikulangara temple, Mavelikkara.

In respect of Fine Arts, the State has an abounding tradition of both ancient and contemporary art and artists. The traditional

Kerala murals are found in ancient temples, churches and palaces across the State. These paintings, mostly dating back between the 9th to 12th centuries AD, display a distinct style, and a colour code which is predominantly ochre and green.

Like the rest of India, religious diversity is very prominent in Kerala. The principal religions are Hinduism, Christianity, and Islam; Jainism, Judaism, Sikhism, and Buddhism have smaller followings. The states historic ties with the rest of the world has resulted in the state having many famous temples, churches, and mosques. The Paradesi Synagogue in Kochi is the oldest in the Commonwealth of Nations.

Recognising the potential of tourism in the diversity of religious faiths, related festivals and structures, the tourism department launched a *Pilgrimage tourism* project.

Major pilgrim tourism attractions include Guruvayur, Sabarimala, Malayatoor, Paradesi Synagogue, St. Mary's Forane (Martha Mariam) Church Kuravilangad built in 105 A.D, Attukal Ponkal and Chettikulangara Bharani.

Advertising Campaigns

Kerala Tourism is noted for its innovative and market-focused ad campaigns. These campaigns have won the tourism department numerous awards, including the *Das Golden Stadttor Award for Best Commercial, 2006, Pacific Asia Travel Association-Gold Award for Marketing, 2003* and the Government of India's *Best Promotion Literature, 2004, Best Publishing, 2004* and *Best Tourism Film, 2001.*

Catchy slogans and innovative designs are considered a trademark of brand Kerala Tourism. Celebrity promotions are also used to attract more tourists to the state. The Kerala tourism website is widely visited, and has been the recipient of many awards. Recently, the tourism department has also engaged in advertising via mobiles, by setting up a WAP portal, and distributing wallpapers and ringtones related to Kerala through it.

Threats to the Tourism Industry

With increasing threats posed by global warming and changing weather patterns, it is feared that much of Kerala's low lying areas might be susceptible to beach erosions and coastal flooding. The differing monsoon patterns also suggest possible tropical cyclones in the future.

Awards

The state has won numerous awards for its tourism initiatives. These include:

- 2005-Nominated as one among the three finalists at the World Travel and Tourism Council's 'Tourism for Tomorrow' awards in the destination category.
- Das Golden Stadttor Award for Best Commercial, 2006

Pacific Asia Travel Association;

- Grand award for Environment, 2006
- Gold award for Ecotourism, 2006
- Gold award for Publication, 2006
- Gold Award for E-Newsletter, 2005
- Honourable Mention for Culture, 2005
- Gold Award for Culture, 2004
- Gold Award for Ecotourism, 2004
- Gold Award for CD-ROM, 2004 and 2003
- Gold Award for Marketing, 2003
- Grand Award for Heritage, 2002

Pacific Asia Travel Writers Association;

- International Award for Leisure Tourism, 2000–2001.

Government of India;

- Best Performing Tourism State, 2005
- Best Maintained Tourist-friendly Monument, 2005
- Best Publishing, 2005
- Best Marketed and Promoted State, 2004.
- Best Maintained Tourist-friendly Monument, 2004
- Best Innovative Tourism Project, 2004
- Best Promotion Literature, 2004
- Best Publishing, 2004
- Best Performing State for 2003, 2001, 2000 and 1999-Award for Excellence in Tourism.
- Best Practices by a State Government, 2003
- Best Eco-tourism Product, 2003
- Best Wildlife Sanctuary, 2003

- Most Innovative Use of Information Technology, 2003 and 2001
- Most Tourist-friendly International Airport, 2002
- Most Eco-friendly Destination, 2002
- Best Tourism Film, 2001.

Outlook Traveller – TAAI;

- Best State that promoted Travel & Tourism, 2000–2001.

Federation of Indian Chambers of Commerce and Industry;

- Award for Best Marketing, 2003
- Award for Best Use of IT in Tourism, 2003.

Galileo-Express Travel & Tourism;

- Award for the Best Tourism Board, 2006
- Award for the Best State Tourism Board, 2003.

Madhya Pradesh

Madhya Pradesh is called the *"Heart of India"* because of its location in the centre of the country. It has been home to the cultural heritage of Hinduism, Islam, Buddhism, Sikhism, Jainism. Innumerable monuments, exquisitely carved temples, stupas, forts and palaces are dotted all over the State.

The temples of Khajuraho are world-famous for their erotic sculptures, and are a UNESCO World Heritage Site. Gwalior is famous for its forts, the Tomb of Rani Lakshmibai, and the Palace of Tansen.

Madhya Pradesh is also known as *Tiger State* because of the tiger population. Famous national parks like Kanha, Bandhavgadh, Shivpuri, Sanjay, Pench are located in MP. Spectacular mountain ranges, meandering rivers and miles and miles of dense forests offering a unique and exciting panorama of wildlife in sylvan surroundings.

Maharashtra

Maharashtra is the second most visited state in India by foreign tourists, with more than 2 million foreign tourists arrivals annually. Maharashtra boasts of a large number of popular and revered religious venues that are heavily frequented by locals as well as out-of-state visitors. Ajanta Caves, Ellora Caves and Victoria Terminus are the three UNESCO World Heritage sites in Maharashtra and are highly responsible for the development of

Tourism in the state. Mumbai is the most cosmopolitan city in India, and a great place to experience modern India. Mumbai famous for Bollywood, the world's largest film industry. In addition, Mumbai is famous for its clubs, shopping, and upscale gastronomy. The city is known for its architecture, from the ancient Elephanta Caves, to the Islamic Haji Ali Mosque, to the colonial architecture of Bombay High Court and Victoria Terminus.

Maharashtra also has numerous adventure tourism destinations, including paragliding, rock climbing, canoeing, kayaking, snorkelling, and scuba diving. Maharashtra also has several pristine national parks and reserves. The Bibi Ka Maqbara at Aurangabad the Mahalakshmi temple at Kolhapur, the cities of Nashik, Trimbak famous for religious importance and the city of Pune the seat of the Maratha Empire and the fantastic Ganesh Chaturthi celebrations together contribute for the Tourism sector of Mahrashtra.

Orissa

Orissa has been a preferred destination from ancient days for people who have an interest in spirituality, religion, culture, art and natural beauty. Ancient and medieval architecture, pristine sea beaches, the classical and ethnic dance forms and a variety of festivals. Orissa has kept the religion of Buddhism alive. Rock-edicts that have challenged time stand huge and over-powering by the banks of the river Daya. The torch of Buddhism is still ablaze in the sublime triangle at Udayagiri and Khandagiri Caves, on the banks of river Birupa. Precious fragments of a glorious past come alive in the shape of stupas, rock-cut caves, rock-edicts, excavated monasteries, viharas, chaityas and sacred relics in caskets and the Rock-edicts of Ashoka. Orissa is also famous for its well-preserved Hindu Temples, especially the Konark Sun Temple.

Orissa is the home for various tribal communities who have contributed uniquely to the multicultural and multilingual character of the state. Their handicrafts, different dance forms, jungle products and their unique life style blended with their healing practices have got world wide attention.

Puducherry

The Union Territory of Puducherry comprises four coastal regions viz-Puducherry, Karaikal, Mahe and Yanam. Puducherry is the Capital of this Union Territory and one of the most popular tourist destinations in South India. Puducherry has been described by National Geographic as "a glowing highlight of subcontinental sojourn". The city has many beautiful colonial buildings, churches, temples, and statues, which, combined with the systematic town planning and the well planned French style avenues, still preserve much of the colonial ambience.

Punjab

Punjab is one of India's most beautiful states. The state of Punjab is renowned for its cuisine, culture and history. Punjab has a vast public transportation and communication network. Some of the main cities in Punjab are Amritsar, Chandigarh, and Ludhiana. Punjab also has a rich religious history incorporating Sikhism and Hinduism. Tourism in Punjab is principally suited for the tourists interested in culture, ancient civilization, spirituality and epic history. Some of the villages in Punjab are also a must see for the person who wants to see the true Punjab, with their beautiful traditional Indian homes, farms and temples, this is a must see for any visitor that goes to Punjab.

Rajasthan

Rajasthan, literally meaning *"Land of the Kings"*, is one of the most attractive tourist destinations in Northern India. The vast sand dunes of the Thar Desert attract millions of tourists from around the globe every year.

Attractions:

- Jaipur-The capital of Rajasthan, famous for its rich history and royal architecture.
- Jodhpur-Fortress-city at the edge of the Thar Desert, famous for its blue homes and architecture.
- Udaipur-Known as the "Venice" of India.
- Jaisalmer-Famous for its golden fortress.
- Barmer-Barmer and surrounding areas offer perfect picture of typical Rajasthani villages.
- Bikaner-Famous for its medieval history as a trade route outpost.
- Mount Abu-Is the highest peak in the Aravalli Range of Rajasthan.
- Pushkar-It has the first and one of the very Brahma temples in the world.

- Nathdwara-This town near Udaipur hosts the famous temple of Shrinathji.
- Ranthambore-Situated near Sawai Madhopur, this town has one of the largest and most famous national parks in India.

Sikkim

Originally known as Suk-Heem, which in the local language means "peaceful home", Sikkim was an independent kingdom till the year 1974, when it became a part of the Republic of India. The capital of Sikkim is Gangtok, located approximately 185 kilometers from New Jalpaiguri, the nearest railway station to Sikkim.

Although, an airport is under construction at Dekiling in East Sikkim, the nearest airport to Sikkim would be Bagdogra. Sikkim is considered as the land of Orchids and mystic cultures and colorful traditions. Sikkim is well known among trekkers and adventure lovers, as West Sikkim has a lot to give them.

Places near Sikkim include Darjeeling also known as the Queen of hills and Kalimpong. Darjeeling, other than its world famous "Darjeeling tea" is also famous for its refined "Prep schools" founded during the British Raj. Kalimpong is also famous for its flora cultivation and is home to many internationally known Nurseries.

Tamil Nadu

Tamil Nadu lies in the southern Indian peninsula, on the shores of the Bay of Bengal. Many great rulers including the Cholas, Pallavas, Pandyas and the Vijayanagara Empire ruled over parts of Tamil Nadu. The state is known for its cultural heritage and temple architecture.

Attractions include Mahabalipuram, famous for its Shore Temple, Kanyakumari, the southernmost tip of India, Auroville, an International Utopian city, Mudumalai Wildlife Sanctuary, Ooty and Kodaikanal, two famous hill stations.

Uttarakhand

Uttaranchal is the 27th state of the Republic of India. It contains glaciers, snow-clad mountains, valley of flowers, skiing slopes and dense forests, and many shrines and places of pilgrimage. *Char-dhams,* the four most sacred and revered Hindu temples:

Badrinath, Kedarnath, Gangotri and Yamunotri are nestled in the Himalayas. Haridwar which means *Gateway to God* is the only place on the plains.

It holds the watershed for Gangetic River System spanning 300 km from Satluj in the west to Kali river in the east. Nanda Devi (25640 Ft) is the second highest peak in India after Kanchenjunga (28160 Ft). Dunagiri, Neelkanth, Chaukhamba, Panchachuli, Trisul are other peaks above 23000 Ft. It is considered the abode of *Devtas, Yakashyas, Kinners,* Fairies and Sages. It boasts of some old hill-stations developed during British era like Mussoorie, Almora and Nainital.

Glaciers Pindari Glacier, Milam Glacier, Gangotri Glacier, Bunder Punch Glacier, Khatling Glacier, Doonagiri Glacier, Dokrani Glacier, Kaphini Glacier, Ralam Glacier Wildlife Reserves Corbett National Park, Rajaji National Park, Asan Conservation Reserve, Nanda Devi National Park, Govind Wildlife Sanctuary, Askot Musk Deer Sanctuary (Askot), Valley of Flowers Adventure Sports Skiing at Mundali, Auli, Dayara Bagyal and Munsiyari. Trekking at Mussoorie, Uttarkashi, Joshimath, Munsiyari, Chaukori, Pauri, Almora, Nainital.

Uttar Pradesh

Situated in the northern part of India, Uttar Pradesh is important with its wealth of monuments and religious fervour. Geographically, Uttar Pradesh is very diverse, with Himalayan foothills in the extreme north, the Gangetic Plain in the centre, and the Vindhya Mountain Range towards the South. It is also home of India's most visited site, the Taj Mahal, and Hinduism's holiest city, Varanasi. The most populous state of the Indian Union also has a rich cultural heritage, and at the heart of North India, Uttar Pradesh has much to offer. Places of interest include Varanasi, Agra, Mathura, Jhansi, Prayag, Sarnath, Ayodhya, Dudhwa National Park and Fatehpur Sikri.

West Bengal

Kolkata, one of the many cities in the state of West Bengal has been nicknamed the City of Palaces. This comes from the numerous palatial mansions built all over the city. Unlike many north Indian cities, whose construction stresses minimalism, the layout of much of the architectural variety in Kolkata owes its origins to European styles and tastes imported by the British and, to a much lesser extent, the Portuguese and French. The buildings were designed and inspired by the tastes of the English gentleman around and the aspiring Bengali Babu (literally, a *nouveau riche* Bengali who aspired to cultivation of English etiquette, manners and custom, as such practices were favourable to monetary gains from the British). Today, many of these structures are in various stages of decay. Some of the major buildings of this period are well maintained and several buildings have been declared as heritage structures.

From historical point of view, the story of West Bengal begins from Gour and Pandua situated close to the present district town of Malda. The twin medieval cities had been sacked at least once by changing powers in the 15th century. However, ruins from the period still remain, and several architectural specimens still retain the glory and shin of those times. The Hindu architecture of Bishnupur in terracotta and laterite sandstone are renowned world over. Towards the British colonial period came the architecture of Murshidabad and Coochbehar.

Historic Monuments

The Taj Mahal is one of India's best-known sites and one of the best architectural achievements in India. Located in Agra, it was built between 1631 and 1653 by Emperor Shah Jahan in honour of his wife, Arjumand Banu, more popularly known as Mumtaz Mahal. The Taj Mahal serves as her tomb.

The Golden Temple is one of the most respected temples in India and the most sacred place for Sikhs. The Golden Temple is located in Amritsar, Punjab, India.

The Bahai temple in Delhi, was completed in 1986 and serves as the Mother Temple of the Indian Subcontinent. It has won numerous architectural awards and been featured in hundreds of newspaper and magazine articles.

Nature Tourism

India has geographical diversity, which resulted in varieties of nature tourism.

- Water falls in Western Ghats including Jog falls (highest in India).
- Western Ghats
- Kerala backwaters

- Hill Stations
- Wildlife reserves.

Wildlife in India

India is home to several well known large mammals including the Asian Elephant, Bengal Tiger, Asiatic Lion, Leopard and Indian Rhinoceros, often engrained culturally and religiously often being associated with deities. Other well known large Indian mammals include ungulates such as the domestic Asian Water buffalo, wild Asian Water buffalo, Nilgai, Gaur and several species of deer and antelope. Some members of the dog family such as the Indian Wolf, Bengal Fox, Golden Jackal and the Dhole or Wild Dogs are also widely distributed. It is also home to the Striped Hyaena, Macaques, Langurs and Mongoose species. India also has a large variety of protected wildlife. The country's protected wilderness consists of 75 National parks of India and 421 Sanctuaries, of which 19 fall under the purview of Project Tiger. Its climatic and geographic diversity makes it the home of over 350 mammals and 1200 bird species, many of which are unique to the subcontinent.

Some well known national wildlife sanctuaries include Bharatpur, Corbett, Kanha, Kaziranga, Periyar, Ranthambore and Sariska. The world's largest mangrove forest Sundarbans is located in southern West Bengal. The *Sundarbans* is UNESCO World Heritage Site.

Hill Stations

Several hill stations served as summer capitals of Indian provinces, princely states, or, in the case of Shimla, of British India itself. Since Indian Independence, the role of these hill stations as summer capitals has largely ended, but many hill stations remain popular summer resorts. Most famous hill stations are:

- Pachmarhi, Madhya Pradesh-It is also known as The Queen of Satpura.
- Araku, Andhra Pradesh
- Gulmarg, Srinagar and Laddakh in Jammu and Kashmir
- Darjeeling in West Bengal
- Munnar in Kerala
- Ooty and Kodaikanal in Tamil Nadu
- Shillong in Meghalaya
- Shimla, Kullu in Himachal Pradesh

- Nainital in Uttarakhand
- Gangtok in Sikkim
- Mussoorie in Uttarakhand.

In addition to the bustling hill stations and summer capitals of yore, there are several serene and peaceful nature retreats and places of interest to visit for a nature lover. These range from the stunning moonscapes of Leh and Ladhak, to small, exclusive nature retreats such as Dunagiri, Binsar, Mukteshwar in the Himalayas, to rolling vistas of Western Ghats to numerous private retreats in the rolling hills of Kerala.

Beaches

India offers a wide range of tropical beaches with silver/ golden sand to coral beaches of Lakshadweep. States like Kerala and Goa have exploited the potential of beaches to the fullest. However, there are a lot many unexploited beaches in the states of Andhra Pradesh, Gujarat, Maharastra, Tamil Nadu and Karnataka. These states have very high potential to be develop them as future destinations for prospective tourists. Some of the famous tourist beaches are:

- Beaches of Vizag, Andhra Pradesh
- Beaches of Puri, Orissa
- Beaches of Digha, West Bengal
- Beaches of Goa
- Kovalam Beach, Kerala
- Marina Beach, Chennai
- Beaches of Mahabalipuram
- Beaches in Mumbai
- Beaches of Diu
- Beaches of Midnapore, West Bengal
- Andaman and Nicobar Islands
- Lakshadweep Islands.

Adventure Tourism

- River rafting and kayaking in Himalayas
- Mountain climbing in Himalayas
- Rock climbing in Madhya Pradesh
- Skiing in Gulmarg or Auli

- Boat racing in Bhopal
- Paragliding in Maharashtra.

Promotional Tactics and Ethics for Tourism

To gain a broad understanding of a tourist organisations promotional requirements.

Activity

In association with your marketing assignment-you are required to complete a promotion strategy for your Bed and Breakfast business. This entails a detailed description of your promotion/media mix chosen and the rationale behind your choice. You are also required to identify the promotional messges you are conveying and how they relate to your target market.

Task

To create a sample of the type or mode of promotion you are intending to use:

- an advert-radio (mp3)
- video
- written advertisement in guidebooks
- brochure
- brand
- internet-web page.

Electronic Word-of-mouth in Hospitality and Tourism Management

Cyberspace has presented marketers with new avenues to improve the efficiency and effectiveness of communication, and new approaches for the acquisition and retention of customers (e.g., Osenton 2002; Wind, Mahajan and Gunther 2002). One aspect of cyberspace is the phenomenon of *online interpersonal influence*.

Because a fundamental principle of consumer behavior is that consumers have the ability to exert powerful influences upon each other, it is only natural that marketers seek to manage interpersonal influence (Dichter 1966; Haywood 1989), and with the spread of electronic technologies, it is not surprising that virtual interactions among consumers have proliferated (Goldsmith 2006). A good example of consumers sharing their hospitality and tourism opinions is the website *tripadvisor.com* – touted [by the company] as "the largest site for unbiased travel reviews [which] gives you the real story about hotels, attractions and restaurants around the world. It boasts more than 1,926,031 unbiased reviews and is updated every minute and every day by real travellers; it contains 'been there, done that' inside information; and 'the best deals for your travel dates'" (tripadvisor.com 2005).

Marketers, who have long sought to harness and manage interactions such as these to their own advantage have recently begun to consider and devise strategies to manage online interpersonal influence. Hospitality and tourism marketers find the issue of critical importance for the following reasons: hospitality and tourism product offerings, as intangible goods, cannot be evaluated before their consumption, thus elevating the importance of interpersonal influence (Lewis and Chambers 2000); many hospitality and tourism products are seen as high-risk purchases, for which the emotional risk of reference group evaluation is an important aspect of the decision making process (Lewis and Chambers 2000); hospitality and tourism products are both seasonal and perishable, raising marketing stress levels for providers; the hospitality and tourism industry is intensely competitive, suggesting that the use of online interpersonal influence may provide important competitive advantages for early adopters; and finally, considering the dearth of hospitality and tourism industry specific literature related to the issue, it would appear that the industry lags behind others in the development and discussion of strategies for managing interpersonal influence in an electronic environment. This paper first reviews related studies on interpersonal influence and WOM. It then provides a conceptual model including sources, mediating variables, and motivations for contributing and seeking WOM. Furthermore, the paper discusses WOM manifestation online and how eWOM differs from the traditional WOM. The paper then outlines challenges and opportunities for the tourism industry and suggests relevant marketing strategies to manage and enhance interpersonal influence online. Finally, the paper touches upon ethical issues related to the industry's use of the current technologies and suggests directions for future research.

Interpersonal Influence and Word-of-mouth

Consumers imitate each other following a social or vicarious learning paradigm (Hawkins, Best and Coney 2004), but perhaps more importantly, they also talk to each other. Described as word-of mouth communication (WOM), the process allows consumers to share information and opinions that direct buyers towards and away from specific products, brands, and services (Hawkins, Best and Coney 2004). Marketing research on WOM dates to the 1960's, and over time WOM definitions have evolved (Carl 2006). In the early years, WOM was defined as faceto-face communication about products or companies between those people who were not commercial entities. Later, Westbrook (1987) described WOM more broadly, to include "all informal communications directed at other consumers about the ownership, usage, or characteristics of particular goods and services or their sellers." While Westbrook didn't specifically define what constitute "informal communications", his writing clearly indicated that these are the communications of interpersonal relationships, as opposed to those through mass-media channels that pass product knowledge from producers/providers to consumers. Recently, Buttle (1998) argued that WOM can be mediated by electronic means. He also noted that "informal communications" might not be all inclusive; arguing the fact that more and more companies had adopted viral marketing practices which blurred the boundary between commercial messages and WOM (Lindgreen and Vanhamme 2005).

Thus, the key defining characteristic of WOM is the perceived independence of the source of the message. This definitional evolution indicates, with information technology today ubiquitous, that WOM is becoming both more pervasive and amorphous. In this paper, the authors accept the broadest of definitions: WOM is the communication between consumers about a product, service, or a company in which the sources are considered independent of commercial influence. Before considering WOM for hospitality and tourism management, there are a few general questions that should be answered to add to our foundation of understanding.

Why do consumers spread WOM? (Westbrook 1987) indicated, in a study that examined usage and post-purchase behavior of automobile and cable television purchasers, that positive and negative feelings associated with a product experience created inner tension and called for a discharge in the form of WOM. Other authors added to these emotions, and noted that a consumer's affective elements of satisfaction, pleasure, and sadness all motivated consumers to wish to share experiences with others.

Dellarocas, Fan, and Wood (2004) studied more than 50,000 rare coin auctions from eBay and found that eBay users, both buyers and sellers, exhibited reciprocity toward those other users who had rated them previously, and that they were more likely to rate their trading partners in order to increase chances of their being reciprocally rated. Further, many people simply enjoy sharing their travel experiences and expertise and such post-trip sharing can be one ot the joys of travel.

Where does WOM originate? The key WOM player is the opinion leader, an active user who interprets the meaning of media message content for others, i.e. opinion seekers. In past studies, opinion leadership has been found to be domain specific (Goldsmith and Flynn 1993). Opinion leaders are interested in particular product fields, make an effort to expose themselves to mass media sources, and are trusted by opinion seekers to provide knowledgeable advice. Numerous such relationships have been reported across a range of fields and products. From politics, Lazarsfeld, Berelson, and Gaudet (1944) noted a two-step communication flow in which political views were more profoundly influenced by communication between voters themselves than they were by the initial influence of the mass media. Research also has found that early adopters (not always, but often opinion leaders) who had satisfactory experience with automobile diagnostic centres led to positive WOM. Duhan, Johnson, Wilcox, and Harrell (1997) conducted a study on the selection of a provider of obstetric services by women of childbearing age. Their results showed that while the originators of WOM can be close friends, family, or relatives (i.e. strong ties), that they can be acquaintances or strangers (weak ties) as well.

What are some variables that mediate WOM? The literature suggest two types of mediating variables: those which influence the message originator and those which influence the listener. There are numerous examples of each in the literature. Gremler, Gwinner, and Brown (2001) studied the behavior of bank customers and dental patients and noted that a positive personal relationship between the company's employees and their customers resulted in a higher likelihood that customers would spread positive WOM about the firm. Dichter (1966), who researched the purchase decisions of more than 10,000 consumers, suggested that consumers with higher product involvement generated increased WOM.

(Derbaix and Vanhamme 2003)) surveyed 100 consumers identified as middle-to upper-middle class on their most recent purchase experience and found that the intensity of 'surprise' in the consumption process was positively correlated with WOM volume. From the listener's perspective, Sundaram and Webster (1999), who conducted a study on air conditioner purchase decisions by undergraduate students, demonstrated that the students' evaluation of an unfamiliar brand was more susceptible to change from WOM than was their attitude toward a familiar brand.

Earlier research by Arndt (1967) on the purchase behavior of discounted food products by married students showed that the degree of sociometric integration (i.e. the consumer's degree of integration into their community) was directly related to their willingness to receive WOM.

An experiment by (Laczniak, DeCarlo and Ramaswami 2001)) focused on the influence of negative WOM on purchase decisions for personal computers. Their results indicated that consumers considered the source of information, particularly negative information, before having a change of opinion about a product or service. Thus, there are myriad variables that can affect the effectiveness of WOM as a means of influencing consumer behavior. It seems that the more we study the phenomenon, the more mediating variables emerge from the research.

What are the expected outcomes from the dissemination of WOM? Unsurprisingly, the overarching conclusion is that favourable WOM increases the probability of purchase, while negative WOM has the opposite effect. Such a finding has remained largely unchanged since shared by Arndt in 1967. A study by Mahajan, Muller, and Bass (1990) extended the earlier work of Arndt (1967) and found that WOM could influence product evaluations. Recently,

Gruen, Osmonbekov, and Czaplewski (2005) studied one specific form of WOM, the online "know-how forum" and determined that online WOM impacted not only the receiver's perceived value of a company's products, but also their loyalty intentions. Thus, the exchange of product information through WOM empowers consumers and lessen producer/consumer information asymmetries, ultimately resulting in an acceleration or deceleration of product acceptance (Bass, 1969).

Applications of Word-of-Mouth

Interpersonal influence flows from opinion leaders to followers, but also spreads as a result of relationships among followers. Marketers hoping to harness these relationships seek to create 'buzz', defined by Thomas (2004) as the "amplification of initial marketing efforts by third parties through their passive or active influence." This can be accomplished through *stimulation* – advertising and other promotion techniques that get consumers talking about brands; and *simulation* – strategies such as a store creating a 'teen fashion panel' or simply the depiction in ads of consumers discussing brands or seeking information from opinion leaders.

Several recent well-documented examples of product proliferation through the power of 'buzz' have included, in the USA, the box office success of *The Blair Witch Project* (Streisand 1999), the meteoric diffusion of BOTOX (Ries and Ries 2002), and the pre-lowcarb cult-like status of Krispy Kreme Doughnuts (Serwer 2003). In Germany, the release of the Harry Potter books was accomplished by relying solely upon reviews to create awareness and demand (Fuchs 2003). An interesting application of 'buzz' in Asia was orchestrated by Adidas.

Looking to overcome the marketing disadvantage of not being an official sponsor of the Japanese Olympic Federation, the company ran a series of unofficial offbeat events, such as World Bus Pulling Championship and vertical 100-metre sprints up the staircases of buildings in Osaka and Hong Kong (*Media Asia 2005)*. For each of these examples, success was attributed not to the product's traditional advertising or public relations campaign, but rather to their promoter's creation of 'buzz' through their use of non-traditional WOM promotional strategies.

Word-of-Mouth in Hospitality and Tourism Industry

Interpersonal communications have long been recognized as influential in the tourism industry. In fact, seminal travel and tourism theories such as Cohen's (1972) 'drifter, explorer, mass tourist' typology, Plog's (1974) 'theory of allocentricity and psychocentricity', and Butler's (1980) 'tourist area life cycle model' are each based upon the observation that it is the innovative and adventurous tourists that discover new destinations or tourism products, who then, acting as opinion leaders, share their experiences with their "less intrepid cousins", thus creating diffusion and marketing momentum for new destinations and innovative travel products.

Recent research in the tourism area has demonstrated the influence of both positive and negative WOM upon tourism products, in studies across a broad range of nations. Among these, Morgan, Pritchard, and Piggott's (2003) New Zealand based research noted that negative WOM can have an overwhelming impact upon a destination's image, as dissatisfied visitors spread unflattering comments related to their experiences. Crick's (2003) Caribbean study similarly warned that when locals display hostile feelings towards tourists, the result is negative WOM and a likely downturn in the industry. O'Neill, Palmer and Charters (2002) studied wine tourism in Australia, and found that visitors' WOM recommendations boost wine sales when vacationing opinion leaders return home and tell others of their experiences; Shanka, Ali-Knight and Pope's (2002) study of destination selection methods found that a majority of Western Australia travel decisions were based upon WOM communications; and Diaz-Martin, Iglesias, Vázquez, and Ruiz (2000) found, in their study of Spanish tourists, that while positive WOM increases expectations, it also makes it that much more difficult to satisfy these expectations, an interesting dichotomy.

Morgan, Pritchard, and Pride (2002) studied Wales tourism marketing, and noted the potential of WOM as an effective tool for spreading the 'visit Wales' message through the Welsh diaspora. In a USA based study, Litvin, Blose and Laird (2004) noted that tourists' restaurant selections were predominantly influenced by the WOM recommendations of opinion leaders, with surprisingly few decisions based on the influences of more formal media. These authors suggested that restaurant marketers seeking the tourist trade shift their emphasis from traditional marketing channels (advertising and public relations) to nontraditional interpersonal marketing strategies. In a cross-cultural study that employed a sample comprised of travellers from the UK, Germany, Japan, Brazil and Taiwan, Crotts and Erdmann (2000) noted that while complaint behavior was found across the full range of their sample that Hofstede's dimension of masculinity helped to explain the likelihood that those of different cultures would pass along their complaint through WOM to other travellers. An interesting hospitality example relates to *Yours is a Very Bad Hotel*, by Farmer and Atchison (2001), a Power Point presentation that discussed what its creators considered to have been a poor lodging experience at a Houston Double Tree hotel property. Per Shea, Enghagen and Khullar (2004), Farmer and Atchison never intended their presentation to be made public, but through the power of electronic communications, the presentation was passed along in rapid fashion until it had spread among business travellers and academics worldwide, generated in excess of 4,000 email responses to Farmer and Atchison, and created an untold amount of negative 'buzz' for both the property and the chain.

Electronic Word-of-mouth and Tourism

With the advancements of Internet technologies, increasing numbers of travellers are using the Internet to seek destination information and to conduct transactions online. According to the Travel Industry Association of America (TIA 2005), 67 percent of US travellers have used the Internet to search for information on destinations or check prices or schedules. Even more impressively, 41 percent of US travellers have booked at least some aspects of their trips via the medium. Germane to this paper, the Internet has enabled new forms of communication platforms which have the ability to further empower both providers and consumers, allowing a vehicle for the sharing of information and opinions both from Business to Consumer, and from Consumer to Consumer. It is within these contexts that we consider the concept of eWOM.

Defining Electronic Word-of-mouth (eWOM)

Based on the definition of WOM by Westbrook (1987), electronic Word-of-Mouth (eWOM) can be defined as all informal communications directed at consumers through Internet-based technology related to the usage or characteristics of particular goods and services, or their sellers. This includes communication between producers and consumers as well as those between consumers themselves – both integral parts of the WOM flow, and both distinctly differentiated from communications through mass media (Goldsmith 2006; Lazarsfeld, Berelson, and Gaudet, 1944).

A Typology of eWOM Media

Several types of electronic media have an impact upon interpersonal relationships. Each possess different characteristics. Some are synchronous, such as Instant Messaging; while others are asynchronous, such as email and blogs. Some communications link one consumer with another, such as email; while others connect a single consumer with many others.

Challenges and Opportunities of eWOM

The digitalization of word-of-mouth has created both new possibilities and challenges for marketers. Per (Dellarocas 2003)): 1) with the low cost of access and information exchange, electronic word-of-mouth can appear in an unprecedented large scale, potentially creating new dynamics in the market; 2) though broader in scope, the technology allows for greater control over format and communication types; and 3) new problems may arise given the anonymity of communicators, potentially leading to intentionally misleading and out-ofcontext messages.

In light of the media's low cost, broader scope, and increased anonymity, it seems likely, as time progresses, that consumers in increasingly larger numbers will either seek or simply be exposed to the advice of online opinion leaders.

More importantly, and different from the ephemeral nature of traditional WOM, eWOM exists in online 'space' which can be accessed, linked, and searched. Given that travellers are relying more and more on search engines to locate travel information (eMarketer 2006), eWOM will inevitably change the structure of travel information, the accessibility of travel information, and subsequently travellers' knowledge and perception of various travel products.

For example, the dominant online search engine Google uses the Page Rank algorithm that utilizes the link structure of the web space and the content of web pages to rank the most authoritative and relevant web pages (Brin and Page 1998). 'Google bombing' is a practice in which savvy users of Google take advantage of the knowledge of Google's algorithm to manipulate search results when the user types a Google query (Tatum 2005). eWOM can actually become a tool that 'Google bombers' may use in manipulating the hyperlink structure of the web space so as to influence the returned results in Google. As such, far different from physical WOM, eWOM can create virtual relationships and communities, with influence far beyond the readers and producers of WOM; it actually creates a new type of reality by influencing readers during their online information searches.

Strategies for Managing eWOM in Hospitality and Tourism

The unique properties and environment of the Internet discussed above necessitate a new view of the dynamics of online eWOM, and new strategies for managing them. These can be classified into two major categories: informational and revenue generating. From an informational perspective, procedures need to be established that allow hospitality and tourism marketers to harvest discussion and feedback created online. Harvested information about the property and destination can then be used to accomplish such tasks as: enhancing visitor satisfaction through product improvement; solving visitor problems; discovering what visitors say – good and bad – about their experiences; analyzing competitive strategies; and monitoring company reputation/image. Of no less importance is the need to manage eWOM for purposes of revenue generation (Kirkpatrick and Roth 2005).

These efforts could be directed toward spreading good WOM about the property and destination – helping potential visitors seeking information by providing reinforcing images and opinions. Encouraging or stimulating good eWOM should result in enhanced business activity. Below are specific strategy suggestions for hospitality and tourism marketers to accomplish these goals in cyberspace. Ethical issues related to the potential abuse of these practices are then briefly considered.

Email (and Instant Messaging)

Email is an asynchronous, one-to-one medium for which privacy is a primary concern. An advantage of a marketer utilizing email versus traditional mail is that email list size does not correlate with emailing costs, as the variable expense of stationery, reproduction, and postage are negated. Once names and email addresses have been obtained, mass emailings that pique interest, or at least do not offend or annoy, become a highly efficient means of communication between a hospitality provider and its past and potential guests. Keeping mailing lists current is both a challenge and a necessity. However the good news is that 'bad' addresses embedded in an emailing list add virtually nothing to distribution costs, other than the minimal time and energy required to process returned email messages.

While lists of names that fit specific geographic or demographic criteria can be purchased, no better prospects exist than past and present clientele. As do airlines and major hotel chains in conjunction with their frequent flyer or guest programs, hotels and car rental agencies should make the collection of email addresses an integral step in their reservation and check-in process. Restaurants, carriage tour companies, and visitor attractions should provide guests with cards asking for their email addresses, offering as possible incentive a free appetizer or future discount. Regular mass emailings and e-newsletters with links to web sites can then be sent to list members hyping future promotions and events. In a paper-based marketing channel, large distribution lists translate into high printing costs. For e-newsletters, the marginal cost of sending a thousand versus a million messages is nil, except for the time involved managing the list. The larger the list size, the greater the potential for reaching potential customers. Email distribution has successfully allowed marketers to sidestep the traditional marketing tradeoff of distribution breadth versus message depth and should be adopted aggressively.

Users, however, distain junk mails and most of them will view email only from trusted sources. Marketers thus need to adopt strategies that provide the receiver a reason to open, perhaps even welcome the provider's email offerings, and to pass them on to others. Marketers can entice email recipients to forward their communications to others (eWOM) by emotionalizing their communications, including an element of surprise, making them humerous, or providing incentives (Lindgreen and Vanhamme 2005). Email communications should also include links to web pages or bulletin boards to further encourage online interaction. Travel is a product that people enjoy reading about and talking about, and travel opinion leaders delighted for opportunities to share their experiences with others. Organizations within the hospitality and tourism industry have an excellent opportunity for success by creating 'buzz' through their effective use of emails.

Websites

The website is an asynchronous, one-to-many medium. While generally a passive means of communication, websites can be used to create the first step of 'buzz' in order to stimulate eWOM among visitors. As does traditional advertising, an effective website should not only share information, but also create a desire to learn more about the product or destination and ideally induce a desire to visit. eWOM can be created online by offering web visitors the ability to access the opinions of satisfied guests. To accomplish this, positive product reviews and the posting of customer comments should be highlighted on the company's web pages. Further, guests should find links to company sponsored bulletin boards where they will be invited to take on the role of opinion leader by expressing their own views and sharing their personal experiences about the destination, hotel, restaurant, etc. Loyal customers should also be encouraged to post links on their personal websites that direct visitors to the tourism provider's website. The key idea is to nurture a community of interest in which visitors and potential visitors talk about the destination product as part of their shared interest in travel. Making it easy for these folks to post their vacation pictures on both the company's web site as well as their own web site encourages eWOM. Travellers, food aficionados, and those with other special interests are eager to share their experiences with others. The hospitality and tourism organization's web page should provide them a ready forum.

Blogs and Virtual Communities, Newsgroups, Chatrooms, Product Review Sites, etc.

These communication media each have their own level of interactivity and communication mode. Blogs and virtual communities, for example, are asynchronous channels that writers and readers access at different times; though an active message board can near synchronous access by its members. Conversely, newsgroups and chat rooms are synchronous. Relevant strategies differ for company sponsored or controlled media, versus public media. For company media, the key is to stimulate usage and to make bulletin boards interesting and lively so that users return often to the site. Allowing and encouraging eWOM on the site through posted comments can provide the host company genuine and untainted consumer feedback, while at the same time providing a service recovery mechanism to reply, rebut, or rebuff negative comments. Further, the electronic forum allows management to demonstrate their caring and concern; providing positive reassurance to potential visitors and guests, as well as to their own employees. Even hate sites (e.g. the anti-United Airlines site 'Untied') provide feedback opportunities to learn more about one's customers (Wolrich 2005) and should be monitored regularly to provide management with important, timely, feedback. Some of these public media are highly active. *Lonely Planet*'s (2006) moderated discussion boards, geared to the budget traveller, has registered 350,000 users. At the higher end of the traveller spectrum, *Condé Nast Traveller's* (2006) "The Perrin Post" travel blog attracts lively discussion on a wide range of travel topics laced with comments by Wendy Perrin, the magazine's Consumer News Editor.

Management, however, must appreciate that postings to bulletin boards, newsgroups and certainly hate sites generally fail to represent anything resembling a random sample of consumers. Research has found that most participants tend to be those with opinions either very favourable or very unfavourable toward the service, with the mid-range majority far less inclined to post their opinions – thus creating a "U" shaped response curve. But while not statistically significant, posted comments can certainly convey a sense of customer satisfaction level in a more neutral environment then can the companysponsored sites. Monitoring allows management to post responses to critical comments, possibly diffusing potential negativity. Importantly, these sites also provide a free and unbiased window through which to glimpse one's competitors' customer satisfaction levels.

The advancement of information technologies, automated web syndication tools such as RSS, and forum monitoring have provided travel marketers feasible and cost-effective ways to assess their customer-perceived service quality and satisfaction, while helping to improve their travellers' overall experiences.

Blogs and Virtual Communities

Blogs (weblogs or online diaries) can be used in a similar manner as discussed above. A good example of the use of blogs to spread positive eWOM was reported by Kaikati and Kaikati (2004) who chronicled Dr. Pepper's use of blogging to create 'buzz' for a new dairy-based soft drink targeted at the youth market. The company invited well-read young bloggers and their parents to their Dallas company headquarters for a product introduction and a week of orientation. In exchange for creating blog diary reports that hyped the new drink, the young recruits were rewarded with promotional materials and free product samples. Similarly, travellers are likely to share their own travel experience and to read of other traveller's trips. Hospitality and tourism companies might consider identifying popular bloggers that appeal to the demographics they wish to attract and inviting these folks for a destination visit or complementary meal, etc. – similar to the familiarization trips that destinations have long provided travel agents, writers, and journalists whose enhanced first-hand product knowledge have made better sellers and stronger advocates of their products.

Virtual communities are groups of online individuals who share interests and interact with one another. Because of the ease of linking web sites, Blogs can be a part of virtual communities along with bulletin boards and chat rooms. Virtual communities vary in the scope of their content from fairly simple lists of resources to complex cyber environments offering net-citizens information and the opportunity to socialize with likeminded individuals. Some of these have arisen spontaneously, while others have been sponsored or managed by companies. Examples would be communities based on shared interests (such as wine-enthusiasts' Virtual Vineyards), or communities held together by product or brand loyalties (e.g., Apple.com/usergroups). In any case, these virtual environments represent fertile territory for the dissemination of eWOM and the creation of 'buzz'.

Some Brief Ethical Concerns

Though the above strategies are presented as positive proactive marketing activities, it is not hard to envision marketers easily overstepping their ethical boundaries. For example, even the most benign strategy, email, presents several ethical concerns. Ease of use and the virtual cost-free (on a variable cost basis) nature of emails can lead to abundant abuse – as most can attest from the amount of junk emails received daily. It is thus important that hospitality and tourism organizations treat the medium as a form of 'permission-granted' marketing, such that all emailings are *requested, respectful, and relevant* (Osenton 2002). Further, when sending emails, the source should be clearly designated and never disguised; unnecessary mailings should be avoided; mailing addresses should not be sold without permission; and 'opt-out' requests should be handled promptly and courteously.

When considering other electronic media, potential abuses are more ominous. Many of these can be classified under the banner of *stealth marketing*. The practice of stealth marketing is defined as "employing tactics that engage the prospect without them knowing they are being marketed" (Neisser 2004). Taylor

(2003) traced its use to the early days of British theater, when the theater company would plant people in their audience, paying them a shilling to stand up and shout "Bravo!" (ergo, the source of the term 'shill' coming to mean a front-man or decoy). A current high profile example was a recent Sony Ericcson's picture-phone campaign that relied upon unsuspecting tourists being handed a picture-phone by an actor posing as a fellow tourist, and being asked to take a picture of the actor. The tourist was shown how simple the phone was to operate and engaged in a discussion about the new technology. The intent was to expose the product during its early adoption stage in order to initiate WOM, and thus create 'buzz'. Though treated negatively during a CBS "60 Minutes" story, the company defended its efforts as a highly successful public relations campaign (Atkinson 2004). Following are some other interesting stealth marketing examples, the ethics of which we leave to the reader's personal judgment:

- aylor (2003) noted that for years liquor companies have provided their sales staff 'walking around funds' to surreptitiously purchase drinks of their company's brands for bar patrons.
- Tobacco companies have hired young attractive smokers to offer new brand cigarettes to others in bars (Kaikati and Kaikati 2004).
- Record companies have employed the tactic of hiring young 'hip' music fans to discuss the company's new releases among themselves in music stores, with the intent of being overheard by shoppers (Kuntz and Weber 1996).

Though the above descriptions and definitions may or may not raise alarm, they are difficult to reconcile with the American Marketing Association's Code of Ethics, which specifically prohibits the deliberate misleading of consumers (AMA 2005).

Online 'stealth marketing' tactics that could tempt hospitality and tourism marketers to promote eWOM and 'buzz' are easily envisioned. The most obvious of these is the use of employees to pose online as consumers in order to post positive comments on behalf of the company. Such postings could be on the company's website forum or on public bulletin boards and newsgroups. To make this effective, employees could be provided with scripted postings to provide a stream of product reviews and comments. As their postings would appear to be from knowledgeable users and not company 'shills', the employees would assume the role of e-opinion leaders, generating enhanced visitorship from opinion seekers who rely upon their expertise. It is important to note how easy the new technologies make implementation of such a strategy, and how virtually undetectable such subterfuge would be to net habitus. Taking this just one step further leads to thinner ethical ice. Equally as easy to implement, and just as hard to detect, would be having employees post negative comments regarding the competition. These could be in the form of harsh restaurant, destination, or property reviews on travel review sites; the posting of complaints to a lack of follow-up to non-existent problems on travel Web Boards; the seeding of negatively toned discussion streams within travel chat rooms; or even be the genesis of new hate sites directed at a targeted competitor.

It does not take much imagination to come up with a list of potential abuses, and even less imagination to consider the damage that could be done by spreading negative eWOM through these readily accessible media. Abuse of online communities would similarly take little effort or imagination. An employee could be encouraged or specifically charged with infiltrating his/her avatar into an e-community. Once an accepted net-citizen, he/she would be in a position to interject or initiate positive comments into conversations regarding his/her employer, and negative comments regarding the competition. If recognized as a knowledgeable traveller and trusted voice within the community, the eWOM disseminated could have significant influence on other members' hospitality and tourism purchase decisions. The serendipitous use of blogs has similar issues. Kaikati and Kaikati (2004) indicated that bloggers who took part in the previously discussed Dr. Pepper offer were criticized by peers for not respecting the purity of their medium. Beyond the issue of 'blog culture', opportunities abound for abuse by bloggers that fail to report their company affiliations. Nobody licenses blogs and their intellectual freedom is one of the medium's principle attractions. However, this same lack of control is an open door for abuse. While we certainly hope that our industry would not indulge in the ethically questionable practices discussed above, it is not hard to envision their temptation. Clearly, the issue of ethics and eWOM calls for intense further study in order to demarcate a well defined boundary between the ethical practice of managing eWOM, and its abuse.

Final Comments

This paper has proposed a conceptual model of WOM and discussed a series of available strategies for harnessing the power of the media for hospitality and tourism providers to stimulate their marketing efforts. The nascent field of eWOM appears to incorporate many of the traditional off-line techniques for managing interpersonal influence (i.e., stimulating and creating opinion leaders), while at the same time creating new techniques enabled by the unique characteristics of cyberspace. Hospitality and tourism marketers must understand that their guests are going online in increasing numbers and that in their electronic universe these consumers are exposed to and are likely influenced by the many sites devoted to the selling or discussion of travel. Tourism marketers should take the lead in understanding and utilizing the emerging technologies, rather than being driven by the adoption of strategies by their competitors.

There has been a significant change in the distribution of travel products over the past decade, and much has been written about the demise of the travel agent. However, while the traditional 'brick and mortar' leisure travel agency has found the new electronic environment challenging, a new generation of intermediaries, such as Expedia, Travelocity, Hotels.com, Cruise Critic, etc. are quite successfully filling the void. In the past, neighborhood travel agents, selling third party products, served as trusted opinion leaders to their clients. This relationship led tourism industry providers to work hard to cultivate relationships with travel agent intermediaries, hoping the travel agent would then be influential in moving incremental

company invited well-read young bloggers and their parents to their Dallas company headquarters for a product introduction and a week of orientation. In exchange for creating blog diary reports that hyped the new drink, the young recruits were rewarded with promotional materials and free product samples. Similarly, travellers are likely to share their own travel experience and to read of other traveller's trips. Hospitality and tourism companies might consider identifying popular bloggers that appeal to the demographics they wish to attract and inviting these folks for a destination visit or complementary meal, etc. – similar to the familiarization trips that destinations have long provided travel agents, writers, and journalists whose enhanced first-hand product knowledge have made better sellers and stronger advocates of their products.

Virtual communities are groups of online individuals who share interests and interact with one another. Because of the ease of linking web sites, Blogs can be a part of virtual communities along with bulletin boards and chat rooms. Virtual communities vary in the scope of their content from fairly simple lists of resources to complex cyber environments offering net-citizens information and the opportunity to socialize with likeminded individuals. Some of these have arisen spontaneously, while others have been sponsored or managed by companies. Examples would be communities based on shared interests (such as wine-enthusiasts' Virtual Vineyards), or communities held together by product or brand loyalties (e.g., Apple.com/usergroups). In any case, these virtual environments represent fertile territory for the dissemination of eWOM and the creation of 'buzz'.

Directions for Future Research

This paper has sought to introduce the topic of eWOM to the hospitality and tourism community by providing a conceptual model of eWOM, discussing its management strategies, and touching upon ethical concerns. It has also briefly raised issues regarding potential abuse. Future research related to the application of eWOM strategies should now move to the practical, with studies designed to measure the cognitive, affective, and behavioural implications upon traveller behavior and the new dynamics created by eWOM. Researchers will have to devise new methods to study online interpersonal influence so that they can test theoretical propositions derived from the existing literature on social influence. The area is likely to provide a rich and interesting stream of exploration. For example, study should be made of what kind of information consumers seek online and how they actually use the information they acquire online from other consumers to make their travel and hospitality decisions. How much weight do they give personal sources versus impersonal sources? Do they acquire different types of information from each type of source, or are all topics equally queried using both sources? When information from personal and impersonal sources is acquired, do consumers maintain these source distinctions, or do they treat all the information as if it came from one source? Lacking face-to-face contact with opinion givers, what cues do consumers use to assign trust to online social influences? If consumers become aware of dubious ethical practices, how do they react? Will they actively attack the unethical sponsor, spread negative eWOM to others, and/or complain to third-part authorities?

Beyond the above macro-oriented questions, on a practical level, managers should initiate their own studies focused on their specific sites to assess the level of current eWOM and test tactics to increase it. Electronic Word-of-Mouth should be made part of an overall marketing and promotion strategy. Since unethical practices can be exposed and publicized by the online community, these should be strenuously avoided, and attacks vigorously defended. Given the powerful influence of eWOM, it should not be ignored or abused, but nourished and managed to improve the efficiency and effectiveness of the hospitality and tourism firm's marketing strategies.

3

World Tourism Organization

The World Tourism Organization (UNWTO), based in Madrid, Spain, is a United Nations agency dealing with questions relating to tourism. It compiles the World Tourism rankings. The World Tourism Organization is a significant global body, concerned with the collection and collation of statistical information on international tourism. This organization represents public sector tourism bodies, from most countries in the world and the publication of its data makes possible comparisons of the flow and growth of tourism on a global scale. The official languages of UNWTO are Arabic, English, French, Russian and Spanish.

Organizational Aims

The World Tourism Organization plays a role in promoting the development of responsible, sustainable and universally accessible tourism, paying particular attention to the interests of developing countries.

The Organization encourages the implementation of the Global Code of Ethics for Tourism, with a view to ensuring that member countries, tourist destinations and businesses maximize the positive economic, social and cultural effects of tourism and fully reap its benefits, while minimizing its negative social and environmental impacts. UNWTO is committed to the United Nations Millennium Development Goals, geared toward reducing poverty and fostering sustainable development.

History

The origin of the World Tourism Organization stems back to 1925 when the International Congress of Official Tourist Traffic Associations (ICOTT) was formed at The Hague. Some articles from early volumes of the Annals of Tourism Research, claim that the UNWTO originated from the International Union of Official Tourist Publicity Organizations (IUOTPO), although the UNWTO states that the ICOTT became the International Union of Official Tourist Propaganda Organizations first in 1934.

Following the end of the Second World War and with international travel numbers increasing, the IUOTPO restructured itself into the International Union of Official Travel Organizations (IUOTO). A technical, non-governmental organization, the IUOTO was made up of a combination of national tourist organizations, industry and consumer groups. The goals and objectives of the IUOTO were to not only promote tourism in general but also to extract the best out of tourism as an international trade component and as an economic development strategy for developing nations.

Towards the end of the 1960's, the IUOTO realized the need for further transformation to enhance its role on an international level. The 20th IUOTO general assembly in Tokyo, 1967, declared the need for the creation of an intergovernmental body with the necessary abilities to function on an international level in cooperation with other international agencies, in particular the United Nations. Throughout the existence of the IUOTO, close ties had been established between the organization and the United Nations (UN) and initial suggestions had the IUOTO becoming part of the UN. However, following the circulation of a draft convention, consensus held that any resultant intergovernmental organization should be closely linked to the UN but preserve its "complete administrative and financial autonomy".

In 1970, the IUOTO general assembly voted in favour of forming the World Tourism Organization (WTO), based on statutes of the IUOTO, and after ratification by the prescribed 51 states, the WTO came into operation on November 1, 1974.

Most recently, at the fifteenth general assembly in 2003, the WTO general council and the UN agreed to establish the WTO as a specialized agency of the UN. The significance of this collaboration, WTO Secretary-General Mr. Francesco Frangialli claimed, would lie in "the increased visibility it gives the WTO, and the recognition that will be accorded to [it]. Tourism will be considered on an equal footing with other major activities of human society". As of 2007, its membership included 150 countries, seven territories and some 350 affiliate members, representing the private sector, educational institutions, tourism associations and local tourism authorities. The frequent confusion between the two WTOs – World Tourism Organization and the Geneva-based World Trade Organization – officially ended on 1 December 2005, when the General Assembly approved to add the letters UN (for United Nations) to the start of abbreviation of the leading international tourism body in English and in Russian. UNWTO abbreviation remains OMT in French and Spanish. UNWTO General Assembly concluded its work at its 16th session in Dakar, Senegal, on 2 December 2005.

Structure

General Assembly

The General Assembly is the supreme organ of the Organization. Its ordinary sessions, held every two years, are attended by delegates of the Full and Associate members, as well as representatives from the Business Council It is the most important meeting of senior tourism officials and high-level representatives of the private sector from all over the world.

Regional Commissions

Established in 1975 as subsidiary organs of the General Assembly, the six Regional Commissions normally meet once a year. They enable member States to maintain contact with one another and with the Secretariat between sessions of the General assembly, to which they submit their proposals and convey their concerns. Each commission elects one Chairman and its Vice-Chairmen from among its Members for a term of two years commencing from one session to the next session of the Assembly.

Executive Council

The Executive Council's task is to take all necessary measures, in consultation with the Secretary-General, for the implementation of its own decisions and recommendations of the Assembly and report there on to the Assembly The Council meets at least twice a yearly the Council consists of Full Members elected by the Assembly in the proportion of one Member for every five Full Members, in accordance with the Rules of Procedure laid down by the Assembly with a view to achieving fair and equitable geographical distributional The term of office of Members elected to the Council is four years and elections for one-half of the

Council membership are held every two years. Spain is a Permanent member of the Executive Conceal.

Committees

World Committee on Tourism Ethics programme Committee on Budget and Finance committee on Market and Competitiveness Committee on Statistics and the Tourism Satellite account Sustainable Development of Tourism Committee on Poverty Reduction Committee for the Review of Applications for Affiliate Membership.

Secretariat

The Secretariat is led by Secretary-General ad interim Tale Rifai of Jordan, who supervises about 110 full-time staff at UNWTO's Madrid Headquarters. He is assisted by the Deputy Secretary-General. These officials are responsible for implementing UNWTO's programme of work and serving the needs of Members. The Affiliate Members are supported by a full-time Executive Director at the Madrid Headquarters. The secretariat also includes a regional support office for Asia-Pacific in Osaka, Japan, financed by the Japanese Government.

Sustainable Tourism: Towards Earth Summit (2002)

Sustainable Tourism – Turning the Tide

There are a myriad of definitions for Sustainable Tourism, including ecotourism, green travel, environmentally and culturally responsible tourism, fair trade and ethical travel. The most widely accepted definition is that of the World Tourism Organisation. They define sustainable tourism as *"tourism which leads to management of all resources in such a way that economic, social and aesthetic needs can be fulfilled while maintaining cultural integrity, essential ecological processes, biological diversity and life support systems."* In addition they describe the development of sustainable tourism as a process which meets the needs of present tourists and host communities whilst protecting and enhancing needs in the future (World Tourism Organisation 1996).

Tourism is one of the world's largest industries. For developing countries it is also one of the biggest income generators. But the huge infrastructural and resource demands of tourism (e.g. water consumption, waste generation and energy use) can have severe impacts upon local communities and the environment if it is not properly managed. To reach this current state, we have witnessed an exponential growth in global tourism over the past half century. 25 million international visitors in 1950 grew to an estimated 650 million people by the year 2000 (Roe et al 1997). Several factors have contributed to this rise in consumer demand in recent decades. This includes an increase in the standard of living in the developed countries, greater allowances for holiday entitlements and declining costs of travel. Tourism is an important export for a large number of developing countries, and the principal export for about a third of these. Statistics for domestic tourism are not so easily available. However it is certain that domestic tourism is also growing rapidly in many Asian and Latin American countries (Goodwin 2000).

World Travel and Tourism Council (WTTC) estimates show that in 2002 travel, tourism and related activities will contribute 11% to the world's GDP, rising to about 12% by 2010. The industry is currently estimated to generate 1 in every 12.8 jobs or 7.8% of the total workforce. This percentage is expected to rise to 8.6% by 2012. Tourism is also the world's largest employer, accounting for more than 255 million jobs, or 10.7% of the global labour force (WTTC 2002).

It is clear that ecotourism, in the strictest sense of the word, still only accounts for a small proportion of the total tourism market. Current estimates are between 3-7% of the market (WTTC, WTO, Earth Council 1996). Taking the WTO's full definition of tourism, there's a risk that ecotourism alone will fail to fully realise the potential to support more sustainable development across the entire sector – suggesting that there may be real benefits trying to make all of the Travel and Tourism industry more sustainable.

Current Global and Regional Trends

Tourism and Travel Statistics and Trends

The magnitude of the tourism industry can be clearly seen from the World Travel and Tourism Council (WTTC) statistics. The WTTC estimates that in the year 2002, travel, tourism and related activities will contribute to approximately 10% of the world's GDP, growing to 10.6% by 2012. The industry is currently estimated to help generate 1 in every 12.8 jobs, 7.8% of total employment. This will rise to 8.6% by 2012 (WTTC 2002).

Tourism has helped to create millions of jobs in developing countries. For example official estimates for 2002 suggest China has 51.1 million jobs associated to tourism and India 23.7 million jobs. In terms of the relative importance of different sectors for job creation, the largest contributors in travel and tourism employment are found in island states and destinations-ranging from 76.3% of the total number of people employed in Curacao, to 34.6% employment in Antigua and Barbuda. The top ten countries with greatest expected relative growth in employment over the next ten years are all developing countries is predicted an annual growth rate of 8.8% in employment and tops the list. The balance of benefits begins to tilt toward the developed countries in terms of visitor exports and capital investments, in absolute terms. The top ten list for visitor exports is led by the US. The rest are all European countries, except for China. On capital investments, US receives an estimated investment of US$ 205.2 million-far ahead of all other countries. Japan with an investment of US$ 42.7 million and China with US$ 42.5 million follow. The expected growth rates for capital investments over the next ten years are significant for developing countries. Turkey has an annualised growth rate of 10.4% (WTTC 2002). Whilst it can be argued that tourism creates an incentive for environmental conservation, tourism is also responsible for damage to the environment. The phenomenal growth of the sector has been accompanied by severe environmental and cultural damage. The projected growth for the industry frequently occurs in destinations that are close to or have exceeded their natural carrying-capacity limits. The consequences are that short term economic gain clearly incurs long term environmental and social costs (European Parliament 2002).

Beyond these environmental aspects, other issues of a more social, cultural and rights-based nature have gained increased attention since the mid-1990's. These include financial leakages, disruptive impacts to local livelihoods and culture, gender bias, sexual exploitation, formal vs. informal sector, domestic vs. international tourism, the growth of "all-inclusive" package tours. Some of the key issues and challenges related to these problems are outlined in the sections below.

Issues: Progress and Challenges

Tourism and the Environment

The natural environment is an important resource for tourism. With increasing urbanisation, destinations in both industrialised and developing countries with significant natural features, scenery, cultural heritage or biodiversity are becoming increasingly popular sites for tourist destinations. Efforts to preserve and enhance the natural environment should therefore be a high priority for the industry and for governments. But the reality is not quite as clear-cut. Environments where past human interaction has been minimal are often fragile.

Small islands, coastal areas, wetlands, mountains and deserts, all now popular as tourist destinations, are five of the six 'fragile ecosystems' as identified by Agenda 21 that require specific action by governments and international donors. The biophysical characteristics of these habitats often render them particularly susceptible to damage from human activities. As the scale of tourism grows, the resource use threatens to become unsustainable. With a degraded physical environment, the destination is in danger of losing its original attraction, increasing the levels of cheaper mass tourism and forcing more "nature-based" tourism to move on to new destinations, which are likely to be even more inaccessible and fragile. Mainstream "ecotourism", as promoted after the Rio Earth Summit, hasn't always enjoyed a good reputation. Tour operators have used the concept merely as a "greenwash" marketing tool. In reality it often meant introducing unsustainable levels of tourism into fragile areas, having scant regard for either the environment or for the residents of the destination areas. As the International Council for Local Environmental Initiatives (ICLEI) pointed out:

> *"Tourism in natural areas, euphemistically called "ecotourism," can be a major source of degradation of local ecological, economic and social systems. The intrusion of large numbers of foreigners with high-consumption and high-waste habits into natural areas, or into towns with inadequate waste management infrastructure, can produce changes to those natural areas at a rate that is far greater than imposed by local residents. These tourism-related changes are particularly deleterious when local residents rely on those natural areas for their sustenance. Resulting economic losses can encourage socially deleterious economic activities such as prostitution, crime, and migrant and child labour"* (ICLEI 1999).

Some of the different kinds of impacts that tourism development and operational activities can have include:

- *Threats to ecosystems and biodiversity* – e.g. loss of wildlife and rare species, habitat loss and degradation.
- *Disruption of coasts* – e.g. shoreline erosion and pollution, impact to coral reefs and fish spawning grounds,
- *Deforestation* – loss of forests for fuel wood and timber by the tourist industry. Also impacting on soil and water quality, biodiversity integrity, reducing the collection of forest products by local communities,
- *Water overuse* – as a result of tourism/recreational activities e.g. golf courses, swimming pools, and tourist consumption in hotels,
- *Urban problems*-Congestion and overcrowding, increased vehicle traffic and resultant environmental impacts, including air and noise pollution, and health impacts,
- *Exacerbate climate change* – from fossil fuel energy consumption for travel, an hotel and recreational requirements,
- *Unsustainable and inequitable resource use*-Energy and water over consumption, excessive production of wastes, litter and garbage are all common impacts.

Further study could be carried out regarding the negative relationship between tourism and environment (Roe et al 1997), however the many examples across the globe indicate this scenario is quite typical and widely recognised, emphasising the need to identify more mutually beneficial approaches in tourism development.

Tourism and Economics

Economic gains have been a major driving force for the growth of tourism in developing countries. The initial period of growth happened in the late 1970's, when tourism was perceived as a key activity for generating foreign exchange and employment by both development institutions, such as the World Bank, as well as by governments (Goodwin 2000).

Despite the negative economic impacts of tourism (such as inflation; dominance by outsiders in land and property markets; inward-migration eroding economic opportunities for domestic industry including the poor) the demand for travel and tourism continues to grow. The WTTC has estimated there was an approximate 40% cumulative growth in tourism demand between

1990 and 2000. This demand was largely driven by economic gains at all levels, including in the communities in remote, and hitherto relatively isolated, destinations (Ashley, 2000). There is significant scope for enhancing the possible gains through addressing a number of issues that can help improve opportunities for entrepreneurs and the communities in the destinations, for the poorer sections within these communities, as well as at the macro level for the national economy. Some of these are options are discussed below.

Financial Leakages

Powerful trans-national corporations (TNCs) continue to dominate the international tourism market. Estimates suggest that about 80% of international mass tourism is controlled by TNCs. These companies have an almost unhindered access to markets and use this to drive down the cost of supplies. The result is high levels of financial leakage, and limited levels of revenue retention in the destination or host countries. Financial leakages tend to occur due to various factors, including importation of foreign building material, skilled labour and luxury products, and packaged travel arranged with TNCs. This is as opposed to locally sourcing the necessary resources. It has been estimated that, on average, at least 55% of tourism expenditure flows back out of the destination country, rising to 75% in certain cases e.g. the Gambia and Commonwealth Caribbean (Ashley et al 2000).

During the seventh UN Commission on Sustainable Development (CSD) meeting (1999), financial leakages was identified as a key area for stakeholders to take action and work together in order to try and assess the situation, as well as seek solutions to better support local communities in host/developing countries. The CSD called upon the UN and the World Tourism Organization, in consultation with major groups, as well as other relevant international organizations, to jointly facilitate the establishment of an ad-hoc informal open-ended working group on tourism to:

- Assess financial leakages and determine how to maximize benefits for indigenous and local communities;
- Prepare a joint initiative to improve information availability and capacity-building for participation, and address other matters relevant to the implementation of the international

work programme on sustainable tourism development (UN CSD 1999).

Impacts on Livelihoods in Destination Communities

In most tourist destinations of developing countries, the livelihood impacts of tourism, takes various forms. Jobs and wages are only a part of livelihood gains and often not the most significant ones. Tourism can generate four different types of local cash income, involving four distinct categories of people:

- Wages from formal employment.
- Earnings from selling goods, services, or casual labour (e.g. food, crafts, building materials, guide services).
- Dividends and profits arising from locally-owned enterprises.
- Collective income: this may include profits from a community-run enterprise, dividends from a private sector partnership and land rental paid by an investor.

Waged employment can be sufficient to lift a household from an insecure to a secure footing, but it may only be available to a minority of people, and not the poor. Casual earnings may be very small, but more widely spread, and may be enough, for instance, to cover school fees for one or more children. Local participation in the industry can be categorised into three different categories; the formal sector (such as hotels), the informal sector (such as vending) and secondary enterprises that are linked to tourism (such as food retail and telecommunications). Experience from Asia suggests that:

- As a destination is developing, accommodation for tourists can be as simple as offering home stays at the early stage, with lodges, guest houses and hotels replacing more basic options as tourism grows, and some of these may include foreign companies. Once luxury resorts start to develop, the scenario becomes more complex with international investors beginning to play a much more dominant role.
- Transport tends to fall into a grey area between formal and informal sectors. Most destinations have taxis, jeeps or other motorised forms of transport, often driven by the owners. As things expand organised associations of owners, operating on a rota system become more common.

- Data about employment in the formal sector is scattered and collection is often not very systematic. There are references of cases where high-status jobs in resorts typically go to non-locals, expatriate staff or foreign-trained nationals. However, there is almost no analysis of who is employed in middle and lower ranking jobs. The potential for employment of local staff seems to improve as one moves away from the luxury resorts into less established areas.
- The informal sector includes activities such as vending, running stalls and collecting fuel wood for the tourist industry. The informal sector often provides an easy entry into the industry for the poor, especially for women. The incomes can be substantial but unreliable as it is often a seasonal activity. However it can still provide a substantial boost to the income of the poor.
- The informal sector tends to get the least attention when interventions are planned, and interventions such as planning permissions are frequently detrimental to this sector. However, there are cases where initiatives such as flexible licensing systems and cooperatives and associations have helped the sector.
- Causal labour and self-employment provides major opportunities for local communities to enhance their livelihood opportunities from tourism. Unlike formal employment, self-employment tends to highlight the entrepreneurial spirit of village communities. Villagers are used to stringing together a livelihood from a diverse variety of sources, often giving them a knack for enterprise. Causal labour includes porters, cooks, guides, launderers, cleaners, caterer and entertainers. Nepal, for instance, has a well-organised labour market to employ porters, cooks and guides on a seasonal basis. An estimate made in 1989 showed that trekking alone generated 0.5 to 1 million person days of employment in a year in Nepal.
- Significant gains also accrue from economic linkages between tourism and other economic sectors such as agriculture, horticulture, animal husbandry and handicrafts.

There continues to be fairly poor quantitative data available regarding the economic gains that can be generated from travel and tourism, particularly data that quantifies the impacts to formal, informal and indirect activities as touched upon above. There is a need for a standardised framework and guidelines for the collection and analysis of comparative data sets, to better identify the possible economic impacts for different segments of the market, as well as to develop policies which better reflect the needs of the informal as well as formal tourism ventures.

Another gap in research about tourism relates to understanding how domestic tourism benefits formal and informal segments in a country and the degree to which the extreme poor gain at all from the industry

- Domestic or regional tourists are particularly important clients for self-employed sellers and owners of small establishments (the skilled poor and not-so-poor). Studies in Yogyakarta (Indonesia) and elsewhere in South East Asia show that domestic and other Asian tourists tend to buy more from local vendors than Western tourists (Shah, 2000).
- Budget and independent tourists, particularly backpackers are also more likely than luxury tourists to use the cheaper guest houses, home-stays, transport and eating services provided by local people. They tend to stay longer at a destination than groups of tourists and interact more with the local economy, but also spend less per day, often bargaining over prices.
- Nature-based tourism (including 'ecotourism') does not necessarily provide more opportunities for the poor than 'mass tourism'. Nature tourism does offer some potential advantages however. It takes place in less developed areas, often involves smaller operators with more local commitment. It involves a higher proportion of independent travellers, and if marketed as 'ecotourism' can stimulate consumer pressure for ensuring domestic socioeconomic benefits. But it remains a niche in the market, can be heavily dependent on imports, and can spread disruption to less developed areas.
- Mass tourism is highly competitive, and usually dominated by large suppliers who have little commitment to a

destination. They are less likely to use local suppliers. However the segment does generate jobs and negative impacts are not always spread beyond immediate localities. Further knowledge is needed about how local economic opportunities can be expanded under such circumstances, as well as to identify how the negative impacts can be minimised in the mass tourism segment.

- Cruises and 'all-inclusives' are rapidly growing segments of the market, but by their nature are unlikely to generate few economic linkages. Some governments are trying to actively reduce this, for example the Gambian Government has recently decided to ban 'all-inclusives' in response to local demands.
- The informal sector is where opportunities for small-scale enterprise or labour by the poor are maximised. For example, at Bai Chay, Ha Long Bay in Vietnam, almost a dozen local families run private hotels, but local involvement in tourism spreads far beyond this, to an estimated 70–80% of the population. Apart from those with jobs in the hotels and restaurants, local women share the running of noodle stalls, many women and children are walking vendors, and anyone with a boat or motorbike hires them out to tourists. However, the informal sector is often neglected by planners.

Tourism and Society/Culture

Tourism developments often stop people from having the right of access to land, water and natural resources. NGO's such as Tourism Concern and Rethinking Tourism have reported on examples worldwide where the articles in the UN Declaration of Human Rights are flouted, and where indigenous rights are lost or exploited. Adverse social impacts also include poor working conditions, low wages, child labour and sex tourism. The International Labour Organisation and International Confederation Free Trade Unions (ICFTU) note that some parts of the tourist industry still degrades labour and drives workers to the lowest levels, exhibiting the worst side of unsustainable production.

Cultural Transformation

Fears of tourism threatening local cultures can be misplaced and many cultures have proved resilient enough to be able to take rapid changes required by tourism in their stride. However it is true that popular destinations are typically transformed at a very rapid pace. Buzzing small towns can replace sleepy one lane bazaars. Areas where once only officials rode in motorised vehicles become a familiar site for traffic jams, and dealing with unknown faces can become a daily occurrence for people whose previous focus had been confined to a few score square kilometres to their home and work.

Communities visited by tourists can (or have to!) adapt surprisingly quickly. For example, they rapidly adopt businesslike attitudes to maximise profits. They are creative in inventing and staging events to entertain and provide information on their culture. These attractions, while usually not explicitly developed to protect back regions (i.e. areas of a host society reserved only for local residents, where tourists are not welcome), can function to deflect the tourist gaze from private space and activities. Host communities take specific, active measures to protect their values and customs. This can either be covert action such as private communal functions, fencing off of domesticities but also overt action such as organised protests and even aggression to protect their interests (Harrison and Price 1996). Tourism development in remote areas can be positive however, bringing with it infrastructure, health services and education facilities. It could be a by-product, or a result of increased incomes, or as is happening increasingly, a result of corporate and customer social responsibility.

Nevertheless, rapid tourism development can come at a price and often creates its own unique problems. Tourism activities can degrade the social and natural wealth of a community. The intrusion of large numbers of uninformed foreigners into local social systems can undermine pre-existing social relationships and values. This is particularly a problem where tourism business is centred in traditional social systems, such as isolated communities or indigenous peoples (ICLEI 1999).

There are also examples in ecotourism segment, of communities becoming marginalised and forced out of traditional lands as protected areas and destinations become established. Involving host and particularly local communities in all stages of tourism development, from planning right through operations, will help to alleviate some of these issues-if their needs and perspectives are properly taken into account. There is growing amount of work in this area and an expanding body of good practice examples but such approaches need to extended. In addition, programmes which aim to train and assist communities adversely affected by tourism development i.e. providing a social safety net need to be openly assessed for their suitability, and promoted where appropriate.

Tourism and Child Prostitution

On the darker side to global tourism, the sex trade and drug tourism remain areas that are poorly reported or regulated, especially where it concerns children. The root causes behind these growing problems may not wholly lie with growth in tourism, but it is significant and should be a real cause for concern throughout the sector. In recent years the industry has started to try and tackle such problems. In 1998 it collaborated with ECPAT (End Child Prostitution and Trafficking in Children for Sexual Purposes) to draw up a Code of Conduct for tour operators in relation to child prostitution and tourism. Signatories to ECPAT's Code of Conduct commit themselves to:

- working against child exploitation in their policy documents;
- training staff on how to combat child exploitation;
- provision of information to customers;
- putting pressure on suppliers by including a clause against the commercial sexual exploitation of children in the contract (with hotels, for example);
- provision of information to key local people and organizations by creating a network in destinations to raise awareness amongst local people.

The Fritidresor Group (FRG), a subsidiary of the Thomson Travel Group, has risen to the challenge by following up on this initiative in a systematic manner. Since 1999 it has designed and conducted workshops, developed an elaborate customer information programme and initiated pilot programmes in five destinations where child abuse is common (Brazil, Cuba, Dominican Republic, India and Thailand). Feedback from ECPAT from one of the pilots has been positive, e.g. the number of paedophiles in Thailand is decreasing. There are concerns, however, that this is happening at the expense of other countries, especially in Central America, where ECPAT has a weaker presence (Tour Operators Initiatives for Sustainable Tourism Development).

Gender

Gender dis-aggregated data for the tourism sector are not easily available. Using the data for restaurant, catering and hotels as proxy, the Gender and Tourism Report prepared by Stakeholder Forum for the CSD in 1999, reached some tentative conclusions. The general picture suggests that the formal tourism industry seems to be a particularly important sector for women (46% of the workforce are women, compared to 34-40% in other general labour markets). However the proportion of women in the tourism workforce varies greatly – from as low as 2% in some countries and up to over 80% in others, depending upon the maturity of the tourism industry. For example, in countries where there is a mature industry, women generally accounted for around 50% of those employed in the industry. Using data from 39 countries, the proportion of women's working hours compared to men's working hours was 89%. Whilst the proportion of women's wages to men's wages is 79% (based on data available from 31 countries). This suggests that women continue to receive disproportionately lower wages than their male counterparts – often in equivalent positions of status in an organisation. Furthermore the statistics, typically do not include the contribution of women employed in the informal sector. Several studies have indicated, whilst this area is frequently ignored, it also tends to be a significant contributor, particularly in developing countries (Hemmati 1999).

Solutions and Partnerships –Towards Sustainable Tourism

Tourism was only specifically mentioned in a few sections of the 1992 Rio Agenda 21, despite its huge economic significance. Agenda 21 for the Travel and Tourism Industry was written in 1996 by the World Trade Organisation, the World Travel and Tourism Council and Earth Council to try and fill this gap. It noted that with a growing standing in the world economy the tourism industry has " a moral responsibility in making the transition to sustainable development. It also has a vested interest in doing so". The document highlights the vital importance of the environment as the main base upon which the market relies.

These and other activities have supported a growing awareness of the positive and negative impacts of tourism, including a growing realisation of the impact that a degrading environment has on the livelihoods of communities living in destination areas. This has contributed towards the initiation of positive actions for mitigating and minimising the more negative aspects. Various different approaches have been explored, especially in the last couple of decades. Emerging from these efforts is a better recognition of the importance of the role of local communities, their valuable knowledge base and understanding of local circumstances, as well as their strong vested interest in preserving a sustainable system. Establishing partnerships with local communities is being increasingly recognised as necessary for sustainable tourism. The trend now is moving towards more integrated approaches, which include communities working with governments. Some broad proposals and responses for moving towards more sustainable tourism, from various stakeholders, are outlined below.

International Institutions, Agreements and Action Plans

UNEP and Tourism

- UNEP and Ecotourism Society have produced a guide *Ecotourism: Principles, Practices and Policies for Sustainability,* highlighting ecotourism's successes and failures.
- UNEP Partnerships with hotel industry have been developed – *Sowing the Seeds of Change,* is an environmental training pack with good practice examples for hotels, published with the International Hotel and Restaurant Association and International Association of Hotel Schools.
- For tourists, UNEP (in partnership with McCann International and the French Government) has produced *It's My Choice – Coral or no Coral?,* a package of communication tools in 5 languages available free to any company or organisation willing to distribute them.
- UNEP with UNESCO World Heritage Centre and support from the United Nations Foundation is also implementing sustainable tourism components in 6 World Heritage Sites in Mexico, Guatemala, Honduras and Indonesia.
- UNEP Global Programme of Action for the Protection of the Marine Environment from Land-based activities (launched in 1995) was revitalized in 2001. A key aim is reducing untreated sewage discharges, often linked to coastal and tourism development.

UNEP has also produced a set of policy guidelines, including the *Principles for Implementation of Sustainable Tourism,* widely distributed to governments and local authorities and used as inputs to some of the multi-lateral environmental agreements. UNEP's Principles on Implementation of Sustainable Tourism (2000) include:

- *Legislative Framework*: Support implementation of sustainable tourism through an effective legislative framework that establishes standards for land use in tourism development, tourism facilities, management and investment in tourism.
- *Environmental Standards*: Protect the environment by setting clear ambient environmental quality standards, along with targets for reducing pollution from all sectors, including tourism, to achieve these standards, and by preventing development in areas where it would be inappropriate.
- *Regional Standards*: Ensure that tourism and the environment are mutually supportive at a regional level through cooperation and coordination between States, to establish common approaches to incentives, environmental policies, and integrated tourism development planning.

International institutions such as UNEP are working in a number of ways (often in partnership) to promote sustainable tourism. This includes a proposal by UN Economic and Social Council to the UN General Assemebly to designate 2002 the "UN International Year of Ecotourism". Though facing some controversy regarding the definition and breadth of the term "ecotourism", the idea was that the year would aim to recognise tourism's potential benefit as both a tool for environmental protection and development. For ecotourism, it is particularly seen as a means to advance three basic goals of the UN Convention on Biological Diversity: To conserve biological diversity; 2. To promote sustainable use of biodiversity to generate income, jobs and business opportunities in ecotourism etc.; 3. To share the benefits of ecotourism developments equitably with local communities & indigenous peoples). Other groups like the World Tourism Organisation do work to try and encourage good practice in the sector. For example the World Tourism Organisation has produced a "Global Code of Ethics for Tourism in 1999 (an extension of the WTO "Manila Declaration on the Social Impacts of Tourism" 1997), as well as a "Compilation of good practices in sustainable tourism", and a practical guide for the development and application of indicators of sustainable tourism, "What Tourism Managers Need to Know".

Business Initiatives

1. International Hotels Environment Initiative (IHEI) – is a charity programme developed by the international hotel industry whose aim is to promote the benefits of environmental management as an integral part of running a successful, efficient hotel business.
2. Benchmarkhotel – An online bench marking tool to help hotels measure and improve their environmental performance (joint initiative of IHEI, WWF-UK and Biffa Award).
3. Tour Operators' Initiative for Sustainable Tourism Development-Tour operators are moving towards sustainable tourism by committing themselves to the concepts of sustainable development as the core of their business activity and to work together through common activities to promote and disseminate methods and practices compatible with sustainable development. The Initiative has been developed by tour operators for tour operators with the support of the United Nations Environment Programme (UNEP), the United Nations Educational, Scientific and Cultural Organization (UNESCO) and the World Tourism Organization (WTO/OMT), who are also full members of the Initiative.

Business Response to Calls for Minimising Tourism Impacts

The Rio Earth Summit 1992 was a major turning point for the tourism industry. Environmental issues subsequently became an important part of the agenda for the industry. However, the approach has not yet generally been an integrating one. Instead the focus has been on minimising environmental impacts that the industry is directly responsible for. There is growing support by lead companies throughout the private sector to implement principles of Corporate Social Responsibility (CSR), Environmental Management and Auditing Systems (EMAS), "Triple Bottom Line" accounting procedures (Environment, Society and Economics) and Sustainability Reporting. Measures are predominately based on adopting a voluntary approach to tackling impacts rather than having regulations/legislation imposed on business by governments. The action plan for the industry, "Agenda 21 for the Travel & Tourism Industry: Towards Environmentally Sustainable Development" contains a number of priority areas for action and suggested steps to achieve them. The importance of partnerships between government, industry and NGOs is stressed, along with the enormous benefits that will be obtained by making the tourism industry more sustainable. The document warns the industry not to underestimate the challenge which requires "fundamental reorientation". However it also makes it clear that the long-term costs of inaction will far outweigh those for starting to act now. Companies are encouraged to set up systems and procedures to incorporate sustainable development issues into core management functions and to identify actions needed to bring sustainable tourism into being. A long-term communications programme was initiated after the document launch to increase awareness and promote regional implementation (WTTC). The 10 priority areas for action are:

- Waste minimization, re-use and recycling
- Energy efficiency, conservation and management
- Management of freshwater resources
- Waste water treatment
- Hazardous substances
- Transport
- Land-use planning and management
- Involving staff, customers and communities in environmental issues
- Design for sustainability
- Partnerships for sustainability.

Voluntary Codes

Pacific Asia Travel Association Traveller's Code: Sustaining Indigenous Cultures;

1. Be Flexible. Are you prepared to accept cultures and practices different from your own?
2. Choose Responsibly. Have you elected to support businesses that clearly and actively address the cultural and environmental concerns of the locale you are visiting?

3. Do Your Homework. Have you done any research about the people and places you plan to visit so you may avoid what may innocently offend them or harm their environment?
4. Be Aware. Are you informed of the holidays, holy days, and general religious and social customs of the places you visit?
5. Support Local Enterprise. Have you made a commitment to contribute to the local economy by using businesses that economically support the community you are visiting, eating in local restaurants and buying locally made artisan crafts as remembrances of your trip?
6. Be Respectful and Observant. Are you willing to respect local laws that may include restrictions of your usage of or access to places and things that may harm or otherwise erode the environment or alter or run counter to the places you visit?

Green Globe Scheme, Standards and Certification

Pressure to incorporate social and cultural issues as well as environmental considerations within industry-backed initiatives has resulted in a number of initiatives. One example is found in the agenda of GREEN GLOBE 21, an institution created in 1994 specifically for developing capacity for environmental management and awareness within the travel & tourism industry and for maintaining a certification process. Issues such as training and employment of local people and local sourcing of goods and services are being incorporated, though in a very tentative manner. 'Where possible' is a key phrase in some of these requirements. The GREEN GLOBE 21 standard was originally designed for a number of institutions, mostly those directly related to the industry such as hotels, airports, cruise ships and car hire companies. Beaches and natural protected areas had also been included. But now certification for communities has been added, bringing in Cumbria (UK) Jersey (Channel Islands) and Vilamoura (Portugal). More than a dozen other destinations (in both developing and developed countries) are in the process of being certified, as well as two countries, Dominica and Sri Lanka. GREEN GLOBE is therefore a source of information on lessons learned from designing and implementing measures to lessen the detrimental impacts upon the environment and local communities. Another major voluntary activity highlighted by many companies is the use of codes of conduct and certification.

However, even the voluntary codes lag far behind activities for environmental performance in the area of social responsibility (UNED 1999). The World Tourism Organisation recently produced a study "Voluntary Initiatives for Sustainable Tourism" examining 104 schemes worldwide and gives recommendations to improve the conditions for voluntary initiatives and achieve better effectiveness in the operation and support of voluntary initiatives. In addition it gives a checklist for the planning and assessing of your own voluntary initiatives and makes recommendations for eco-labelling. The report states that voluntary practice has not yet had a significant impact on the mass market. The report recognises that "their current impact has been minimal across the sector as a whole". It finds that 78% of tourism certificates focus on tourism within Europe and not further afield. However the report also says that *"they are revealing tremendous potential to move the industry towards sustainability, but not without careful nurturing and support from key industry partners"* (WTO 2000).

When it comes to building more mainstream corporate responsibility, the vast majority of tourist companies state that whilst they would like to do something they feel they are unable to do so because of being faced with 'cut throat' business competition. They argue that the costs involved in acting more responsibly would drive them out of the market, especially if they take unilateral action without wider industry support. Industry surveys have identified the need for establishing mandatory regulations, making it compulsory for everyone to meet the same standards and thereby incur similar costs. Legal and fiscal regulation of corporate sector includes market-based tools such as carbon trading, as supported through the Kyoto Protocol of the UN Framework Convention for Climate Change. Also environmental standards legislated by governments on water quality and waste management, labelling standards, are growing but need to be more widely implemented and effectively enforced.

NGOs are increasingly engaging with the travel sector. They have been playing an active role in addressing problems such as financial leakages and in trying to encourage greater corporate responsibility. Key activities involve consumer education about the potential impacts of tourism and about how local communities might benefit more from the industry. They actively lobby policy-makers on associated issues of trade liberalisation, fair trade and globalization. There has also been a concerted effort to set up common certification standards, independent of the industry, along the lines of Fair Trade certification or eco-labelling. Initiatives include the International Fair Trade in Tourism Network, established by Tourism Concern (London-based) in 1999 and a feasibility study for setting up a Sustainable Tourism Stewardship Council being conducted by the Rainforest Alliance, New York.

The Sustainable Tourism Stewardship Council

The Sustainable Tourism Stewardship Council (STSC) is proposed as a global accreditation body for sustainable tourism and ecotourism certifiers. If this body is found feasible, it will set international standards for certification of tourism industry organizations that want to claim being sustainable or practicing ecotourism. The current project will investigate the viability of such body by consulting a wide range of stakeholders.

Why an accreditation body? The STSC will respond to the market demand to have international, comparable standards to identify and purchase sustainable holidays and to minimize false claims. There are over 100 certification schemes in tourism, many of them underfunded and generally not able to reach the international tourism market. Bringing certification schemes with high standards under one umbrella will give them competitive advantage in marketing, planning and managing their schemes; this in turn will benefit the companies they certify. Stewardship councils have been successfully implemented in industries such as forestry, organic farming, fishing and social accountability, acting as a catalyst for sustainable business to business and business to consumer purchasing.

Initiatives for Assisting Local Communities to Realise Tourism Opportunities

During the 1990's a number of initiatives emerged which aimed to help communities in destination countries make the most from opportunities provided by tourism. Many have been self initiated, locally and have continued to expand under their own steam, sometimes attracting external technical and/or financial assistance on their own terms. In others, external agents have acted as catalysts.

The nature of the activities have been broad, ranging from small one-village initiatives for organising handicrafts production to building powerful networks of small accommodation providers and creating a marketing network for them. Over time, and by learning from experience and sharing knowledge, these initiatives have tended to become more complex and inclusive. Effective multi-stakeholder processes have evolved from the ground. Backed with success and experience at the ground level and on a significant scale, lessons learnt here have the potential for wide and rapid replication. This also requires support from the international community for creating space and resources to assist the players who have been the active leaders of these processes so far to take the lead in formulating a strategy.

Local Authorities

Another World Tourism Organisation report, this time focusing on the role of local authorities noted that local authorities have a key role to play in many aspects of tourism development and operations. As countries becomes more decentralised, they are taking on more in this area and realising that the sector may assist local areas in achieving development. Community involvement is also referred to as a key part of this process – to ensure that they participate in planning and development processes and therefore increase their chances of achieving greater benefits from tourism e.g. employment, income, establishing tourism related enterprises. The report notes that many local authorities lack in experience for planning, nurturing and developing tourism however. This can result in wasted resources and opportunities. The report states that proper planning, efficient implementation and effective management are all essential to optimise the benefits of tourism (WTO 1998).

The statement by the International Council for Local Environmental Initiatives (ICLEI) during the seventh session of the CSD said that *"in addition to their direct roles in the development process, perhaps the most important role that local authorities can play in a global economy is that of facilitator among the diverse interests seeking to influence the direction of local development"*. ICLEI also stated that *"solutions to adverse tourism impacts are to be found in the shared interest of local communities, tourism businesses, and tourism consumers to maintain the natural wealth and social heritage of the tourist destination"*. Thus a major challenge for "sustainable tourism" will be the creation of tangible and working local partnerships. One way to approach this will be through the principles espoused in Local Agenda 21. These principles should be applied, through partnerships, to evaluate and improve efforts to address sensitive tourism development issues, including:

- Inequitable distribution of tourism revenues and "financial leakages"
- Displacement of pre-existing local settlements by tourism developments
- Equal access to local coastal and recreational resources
- Conflict over use and long-term protection of those areas
- Concerns related to lack of foreign tourist sensitivity to cultural traditions and sites.

Governments

It is fairly disappointing to say that many Governments have been slow to take the lead in ensuring the progress of sustainable tourism and much more work could be done by them to engage more pro-actively with this sector than in the past. Further engagement includes action at all levels, from international forums and negotiations, down to development of tourism plans and policy, and the enforcement of key regulation at national and local levels.

A study for the European Union made some useful recommendations for governments to take action in support of sustainable tourism. In addition, it recommends production of regional and national tourism strategies, as well as the development and exchange of knowledge through regional networks on sustainable tourism, engaging stakeholders as well as government ministries (European Parliament 2002).

Pro-Poor Tourism (PPT) Strategies

PPT is an approach that is gaining recognition by national governments and local authorties. Although PPT is still relatively new and has not been widely applied in practice, existing case studies reveal a number of lessons. These include:

- PPT requires diverse activities from micro to macro levels-including product development, marketing, planning, policy, and investment. It goes well beyond community tourism.

- A lead advocate for PPT is useful, but involving other stakeholders is critical. PPT can be incorporated into the tourism development strategies of government or business.
- Location: PPT works best where the wider destination is developing well.
- PPT strategies often involve development of new products, particularly products linked to local culture. These products should be integrated with mainstream markets where possible.
- Ensuring commercial viability is a priority. This requires understanding demand, product quality, marketing, investment in business skills, and involving the private sector.

Support Local Agenda 21

- Design national and international investment, and development assistance programs for local authorities
- Support locally relevant mechanisms to monitor and evaluate progress.
- National governments should ensure the full implementation of Local Agenda 21 Sustainable Development Plans by local authorities-through the development of a national action plan, and provision of resources and expertise.
- Establish Local Agenda 21 best practice networks-to facilitate knowledge transfer across countries.
- Application of strategic environmental assessments and environmental impact assessments. These assessments should be made public, for use by all stakeholders. The integrity of both SEAs and EIAs should be maintained by the use of impartial and informed entities, such as research institutes and universities.
- Land-use planning and development control-The precautionary principle should be applied at the local and regional level. Carrying capacity studies conducted in all tourist destinations prior to further expansion.
- Integrated Coastal Zone Management strategies-Resources should be allocated to programmes for fostering ICZM projects. The release of funds for coastal areas should be dependent up-holding the principles of ICZM.

Promote Tourism in Natural and Cultural Heritage Sites

- Tourism in protected areas-Management plans for each specific area should be given full attention by national governments, and adequate resources and expertise made available to develop competent plans.
- Rural tourism-Measures should be taken to support development of rural tourism as a key component of sustainable development in rural areas. Rural destinations should be encouraged to adopt the principles of Integrated Quality Management, involving local communities in measures to manage and develop rural products in line with market needs, plus maximizing the proportion of income retained in the community. Loss of biodiversity and cultural heritage caused by tourism should be offset by resources at the regional level to mitigate habitat fragmentation and maintain and restore the regional landscape.
- Eco-tourism-Ecotourism should be encouraged and regulated through use of eco-labels and certification schemes, to guarantee better environmental performance and progress towards sustainable development. If an activity is to be conducted in a designated protected area, then an Environmental Impact Assessment should be undertaken in advance by the responsible agency, and plans amended according to the outcomes of the assessment.
- Tourism in heritage sites-Projects combining preservation and promotion of cultural heritage sites should be supported, provided that proposals are of a high quality and are based on a sound visitor management plan.

Making Tourism Enterprises more Sustainable

- Information, training and advice-stimulate and support the development of specialist information networks for sustainable tourism and provide the technological capacity to manage such networks efficiently. Sustainable tourism internet training modules should be developed for specific industry players.
- Quality marks and labelling-Research the best ways fc evolving product and service certification, through

examination of which sectors to target, and of mandatory vs. voluntary certification. Use existing know-how and experience to achieve recognition and acceptance by the sector and consumers. High priority should be given to promoting the image of eco-labels, equating "environmentally friendly" with quality.

- Financial incentives-Set up a comprehensive enquiry into green taxes for the tourism industry, taking into account both the opportunity for punitive taxes via the polluter pays principle and tax breaks for certified good practice. Greater stakeholder consultation should be conducted to investigate how the industry can access suitable funding schemes. Monitoring of projects should focus on the sustainability criteria built into a project, and ensure compliance of commitment to sustainability.

Raising Public Awareness

- *Stakeholder Participation*-Reinforce current increasing environmental awareness with greater stakeholder access to information, though improvements in government educational programmes and the refinement of the availability and content of information services.

Economic measures should expand both formal and casual earning opportunities.

- Non-financial benefits (e.g. increased community participation, access to assets) can reduce market vulnerability.
- PPT is a long-term investment. Expectations must be prudent and opportunities for short-term benefits investigated.
- External funding may be necessary to cover substantial transaction costs of establishing partnerships, developing skills, and revising policies (Ashley et al 2001).

Conserving and Documenting Biodiversity

The scientific community has played a role in promoting conservation and research on biodiversity through tourism. One example is Earthwatch, an organisation that supports scientific research through volunteer tourists and funding. In the UK, Earthwatch has a programme which sponsors teachers to be volunteers, and as a result has encouraged greater environmental education in schools in the UK. Another example is the Monteverde Cloud Forest Preserve (MCFR) in Costa Rica, combining private initiative, conservation, education and a spirit of internationalism.

The Monteverde Cloud Forest Preserve

Located high up in the Tilarian Mountains of Costa Rica, the Monteverde Cloud Forest Preserve is climatically influenced by both the Atlantic and the Pacific. The result is a unique bio-sphere with six major eco-zones or microclimates harbouring over 100 species of mammals, 400 bird and 120 reptile species and 2500 plant species.

The primary forest cover was still extensive in the 1950s, but the area came under pressure expanding agricultural practices. Around this time a group of Quaker families emigrated from the US, in the search of an "alternative" lifestyle. They bought 1400 ha of land, setting aside 554 hectares as a watershed and dividing the rest amongst themselves for cultivation.

A decade later, scientific studies began to attract tourists into the area, coinciding with a growth in the conservation movement. In 1972, a Costa Rican NGO-the Tropical Science Centre-acquired 328 hectares for a reserve in Monteverde. And in 1974 they reached an agreement with the Quakers to manage the watershed area. This was the beginning of the MCFR, which now covers a 100 sq. km area.

Community Based Wildlife Tourism

In Africa, Community Based Wildlife Tourism (CBWT) has succeeded in conserving the environment as well as empowering communities. The principle behind CBWT is simple-the benefits to wildlife must exceed the costs. In reality this is not so straight forward. A number of the caveats and complexities necessary for success have been identified through experiences on the ground:

- The link between tourism resource and wildlife conservation is not always obvious. It has to be emphasised through education, dialogue and negotiations. Financial incentives will be ineffective in the absence of institutions and capacity for sustainable management. Hence, responsibility for wildlife management and institutional capacity should take precedence over the benefits.

- Equitable distribution of local earnings from tourism is critical and they should be widely shared within the community managing tourism resources.
- Even if tourism creates incentives for wildlife conservation, wider impacts on ecosystems or biodiversity maintenance should also be considered (Ashley 1998).

ICT and Alternative Technologies

The growing use of Information Communication Technology has been cited as a way to cut down on "unnecessary travel", particularly for work-related travel e.g. through using video conferencing instead of travelling to meetings all the time (IIIEE 2002). However for recreational tourism, the main focus of this paper, the link is less obvious. There are, however, numerous examples of web-based guides and tools, aiming to support sustainable tourism, that are springing up all over the place, a few of which have been cited in this paper. A recent study, for the Global Information Society International Research Programme, identified a number of ways that ICT can support tourism as well as protection of biodiversity:

- Helping to establish global tourism/biodiversity databases to enable more effective planning and monitoring in an inter-related and comprehensive way,
- Encouraging global exchange of information and expertise among professionals and stakeholders,
- Allowing small operators and others to be included in discussion and to gain greater access to data,
- Encouraging direct dialogue, including that of marketing and promotion, between sites and tourists, and between tourist providers and tourists,
- Generally improving consumer and operator awareness of impacts and outcomes of tourism (Boniface 2000).

The study indicated that it is the immediacy of ICT, its capacity to retain and distribute information and its flexibility that are some of its strongest benefits. Another is that ICT can assist the creation of new connections and networks between practitioners, operators and tourists across the globe. Such groups are important to help learn and exchange good practice in sustainable tourism.

Alternative technologies are another important area. Organisations which combine alternative technology with "learning by living" holidays are growing in number. They include activities like agro-ecotourism, which link tourism, education and promoting traditional conservation and sustainable use practices. Tourists are taught new skills for sustainable living, such as organic farming, using alternative renewable energies, through visiting eco-villages, alternative technology centres and traditional communities (ITDG 2002).

Education, Capacity Building and Participation

Education is the key to changing tourist behaviour. Some examples, such as marketing and publicity campaigns by tour operators, have alsready been cited. Other opportunities also exist, such as learning about sustainability in tourism through job training. These activities should be a shared responsibility between government, private sector operators and trade associations, as well as local tourist organisations, formal training institutions, unions and representative bodies (ICFTU 1999).

The Way Forward – Responsible Tourism

Recognising the substantial impacts of tourism yet also its potential to help implementation of Sustainable Development, the CSD addressed sustainable tourism for the first time in 1999. Many of the issues raised are already considered within this paper but a direct result was the designation of 2002 as UN 2002 UN International Year of Ecotourism (IYE). IYE has not been without its critics (e.g. Third World Network, Rethinking Tourism) who expressed real concerns about assuming that Ecotourism was already a "success", when even the World Bank (who has been supporting ecotourism for over a decade) suggests that few projects have actually generated substantial income for local communities (Vivanco 2002). The Quebec Declaration on Ecotourism is expected to become a major point of reference for future discussion about ecotourism but "much work remains to be done, notably in the fight against poverty" (WTO 2002). Promoting a broader and more inclusive approach towards seeking sustainable tourism development and capacity building will be key. According to UNEP some of the conditions for a successful transition towards sustainable tourism include:

- Involvement of stakeholders: Increase the long-term success of tourism projects by involving key stakeholders in the development and implementation of tourism plans,

- Information exchange: Raise awareness of sustainable tourism and its implementation by promoting exchange of information, between governments and stakeholders, on best practice for sustainable tourism, and establishing networks for dialogue on implementation of Sustainable Tourism Principles;
- Capacity Building: Ensure effective implementation of sustainable tourism, through capacity building programmes to develop and strengthen human resources and institutional capacities in government at national and local levels, and amongst local communities; and to integrate environmental and human ecological considerations at all levels.

Conclusions

As we've seen ecotourism is just one approach towards seeking sustainable tourism. Responsible and pro-poor tourism are emerging as new specialist approaches. And new initiatives which aim to push the mainstream tourism industry are building. One example is a new alliance between the World Tourism Organisation and UNCTAD aimed at "poverty alleviation through tourism". The initiative was announced in July 2002 and it will be presented at the Johannesburg Summit in an attempt to gain wider support. Model projects and successful multi-stakeholder initiatives, albeit on a small-scale, are also beginning to grow. Even these few examples perhaps prove that tourism has the potential to meet many of the objectives of sustainable development – to revitalize economies, support local communities, protect the environment and even generate cost savings and efficiency gains for tourism companies.

Promotion of sustainable tourism, through the development of policy tools, capacity building and awareness-raising programmes, local involvement, guidelines for good practice and actual implementation remain essential goals. Sustainable tourism should aim to directly support poverty eradication and sustainable production and consumption – in line with the general aims of Agenda 21. Making progress on a larger scale will be a fine balancing act and will require a massive "sea-change" in approach from the entire Travel and Tourism industry but it is an approach that is clearly worthy of support from all stakeholders interested and involved in the industry.

4

Sustainable Development of Tourism—WTO

The New Realities of Tourism in an Era of Global Climate Change

Compelling evidence indicates that global climate has changed compared to the preindustrial era and is anticipated to continue to change over the 21st century and beyond. The Intergovernmental Panel on Climate Change (IPCC) declared that "[...] *warming of the climate system is unequivocal.*" The global mean temperature has increased approximately 0.76°C between 1850–1899 and 2001–2005 and the IPCC concluded that most of the observed increase in global average temperatures since the mid-20th century is very likely (> 90% probability) the result of human activities that are increasing greenhouse gas concentrations in the atmosphere. Discernible human influences now also extend to other aspects of climate, including ocean warming, continental-average temperatures, temperature extremes and wind patterns. Widespread decreases in glaciers and ice caps and warming ocean surface temperature have contributed to sea level rise of 1.8 mm per year from 1961 to 2003, and approximately 3.1 mm per year from 1993 to 2003. The biological response of ecosystems and individual species has been recorded on every continent.

The IPCC has projected that the pace of climate change is very likely (> 90% probability) to accelerate with continued greenhouse gas (GHG) emissions at or above current rates, with the best estimate that globally averaged surface temperatures will rise by

1.8°C to 4.0°C by the end of the 21st century. Even if atmospheric concentrations of GHGs were stabilized at current levels, the Earth would continue to warm as a result of past GHG emissions and the thermal inertia of the oceans. The biological response to this continued warming and sea level rise would continue for several centuries.

Future changes in temperatures and other important features of climate will manifest themselves differently across the regions of the world. According to the IPCC, it is very likely that hot extremes, heat waves and heavy precipitation events will continue to become more frequent. It is likely that future tropical cyclones (typhoons and hurricanes) will become more intense, with larger peak wind speeds and more heavy precipitation associated with ongoing increases of tropical sea surface temperatures. There is less confidence in projections of a global decrease in numbers of tropical cyclones. The extension of the regions that will be primary affected by these extreme events with major tourism destinations highlights the need for awareness and preparedness for natural hazards at the local level through systematic capacity building and strategies for disaster risk management. Extratropical storm tracks are projected to shift poleward, with consequent changes in wind, precipitation and temperature patterns, continuing the broad pattern of observed trends over the last half-century. Observed decreases in snow cover are also projected to continue.

The environmental and economic risks of the magnitude of climate change projected for the 21st century are considerable and have featured prominently in recent international policy debates. The IPCC concluded with very high confidence that climate change would impede the ability of many nations to achieve sustainable development by mid-century. The Stern Review on the Economics of Climate Change found that the costs of taking action to reduce GHG emissions now, are much smaller than the costs of economic and social disruption from unmitigated climate change.

Our lifestyles, economies, health and social well-being are all affected by climate change, and although the consequences of climate change will vary on a regional basis, all nations and economic sectors will have to contend with the challenges of climate change through adaptation and mitigation. Tourism is no exception and in the decades ahead, climate change will become an increasingly pivotal issue affecting tourism development and management. With its close connections to the environment and climate itself, tourism is considered to be a highly climate-sensitive economic sector similar to agriculture, insurance, energy, and transportation. The regional manifestations of climate change will be highly relevant for tourism destinations and tourists alike, requiring adaptation by all major tourism stakeholders. Indeed, climate change is not a remote future event for tourism, as the varied impacts of a changing climate are becoming evident at destinations around the world and climate change is already influencing decision-making in the tourism sector.

At the same time, the tourism sector is a non-negligible contributor to climate change through GHG emissions derived especially from the transport and accommodation of tourists. Tourism must seek to significantly reduce its GHG emissions in accordance with the international community, which at the "Vienna Climate Change Talks 2007" recognized that global emissions of GHG need to peak in the next 10– 15 years and then be reduced to very low levels, well below half of levels in 2000 by mid-century. * The tourism sector can not address the challenge of climate change in isolation, but must do so within the context of the broader international sustainable development agenda. The critical challenge before the global tourism sector is to develop a coherent policy strategy that decouples the projected massive growth in tourism in the decades ahead from increased energy use and GHG emissions, so as to allow tourism growth to simultaneously contribute to poverty alleviation and play a major role in achieving the United Nations Millennium Development Goals (MDG). "*Climate change as well as poverty alleviation will remain central* issues for the world community. Tourism is an important element in both. Governments and the private sector must place increased importance on these factors in tourism development strategies and in climate and poverty strategies. They are interdependent and must be dealt with in a holistic fashion."

Francesco Frangialli, UNWTO Secretary-General (2007) Tourism can play a significant role in addressing climate change if the innovativeness and resources of this vital global economic sector are fully mobilized and oriented towards this goal. The concern of the tourism community regarding the challenge of climate change has visibly increased over the last five years. The

World Tourism Organization (UNWTO) and several partner organizations, including UNEP, convened the First International Conference on Climate Change and Tourism in Djerba, Tunisia in 2003. This event was a watershed in terms of raising awareness about the implications of climate change within the international tourism community.

The Djerba Declaration recognized the complex inter-linkages between the tourism sector and climate change and established a framework for future research and policy making on adaptation and mitigation. A number of individual tourism industry associations and businesses have also shown leadership on climate change, voluntarily adopting GHG emission reduction targets, engaging in public education campaigns on climate change and supporting government climate change legislation.

"Far sighted action by the US$ 880 billion international tourism industry will send important signals to governments, industries and the public that mitigation and adaptation to the climate change challenge make economic and environmental sense. It is the kind of leadership that can encourage others to look not only to their exposure and to the risks posed by climate change, but also to the abundant opportunities and benefits of cost effective action." Achim Steiner, UN Under-Secretary General and UNEP Executive Director (2007) The scientific community has also responded, doubling the number of scientific publications that examine the interactions of tourism and climate change between 1996–2000 and 2001–2005 and significantly advancing the place of tourism in the IPCC 4th Assessment Report (AR4) relative to previous assessments. In 2006, the World Meteorological Organization (WMO) established an Expert Team on Climate and Tourism in collaboration with the UNWTO, with the broad mandate to advance the application of weather and climate information in the tourism sector and understanding of the implications of climate change.

Impacts and Adaptation at Tourism Destinations

The tourism industry and destinations are clearly sensitive to climate variability and change. Climate defines the length and quality of tourism seasons and plays a major role in destination choice and tourist spending. In many destinations tourism is closely linked with the natural environment. Climate affects a wide range of the environmental resources that are critical attractions for tourism, such as snow conditions, wildlife productivity and biodiversity, water levels and quality. Climate also has an important influence on environmental conditions that can deter tourists, including infectious disease, wildfires, insect or water-borne pests (e.g., jellyfish, algae blooms), and extreme events such as tropical cyclones.

There are four broad categories of climate change impacts that will affect tourism destinations, their competitiveness and sustainability.

Direct climatic impacts: Climate is a principal resource for tourism, as it codetermines the suitability of locations for a wide range of tourist activities, is a principal driver of global seasonality in tourism demand, and has an important influence on operating costs, such as heating-cooling, snow-making, irrigation, food and water supply, and insurance costs. Thus, changes in the length and quality of climate-dependent tourism seasons (i.e., sun-and-sea or winter sports holidays) could have considerable implications for competitive relationships between destinations and therefore the profitability of tourism enterprises. Studies indicate that a shift of attractive climatic conditions for tourism towards higher latitudes and altitudes is very likely. As a result, the competitive position of some popular holiday areas are anticipated to decline (e.g., the Mediterranean in summer), whereas other areas (e.g., southern England or southern Canada) are expected to improve. Uncertainties related to tourist climate preference and destination loyalty require attention if the implications for the geographic and seasonal redistribution of visitor flows are to be projected. There are well established vulnerabilities among winter sports destinations to projected declines in natural snowfall. Even with increased snow-making, contractions in the ski industry are very likely in the European Alps, Eastern and Western North America, Australia, and Japan, although projected impacts on destinations in these nations vary in magnitude and over different time horizons.

The IPCC has concluded that changes in a number of weather extremes are probable as a result of projected climate change, including: higher maximum temperature and more hot days over nearly all land areas (very likely), greater tropical storm intensity and peak winds (likely), more intense precipitation events over many land areas (very likely), and longer and more severe droughts in many mid-latitude continental interiors (likely). Such changes will affect the tourism industry through increased infrastructure damage, additional emergency preparedness requirements, higher operating expenses (e.g., insurance, backup water and power systems, and evacuations), and business interruptions.

Indirect environmental change impacts: Because environmental conditions are such a critical resource for tourism, a wide-range of climate-induced environmental changes will have profound effects on tourism at the destination and regional level. Changes in water availability, biodiversity loss, reduced landscape aesthetic, altered agricultural production (e.g., wine tourism), increased natural hazards, coastal erosion and inundation, damage to infrastructure and the increasing incidence of vector-borne diseases will all impact tourism to varying degrees. In contrast to the varied impacts of a changed climate on tourism, the indirect effects of climate induced environmental change are likely to be largely negative. Mountain, island, and coastal destinations are considered particularly sensitive to climate-induced environmental change, as are nature-based tourism market segments. UNESCO has also identified several World Heritage Sites that are critical tourist destinations, to be vulnerable to climate-induced environmental change (e.g., Venice, Italy – sea level rise, Great Barrier Reef, Australia – coral bleaching and mortality, Glacier-Waterton International Peace Park, USA and Canada – glacier retreat, Chan Chan Archaeological Zone, Peru – El Nino-Southern Oscillation (ENSO) caused flooding and eroding). While our understanding of the impacts of climate change for various destination types has improved since the Djerba Conference, it is important to emphasize that there remain major regional gaps in our knowledge of how climate change will affect the natural and cultural resources critical for tourism in Africa, the Caribbean, South America, the Middle East and large parts of East Asia.

Impacts of mitigation policies on tourist mobility: National or international mitigation policies – that are policies that seek to reduce GHG emissions – are likely to have an impact on tourist flows. They will lead to an increase in transport costs and may foster environmental attitudes that lead tourists to change their travel patterns (e.g., shift transport mode or destination choices). There has been substantial recent media coverage on this topic, specifically as it relates to air travel. Long-haul destinations can be particularly affected and officials in Southeast Asia, Australia-

New Zealand, and the Caribbean have expressed concern that mitigation policies could adversely impact their national tourism economy. On the other hand, emission scenario projections developed for this report indicate that opportunities may arise for low carbon emission transport modes like coach and rail. This may also help to revitalize destinations that are nearer to the main markets.

Indirect societal change impacts: Climate change is thought to pose a risk to future economic growth and to the political stability of some nations. The Stern Report on the Economics of Climate Change concluded that although a global warming of only 1°C might benefit global GDP, greater climate change would eventually damage economic growth at the global scale, including the stark conclusion that unmitigated climate change could cause a reduction in consumption per capita of 20% later in the 21st century or early 22nd century. Any such reduction of global GDP due to climate change would reduce the discretionary wealth available to consumers for tourism and have negative implications for anticipated future growth in tourism; however there has been no in-depth interpretation of the Stern Report 54 for the tourism sector.

Our actions over the coming few decades could create risks of major disruption to economic and social activity, later in this century and in the next, on a scale similar to those associated with the great wars and the economic depression of the first half of the 20th century.

Climate change is considered a national and international security risk that will steadily intensify, particularly under greater warming scenarios. Climate change associated security risks have been identified in a number of regions where tourism is highly important to local/national economies.

Destination vulnerability hotspots: The integrated effects of climate change will have far-reaching consequences for tourism businesses and destinations. Importantly, climate change will generate both negative and positive impacts in the tourism sector and these impacts will vary substantially by market segment and geographic region. The implications of climate change for any tourism business or destination will also partially depend on the impacts on its competitors. A negative impact in one part of the tourism system may constitute an opportunity elsewhere.

Consequently, there will be 'winners and losers' at the business, destination and nation level. Due to the very limited information available on the potential impacts of climate change in some tourism regions, this qualitative assessment must also be considered with caution.

Until systematic regional level assessments are conducted a definitive statement on the net economic or social impacts in the tourism sector will not be possible. Furthermore, the outcome most likely will depend on the extent of climate change. The impact on the tourism sector may strongly parallel that of the global economy, where a 1°C temperature rise may result in a net benefit for the world economy, but greater increases increasingly show net declines.

Destination level adaptation: It is now recognised that regardless of the emissions reduction efforts, there is an inevitable need for societies around the world to adapt to unavoidable changes in climate. It is essential to emphasize that regardless of the nature and magnitude of climate change impacts, all tourism businesses and destinations will need to adapt to climate change in order to minimize associated risks and capitalize upon new opportunities, in an economically, socially and environmentally sustainable manner.

Tourists have the greatest adaptive capacity (depending on three key resources: money, knowledge and time) with relative freedom to avoid destinations impacted by climate change or shifting the timing of travel to avoid unfavourable climate conditions. Suppliers of tourism services and tourism operators at specific destinations have less adaptive capacity. Large tour operators, who do not own the infrastructure, are in a better position to adapt to changes at destinations, because they can respond to clients demands and provide information to influence clients' travel choices. Destination communities and tourism operators with large investment in immobile capital assets (e.g., hotel, resort complex, marina or casino) have the least adaptive capacity.

The dynamic nature of the tourism industry and its ability to cope with a range of recent major shocks, including SARS, terrorism attacks in a number of nations, or the Asian tsunami, suggests a relatively high adaptive capacity within the tourism industry overall. The capacity to adapt to climate change is thought to vary substantially between sub-sectors, destinations, and individual businesses within the tourism industry.

> *"It is vital for tourism destinations [...] to anticipate the coming changes and to draw their consequences, starting now. [Adaptation] is a long-term project that must be anticipated and carefully prepared beforehand; it is not easy to see this through successfully, because it entails, all at the same time, modifying economic circuits, introducing new technologies, carrying out intensive training, investing in the creation of new products, [...] changing the minds of public authorities, entrepreneurs, host communities and tourists."*

Francesco Frangialli, UNWTO Secretary-General (2007)

The tourism sector has been adapting its operations to climate zones worldwide, using a diverse range of technological, managerial, educational, policy and behavioural adaptations to deal with climate variability. However, adaptation has figured less prominently in climate change research on tourism than in some other economic sectors (e.g., agriculture). There has been a range of research activities focusing on climate change impacts for destinations or specific tourism sectors (e.g., ski operations), but they generally have not identified properly the range of adaptation options available to tourism stakeholders. Due to a lack of integration of adaptation measures in impact analysis studies, the perspectives on projected impacts may be misleading.

Much more needs to be done to incorporate adaptation into future impact assessments in the tourism sector given its high adaptive capacity. Second, knowledge of the capability of current climate adaptations to cope successfully with future climate change remains rudimentary. An important lesson learned from Hurricane Katrina and the extremely warm winter of 2006–2007 in the European Alps is that adaptations can be overwhelmed by events unexpected and beyond the range of experience of the tourism sector. Such events should be anticipated under climate change, and consequently there is a critical need for the tourism sector to evaluate the effectiveness of current adaptations under projected climate conditions. In an era of global climate change, it will no longer be sufficient to rely on past experience. The information requirements for effective, anticipatory climate change adaptation will be substantial and therefore adaptation is a critical area for future research.

Climate change is slowly entering into decision-making of a range of tourism stakeholders (e.g., investors, insurance companies, tourism enterprises, governments, and tourists); studies that have examined the climate change risk appraisal of local tourism officials and operators have consistently found relatively low levels of concern and little evidence of long-term strategic planning in anticipation of future changes in climate.

There is also some evidence that local tourism operators may be overestimating their adaptive capacity (e.g., capacity to make snow under the warmest scenarios). The incorporation of adaptation to climate change into the collective minds of private and public sector tourism decision-makers ('mainstreaming') remains several steps away. Consequently, there is a real need for effective communication between the climate change science community and tourism operators at the regional and local scale, particularly with respect to the development of climate change scenarios and indicators catered toward local tourism decision-making.

Implications of Climate Change for Tourism Demand Patterns

Climate, the natural environment, and personal safety are three primary factors in destination choice, and global climate change is anticipated to have significant impacts on all three of these factors at the regional level. Tourists also have the greatest capacity to adapt to the impacts of climate change, with relative freedom to avoid destinations impacted by climate change or shifting the timing of travel to avoid unfavourable climate conditions.

As such, the response of tourists to the complexity of destination impacts will reshape demand patterns and play a pivotal role in the eventual impacts of climate change on the tourism industry. Understanding and anticipating the potential geographic and seasonal shifts in tourist demand will remain critical areas of research in the future.

The evidence available from studies that have explored the potential impact of altered climate conditions for tourist demand suggests that the geographic and seasonal redistribution of tourist demand may be very large for individual destinations and countries by mid-to late-century. Anticipated impacts include a gradual shift in preferred destinations to higher latitudes and to higher elevations in mountainous areas. Tourists from temperate nations that currently dominate international travel (e.g., Northern Europe) are expected to spend more holidays in their home country or nearby, adapting their travel patterns to take advantage of new climatic opportunities closer to home.

Tourism seasons will be altered with possibly more tourists travelling in shoulder seasons, or in winter seasons, as climate will be more appealing. This shift in travel patterns may have important implications, including proportionally more tourism spending in temperate nations and proportionally less spending in warmer nations now frequented by tourists from temperate regions. The direct effect of climate change might be significant enough to alter major intra-regional tourism flows where climate is of paramount importance, including Northern Europe to the Mediterranean and the Caribbean, North America to the Caribbean, and to a lesser extent North East Asia to Southeast Asia.

However, the net effect of a change in climate on tourist demand at the global scale is expected to be limited, as there is no evidence to suggest that a change in climate will directly lead to a significant reduction of the global volume of tourism. It is important to emphasize that it is the holistic impact of climate change on tourism environments that tourists will respond to, not just changes in climatic conditions.

Tourism demand at the regional scale will also be affected by the range of indirect environmental and social impacts brought about by global climate change. The indirect impacts of global climate change are anticipated to influence tourist demand for specific destinations and perhaps at the regional level where political destabilization may occur, but not affect tourism demand at the global level, unless, as some economic analyses indicate, global economic growth were to be adversely affected by climatic change.

The perceptions of future impacts of climate change are likely to play the central role in the decision-making of tourists and tourism investors alike, as perceptions of climate conditions or environmental changes are just as important to consumer choices as the actual conditions. Perceptions of climate change impacts in a region are often heavily influenced by the nature of media coverage. Speculation and misinformation about the impacts of climate change on tourism destinations already abounds in the media, particularly with regard to the demise of the ski industry and extreme summer temperatures in the Mediterranean region. The combination of increased awareness of the potential environmental impacts of air travel, as reflected in a number of recent public opinion polls, and national or international mitigation policies that increase the costs of travel, will also have important implications for shaping tourist demand. Current understanding of how price increases for travel may alter tourist mobility remains low.

Past studies that have analysed the price sensitivity of air passengers, for example, show moderate inelasticity (–0.7). Recent market surveys have also identified highly varied willingness to pay to offset the environmental consequences of air travel. The perception of transport, and in particular air travel, in relation to its carbon footprint is also likely to be an important influence on tourists' responses to price changes. Information on tourist climate preferences and key thresholds (i.e., temperature limits for a beach holiday), tourist perceptions of the environmental impacts of global climate change at destinations (i.e., perceptions of coral bleaching, diminished or lost glaciers, degraded coastlines, reduced biodiversity or wildlife prevalence), and tourist perceptions of the environmental impacts of tourism related travel and their willingness to pay to reduce this impact, remain important knowledge gaps that need to be addressed if potential long-range shifts in tourist demand are to be more accurately projected. There is also limited understanding of how climate change impacts will interact with other longer term social and market trends influencing tourism demand (e.g., globalization and economic fluctuations, fuel prices, aging populations in industrialized countries, increasing travel safety and health concerns, increased environmental and cultural awareness, advances in information and transportation technology).

Emissions from Global Tourism: Status and Trends

The contribution of tourism to human-induced climate change has never been comprehensively assessed. This report represents the first attempt to calculate emissions of CO2 from three main tourism sub-sectors – transportation, accommodations, and activities – as well as the contribution to radiative forcing (i.e. including all greenhouse gases) for the year 2005. Tourism in this report refers to "[...] *the activities of persons traveling to and staying in places outside their usual* environment for not more than one consecutive year for leisure, business and other purposes not related to the exercise of an activity remunerated from within the place *visited.*"

Existing databases on tourism are not directly suitable for emission inventories, so the UNWTO prepared a specific database for this project with data provided for the baseline year of 2005. In order to refine calculations of GHG emissions from the tourism sector and effectively monitor progress on GHG emission reductions in the future, a strategic reassessment of the current system of tourism statistics will be required so that appropriate data are collected at the necessary spatial and temporal resolutions.

While CO_2 is the most important greenhouse gas from human activities, other greenhouse gases also make significant contributions to global warming. In the tourism sector, this is particularly relevant for emissions from aviation, which, at flight altitude, has an enhanced impact on global warming. Radiative forcing is thus used to calculate the entire contribution of tourist (air) travel to global warming.

Radiative forcing measures the extent to which emissions of greenhouse gases raise global average temperatures now or at a specified year in the future (estimates of tourism contribution to radiative forcing will be analyzed in the full report). International and domestic tourism emissions from three main sub-sectors are estimated to represent between 3.9% and 6.0% of global emissions in 2005, with a best estimate of 4.9%.

The analysis also showed that emissions can vary greatly per tourist trip, between a few kilograms of CO_2 up to 9 t CO_2 for long-distance, cruise-based journeys. A globally averaged tourist journey is estimated to generate 0.25 t of CO_2 emissions. A small share of tourism trips was found to cause the main share of emissions; while the aviation based trips account for 17% of all tourism trips, they cause about 40% of CO_2 emissions from tourism. Long-haul travel by air between the five UNWTO world tourism regions represents only 2.2% of all tourist trips, but contributes 16% to global tourism-related CO_2 emissions. In contrast, international tourist trips (i.e., overnight tourist trips) by coach and rail, which account for an estimated 16% of international tourist trips, stand only for 1% of CO_2 emissions generated by all international tourist trips (transport emissions only).

These results show that mitigation initiatives in the tourism sector will need to strategically focus on the impact of some particular forms of tourism (i.e., particularly those connected with air travel) if substantial reductions in CO_2 emissions are to be achieved. This also implies that climate change mitigation should primarily focus on a minor proportion of tourist trips.

Mitigation Policies and Measures

Climate change mitigation relates to technological, economic and socio-cultural changes that can lead to reductions in greenhouse gas emissions. Tourism-related emissions are projected to continue to grow rapidly under 'business-as-usual' conditions in contrast to the substantial emission reduction targets the international community agreed was required in the latest round of UNFCCC negotiations ("Vienna Climate Change Talks 2007"), where it was recognized that global emissions of GHG need to be reduced to well below half of the levels in 2000 by mid-century.

Mitigation is thus of particular importance in tourism; however, mitigation policies need to consider a number of dimensions, such as the need to stabilize the global climate, the right of people to rest and recover and leisure, and attaining the United Nations Millennium Development Goals.

As the emission reductions required for tourism to contribute meaningfully to the broader emission reduction targets of the international community are substantial, mitigation should ideally combine various strategies, such as voluntary, economic, and regulatory instruments. These can be targeted at different stakeholder groups, including tourists, tour operators, accommodation managers, airlines, manufacturers of cars and aircraft, as well as destination managers. Instruments could also be applied with different emphasis in different countries, so as not to jeopardize the development and poverty reduction opportunity offered by tourism in developing countries. It is clear that for those actors being pro-active in addressing climate change, mitigation offers a range of business opportunities. Given current societal trends, it seems that there will be new, permanent and growing markets for environmentally oriented tourists and many opportunities to develop new low-carbon tourism products.

Four major mitigation strategies for addressing greenhouse gas emissions from tourism can be distinguished:

- reducing energy use;
- improving energy efficiency;
- increasing the use of renewable energy, and;
- sequestering carbon through sinks.

This report has systematically investigated the various options with regard to technological improvements, environmental management, economic and policy measures, and behavioural change, arriving at a number of conclusions:

Reducing energy use is the most essential aspect of mitigation, which can be achieved by altering destination development and marketing (tour operators), destination choices (tourists) as well as shifts in transport use from car and aircraft to rail and coach. Changing management practices can be of importance for business tourism (videoconferencing). Tour operators play a key role in this process, as they bundle products into packages that are advertised to and purchased by tourists. Tour operators can also increase length of stay, which would very effectively reduce the carbon footprint per tourist day and increase economic opportunities for destinations.

It has to be considered however that current tourism trends show an increase of short stays. Overall, tour operators have a considerable influence on creating demand for less carbon intensive journeys by creating attractive products that meet tourists' needs and desires.

Regarding the most important sector, aviation, the industry favours emission trading over the taxation of fuel or emissions. Aviation is likely to soon enter the European Union Emission Trading Scheme, which will increase the speed at which new technologies are introduced. An even better alternative might be to create an emissions trading scheme entirely for aviation. More efficient technology would be introduced faster, while the profitability of the aviation sector could grow rapidly, as prices for tickets can be increased despite stable costs for operating aircraft.

Improving energy efficiency can be another mechanism to decrease energy demand. New technology will significantly reduce the emissions of aviation in a 'business-as-usual' scenario, simply because it saves fuel-costs and improves aircraft performance. Reductions in emissions per pkm are likely to be in the order of 32% between 2005 and 2035. Additional efforts to bring aviation technology to the theoretical limit (50% reduction of emission factors between 2005 and 2035), would contribute to an overall reduction of total emissions from tourist travel (excluding same-day, including all transport modes) by 14% with respect to the 'business-asusual' scenario.

The same overall emissions reduction (14%) may be achieved with strong reductions in the accommodations sub-sector. New technology within car transport has a potential of reducing 7% of all tourist emissions. Note however, that the introduction of new air transport technology takes decades as the market introduction of new technologies is slow, because fleet renewal stretches overseveral decades due to the long operational life of aircraft. The more rapid introduction of new technologies is thus dependent on environmentally pro-active management decisions that need to be aided by government policy, such as emission trading.

This study found that virtually all sources of renewable energy are relevant for tourism, including wind, photovoltaic, solar thermal, geothermal, biomass and energy regeneration from waste. Several studies have explored the extent to which renewable energy sources can be used for tourism, in particular in island destinations where energy supply based on fossil fuels is expensive and at risk of supply interruptions.

These studies come to the conclusion that the use of renewable energy sources is generally economical and technically feasible. For example, in a vast number of destinations in the tropics, investments in solar energy can pay off in as little as two years. Biofuels are another option to contribute to more sustainable transport systems, even though it should be noted that several problems remain unsolved, particularly relating to the sustainability and efficiency of biofuel production and increasing competition over land, especially arable land area. Also the maximum share of biofuels for use in (all) transport is estimated at less than 10%.

CO_2 can also be stored in biomass (e.g., through afforestation and avoided deforestation), in aquifers or oceans, and in geological sinks (e.g., depleted gas fields). Within the tourism industry, this is currently practiced through carbon compensation or carbon offsetting, which means that an amount of greenhouse gas emissions equal to that caused by a certain activity (i.e., a flight), will be reduced elsewhere (i.e., through the planting of additional trees). There is still a lot of confusion among tourists about what carbon offsetting is, and there is also evidence that particularly hyper-mobile travellers, who account for the major share of the distances travelled and emissions caused, are not ready to support voluntary carbon offsets.

There is also a risk that carbon offsetting, which has been initiated as a voluntary form of carbon reductions, is now becoming the means used by the industry to 'reduce' emissions. This effectively means that producer responsibility is turned into customer responsibility, which may be problematic if no action to reduce fuel use is taken.

As such, carbon offsetting can be seen as a controversial solution to climate protection, because it potentially diverts from the real causes of the problems and therefore bypasses the structural and technological changes that need to be made to achieve long-term greenhouse gas reductions in the tourism sector. Nevertheless, carbon offsetting does have a role to play in future mitigation efforts in tourism.

In the framework of this report, the expert team developed several scenarios considering different mitigation options, in order to estimate how emission pathways in the global tourism sector might develop in the future. In case of the 'business-asusual' scenario (which takes into account the UNWTO's *Tourism 2020 Vision* forecast of an average 4% annual growth of international tourist arrivals up to 2020) it was estimated that CO_2 emissions in the global tourism sector may experience a growth of 161% by 2035.

- If maximum assumed technological efficiencies were achieved for all transport modes, accommodations and activities, this may result in 38% lower emissions.

- Reducing energy use by a combination of transport modal shifts, shifts to shorter haul destinations and increasing average length of stay may result in emission reductions by 44%.

Considering the projected dynamic growth of tourism activities, there is a large task ahead if tourism is to reduce its emissions to the same extent as other economic sectors. For an effective reduction of emissions, the tourism sector needs to apply a combination of mitigation measures. Under the most effective mitigation projection, using a combination of both above measures, the 'business-as-usual' scenario emissions in 2035 could be reduced by 68%, thus achieving a 16% reduction of emissions with respect to the emissions in 2005.

The Way Forward to Adaptation and Mitigation in Tourism

Concern about climate change is increasing worldwide and the IPCC has made it clear that global climate change is only just beginning. The impacts of climate change on the tourism sector will steadily intensify, particularly under higher emission scenarios. Climate change would redistribute climate resources for tourism geographically and seasonally and poses a risk to ecosystems worldwide.

The nature and intensity of climate change impacts will differ for tourism destinations around the world. The most vulnerable regions are in developing countries, which generally also have less adaptive capacity, and this will be a particular challenge for their tourist destinations and their host communities. Climate change impacts on the tourism sector could influence other economic sectors, such as agriculture and local business networks supplying tourism. Conversely, the tourism sector must also be cognizant of the implications of climate change adaptation in other economic sectors, which could have significant impacts on tourism. As the financial sector incorporates a company's climate change strategy, or lack of one, into its investment criteria, it will influence credit rating and insurance rates. Climate change mitigation requires the transformation of energy and transportation systems worldwide, with implications for the cost of travel and tourist mobility. Climate change also has the potential to have an adverse effect on the global economy and poses a security risk in some regions.

Consequently, climate change is anticipated to have profound implications that could fundamentally transform aspects of the global tourism sector.

> *"Given that climate change is expected to pose an increasing threat to tourism operations in many destinations [...], WMO urges governments and the private sector to increasingly use climate information generated through National Meteorological and Hydrological Services [...], and to take additional steps towards incorporating climate considerations in tourism policies, development and management plans."*

The unmistakable conclusion of this report is that the significance of climate change to tourism is not in some distant and remote future. Climate change is already influencing decision-making within the tourism sector, including tourists, forward looking tourism businesses and investors, and international tourism organizations. The next generation of tourism professionals will need to contend with virtually all of the broad range of impacts outlined in this report.

Tourism can and must play a significant role in addressing climate change as part of its broader commitment to sustainable development and the United Nations Millennium Development Goals. Tourism as a non-negligible contributor to climate change has the responsibility to reverse the growth trajectory of its GHG emissions over the next three decades to a more sustainable emissions pathway consistent with the actions of the international community. The climate change mitigation potential is thought to be relatively high in the tourism sector because efforts to lower energy consumption and GHG emissions in the sector are still largely in their infancy, and thus far have been generally taken without any vision of a coordinated sector-wide strategic response. 106 Also in this study it is shown that several combinations of strong efforts, including decoupling of the growth of tourism from the growth of tourism transport volumes and technological innovation, may significantly reduce emissions in 2035, without jeopardizing the growth of world tourism in number of trips or guest-nights.

Regardless of the success to reduce GHG emissions by the international community, there will undoubtedly also be costs associated with climate change adaptation. These costs cannot be borne solely by those affected, especially as those most affected are likely to be those less able to take action to cope with the changes (e.g., LDCs, SIDS and local tourism SMMEs). The capacity of the tourism sector to adapt to climate change is thought to be relatively high due to its dynamic nature and therefore there will be important opportunities for tourism to reduce the vulnerability of communities to climate change.

The United Nations Secretary General Ban Ki-moon has called for action by the international community on climate change to be taken in close coordination with action on poverty alleviation and the Millennium Development Goals. The IPCC further contends that there are significant synergies that can be exploited in bringing climate change to the development community and critical development issues to the climate change community. There is an important opportunity for the tourism sector to show leadership in the development of a coherent policy agenda that integrates both development and climate change perspectives.

This is the time now for the tourism community to cellectively formulate a strategy to address what must be considered the greatest challenge to the sustainability of tourism in the 21st century.

5

Tourism in Protected Areas: A Financial Analysis

The Global Mandate for Protected Areas

A protected area is "an area of land and/or sea especially dedicated to the protection and maintenance of biological diversity, and of natural and associated cultural resources, and managed through legal or other effective means" (IUCN, 1994). A protected area may be a wetland, a tropical or deciduous forest, a cultivated landscape of value, an alpine region, a savannah, a marine area or any number of other types of natural or partially modified ecosystems – or indeed any combination of types of ecosystems. In addition to covering an array of ecosystem types, protected areas are defined in a number of different ways relevant to the objectives and values for which they are managed.

Traditionally one of the most widely used and, arguably, most effective tools for achieving conservation goals, protected areas today play a significant role in supporting local, national, and international biodiversity policies. They also serve as places for scientific research, wilderness protection, maintenance of environmental services, education, tourism and recreation, protection of specific natural and cultural features, and sustainable use of biological resources.

The importance of protected areas is emphasised by international conventions and programmes such as the CBD, the World Heritage Convention (WHC), the Ramsar Convention on Wetlands, the UN Law of the Sea Convention, UNESCO's Man and the Biosphere (MAB) Programme of the United Nations

Educational, Scientific and Cultural Organisation (UNESCO) and the global programme of WCPA. Together these agreements and programmes are the backbone of international policy on the establishment and management of protected areas for biodiversity conservation and the sustainable use of natural and cultural resources. The CBD is a particularly important endorsement of protected areas in that: it is globally accepted, with over 170 signatory nations adopting its objectives of conserving biodiversity, sustainably using biological resources, and equitably sharing benefits arising from this use

Category I

An area of land and/or sea possessing some outstanding or representative ecosystems, geological or physiological features and/or species available primarily for research and/or environmental monitoring. A wilderness area is a large area of unmodified or slightly modified land and/or sea retaining its natural character and influence without permanent or significant habitation which is protected and managed so as to preserve its natural condition.

Category II

A natural area of land and/or sea designated to (a) protect the ecological integrity of one or more ecosystems for present and future generations; (b) exclude exploitation or occupation inimical to the purposes of the area; and (c) provide foundation for spiritual, scientific, educational, recreational, and visitor opportunities all of which must be environmentally and culturally compatible.

Category III

An area containing one or more specific natural or natural/cultural feature which is of outstanding or unique value because of its inherent rarity, representative or aesthetic qualities or cultural significance.

Category IV

An area of land and/or sea subject to active intervention for management purposes so as to ensure the maintenance of habitats and/or to meet the requirements of specific species.

Category V

An area with coast and sea, as appropriate, where the interaction of people and nature over time has produced an area with significant aesthetic, ecological and/or cultural value and often with high biological diversity. Safeguarding the integrity of this traditional interaction is vital to the protection, maintenance and evolution of such an area.

Category VI

An area containing predominantly unmodified natural systems managed to ensure long term protection and maintenance of biological diversity while providing at the same time a sustainable flow of natural products and services to meet community needs.

- it defines biodiversity broadly as the variability among living organisms at the genetic, species and ecosystems levels; and
- it presents a powerful array of actions and tools for implementing a global biodiversity agenda. The CBD envisions a major role for protected areas in national plans for biodiversity. Article 8 calls for the establishment and maintenance of systems of protected areas. As experts, IUCN has given advice on the focus and design of national systems of protected areas – see Davey, A. G. (1998). Article 8 establishes global priorities and policies for the *in-situ* conservation of biodiversity and obliges Parties:
- to establish systems of protected areas or areas where special measures need to be taken to conserve biodiversity;
- to develop guidelines for the selection, establishment and management of protected areas or areas where special measures need to be taken to conserve biodiversity;
- o regulate or manage biological resources important for the conservation of biodiversity whether within or outside protected areas, with a view to assuring their conservation and sustainable use;
- to promote environmentally sound and sustainable development in areas adjacent to protected areas with a view to furthering protection of these areas; and
- to provide financial and other support for *in-situ* conservation.

The central role of protected areas in Article 8 is reflected in the decisions of the Conference of the Parties (COP). These emphasise the importance of protected areas in achieving biodiversity goals for forest, marine, coastal, and other ecosystems.

For example, the third COP (November 1996) recommended that strategies for sustainable forest management be based on an ecosystem approach, which integrates conservation measures such as protected areas and the sustainable use of biological resources. The WHC also provides a global foundation for protected areas by encouraging the identification, protection and preservation of the cultural and natural heritage around the world. The WHC is a mechanism for ensuring that globally important sites are protected and properly managed. Under the WHC, countries submit sites for inclusion on the World Heritage List of sites which are then eligible for funding from the World Heritage Fund. Thus this Convention provides countries with an incentive to create and maintain protected areas of global significance.

Further agreements and action in the international arena also support protected areas. The UN Law of the Sea provides the framework for establishing marine protected areas by allocating rights to territorial seas. The Ramsar Convention encourages mutual commitment from signatories in the designation of wetland protected areas important to waterfowl and which can also promote the "wise use" of wetland ecosystems.

UNESCO's MAB Programme recognises protected areas as key components in the design and management of biosphere reserves and important tools for meeting sustainable use objectives. Through the implementation of the biosphere reserve concept, the programme provides an international framework to: (a) conserve natural and cultural diversity; (b) promote models of land management and of approaches to sustainable development; and (c) improve knowledge on the interaction between humanity and nature through research, monitoring, education and training. IUCN's WCPA is the major global network of protected area specialists. The mission of WCPA is "to promote the establishment and effective management of a representative worldwide network of terrestrial and marine protected areas", as an integral contribution to the IUCN mission. The mission of IUCN is "to influence, encourage and assist societies throughout the world to conserve the integrity and diversity of nature and to ensure that any use of natural resources is equitable and ecologically sustainable". The main purposes of protected area management, as outlined by the WCPA, are: scientific research, wilderness protection, preservation of species and genetic diversity, maintenance of environmental services, protection of specific natural and cultural features, tourism and recreation, education, sustainable use of resources from natural ecosystems, and maintenance of cultural traditions and attitudes.

The need for Innovative Approaches

Strong as this international mandate may be, global conventions and programmes alone are not enough to ensure the continued existence of, and sufficient funding for, protected areas. In times of fiscal austerity and tightening government budgets – especially in developing countries which are home to much of the world's biodiversity – traditional funding sources for protected areas are increasingly under threat. Innovative alternatives to these traditional sources are needed in order to secure the long term viability of protected areas. In addition to strengthening traditional funding, finding additional funding sources has the added benefit of diversifying a protected area's income sources. This makes the protected area more viable and helps it to withstand times of economic hardship.

Where does a protected area manager look for alternative funding sources? What do these potential supporters want from the protected area? And what does the protected area manager communicate to these supporters? Valuation can help the protected area manager find the answers to these questions, and more.

The process of valuation provides protected area managers with information about the protected area's goods and services, the values which people (potential supporters or customers) place on those, which values are being captured and which are not, and which groups could derive more benefits through alternative uses of the protected area and are therefore inclined to be a 'threat' to the protected area. In this way, valuation provides useful information for management and financing decisions regarding protected areas.

A thorough scoping stage of a valuation study identifies the array of benefits flowing from the protected area and the people who value those benefits. This information is likely to expose those who are not contributing to the protected area but derive benefits from it (and are therefore potential sources of funding), as well as those who are excluded from deriving benefits from the protected area but are being asked to 'pay' for the protected area, e.g. through taxes, property loss or foregone opportunities. For instance, a protected area manager searching for additional financing may realise, in the preliminary stages of a valuation study, that the protected area is not capturing any of the value held by bird watchers using the area. To capture this, the manager might decide to start renting out binoculars and bird-books or to start a fund directed at donations from bird-watchers earmarked for bird conservation efforts. On the other hand, if the bird-watchers are a low-income group and unlikely to be able to pay for the benefits they receive, the protected area manager may approach a potential donor, such as the Royal Society for the Protection of Birds or the Ramsar small projects fund, which may be willing to be a benefactor for the bird-watching group. By knowing the benefits and the groups receiving these benefits, alternative avenues for funding protected areas are indicated.

In another instance, a protected area manager might find that neighbouring people are not deriving any benefits from the protected area and, in fact, have been forced to forego opportunities of using the land for agriculture, forestry or other uses due to the establishment of the protected area. This manager needs to look for alternative management practices that enable the protected area's neighbours to derive some benefit from the presence of the area without compromising its overall conservation objectives, thereby reducing the pressure to convert the land to other uses. Alternatives may be to open the protected area to sustainable harvesting of forest products or to develop local capacity to service tourists visiting the protected area. In this case, identifying marginalised groups and the benefits that they have foregone helps the manager solve conflicts and thus reduce threats.

The possibility of looking for alternative management practices depends on different factors that should be considered as part of the valuation process:

- What is the management category for the area? A Category V or VI protected area has the potential to accommodate a wide range of uses by zoning the resources within the area. A Category I area offers a much more limited array of use options such as research.
- Is the protected area well managed? Capturing the values attributed to a protected area in turn requires the capacity to manage that area to maintain these values.

- Is the protected area attractive enough? As this paper explains there are a number of different kinds of values attributable to protected areas. Tourism and recreation values are particularly attractive to managers because they are relatively easy to capture and because they can be a source of significant funds.

A New Vision for Protected Areas

But some areas may not have the ability to draw tourists. An economic valuation study conducted at a national level can indicate which areas are most able to obtain funding from tourists and which are not. A system of cross-subsidisation, or a separate funding strategy, can then be used to support wildlife which may be biologically important, but with little appeal to tourists. Such management and finance decisions are not limited to the local protected area manager. Often decisions, such as increasing access fees and the opening up of areas for new tourist concessions, are considered under national or provincial laws and regulations on protected areas. The valuation process, however, can inform decisions taken at national and international levels and should provide recommendations on how to enhance the national legal framework for protected areas management. All governments have limited resources to spend on services for their citizens and must make decisions about how and where to spend these resources. Sectors within government compete for a share of the fiscal budget. Thus protected areas compete with development programmes, health and welfare services, education, and the military, and so forth. Valuing protected areas can provide the economic reasons, to complement the biodiversity ones, why governments – and others – should invest in them.

The 'Client' Approach

Governments, donors, tourists and local people decide what goods and services to buy with their money. In economic terms, such groups are the real or potential 'customers' of the goods and services of protected areas: they are the 'clients' of the protected area. Since protected areas supply goods and services in a generally competitive marketplace they are, in an economic sense, businesses facing a complex array of customers who may wish to spend their limited funds elsewhere. A business is in business to make profits. It makes profits by selling goods and services to customers at a price marginally higher than the cost of producing these goods and services. Though a protected area is in the business of providing biodiversity services, it can use a business approach – profit-centred and entrepreneurial so as to maximise its financial capacity to achieve conservation aims.

To illustrate this client approach, consider some examples of protected areas – a wildlife sanctuary in South Asia, a savannah park in southern Africa, a forest reserve in South America, a protected landscape in Europe or a marine protected area in the South Pacific. All such areas provide a stream of goods and services (benefits) to a host of customers (those who hold a value for the benefits).

What benefits do such protected areas generate and to whom? Are these benefits and their distribution sufficient to ensure that the protected area will be conserved? In particular, do these benefits result in adequate financial flows to maintain the protected area? If not, what measures are needed to generate revenues for managing this protected area and achieve the conservation and development objectives of the protected area?

Think of the customers of the protected area. Think of its neighbours and those living within it as customers. What goods and services do they want from the protected area? Timber to convert into charcoal for fuel? Non-timber products such as fruits and honey? Medicinal plants? Thatching grasses? Do they want access to lands for grazing their livestock or to watering holes during the dry season? Do they want to have access to coral reefs for seafood? What measures are necessary to ensure that the uses they make of protected area resources are sustainable and that they pay for the goods and services provided by the protected area?

Economic Values of Protected Areas

Should the neighbouring or resident community be involved in a collaborative management scheme? Can a system of tradable harvesting permits for timber, honey, fish or grasses be developed? What about access rights for grazing, hunting, or watering? How can support be maintained for traditional land use practices which conserve biodiversity?

Alternatively, think of neighbours or residents as a direct threat to the protected area. Their interest in protected area land for intensive farming or ranching may outweigh their interest in conserving the protected area. Is it in their immediate economic interest to convert the protected area to other uses that threaten biodiversity? If so, why? Are there existing measures, such as agricultural or prospecting subsidies or poorly-defined access rights to wild resources, which threaten biodiversity? Are such "perverse incentives" actually encouraging neighbours to destroy the protected area? Are there positive incentives which can be put in place instead?

Now think of commercial customers of the protected area. What goods and services can be harvested sustainably from the protected area and sold on the open market? Tourism, of course, is often an important non-consumptive service. What about the commercial sales of timber and non-timber products, including medicinal and ornamental plants, honey, bush meat, and so on? Does the protected area offer opportunities for hunting or fishing? Is it a prime site for bio-prospecting? Are there potential genetic resources to be harvested? How can such commercial operations be structured to generate revenues for the protected area so as to support the overall goal of biodiversity conservation?

Additionally, there are probably downstream or indirect customers of the protected area. What benefits accrue to downstream communities and enterprises or more generally to the entire country or region? If the protected area serves as a watershed, it provides benefits to downstream water users including farmers, ranchers, miners, manufacturers and villagers. If it is an area visited by people from cities nearby, then it offers a range of benefits (recreational, educational etc.) to urban dwellers. These groups have a stake in conserving the protected area, but do they have any means to express that interest? What measures will encourage and enable them to support the protected area? Can fiscal measures be used to collect revenues from these downstream customers?

Also, consider the global customers of this protected area. Within the mandates of global environmental agreements, the protected area may provide several global benefits. These could include biodiversity conservation, carbon sequestration, habitat for endangered species and migratory species, replenishing fish stock for traditional and commercial fisheries, mitigation of natural disasters and impacts related to climate change, and so on. What measures will enable the global community to support the protected area? Can the Global Environmental Facility (GEF) be used as a means of finance in such cases?

In short, a protected area can provide a diverse array of biological goods and services to a diverse array of customers. Bringing an entrepreneurial, private sector perspective to protected area management – in the first instance, by thinking of customers for protected area products – can help the protected area to sell goods and services in a way

A New Vision for Protected Areas

That will strengthen the ability of the protected area to support the conservation of biodiversity and sustainable use of natural resources. Valuation is a tool which can help protected area managers to start thinking like a business manager by providing a structured approach for identifying real and potential customers, estimating appropriate prices for goods and services, and signalling ways of capturing those prices.

Economic Values of Protected Areas

Identifying a protected area's goods and services, determining who values those goods and services, and measuring these values is not always a straightforward process. The goods and services include recreation and tourism, plant and wildlife habitat, genetic resources, water supply, protection against natural disasters, and so on. Many of these goods and services are not traded on commercial markets and therefore have no evident market value. The values of non-market goods and services need to be measured and expressed in monetary terms, where possible, so that they can be weighed on the same scale as commercially traded components.

The concept of total economic value (TEV) is now a well-established and useful framework for identifying the various values associated with protected areas. The total economic value of a protected area consists of its use values and non-use values. A protected area's use values are in turn made up of its direct use values, indirect use values, and option values. Non-use values include bequest values and existence values.

The difference between economic valuation and financial analysis should be made clear at this stage. Economic valuation, based on economic value, measures market and non-market values that people hold for a protected area. Financial analysis is a subset of economic valuation and measures the flow only of money through a protected area. Though financial analysis is a very useful tool, it may not be the most appropriate for all situations. This guide uses economic valuation as a framework because it captures a broader array of values.

The direct use values of a protected area are values derived from the direct use of the protected area for activities such as recreation, tourism, natural resource harvesting, hunting, gene pool services, education and research. These activities can be commercial, meaning they are traded on a market (resource harvesting, tourism and research), or non-commercial, meaning there is no formal or regular market on which they are traded (fuelwood collection and informal grazing). The value of commercial uses will generally be a straight-forward process of directly obtaining market-priced values. However, if these prices are administratively set, they may not reflect the true value for the product. Valuing non-commercial uses is more complex and entails a range of techniques which solicit values for goods and services of a roughly comparable nature from other markets.

The indirect use values of a protected area are values derived from the indirect uses of the protected area. Indirect uses are largely comprised of the protected area's ecological functions such as watershed protection, breeding habitat for migratory species, climatic stabilisation and carbon sequestration. Protected areas also provide natural services, such as habitat for insects which pollinate local crops or for raptors which control rodent populations. Indirect use values are often widely dispersed and thus go unmeasured by markets. Alternative valuation techniques discussed later are necessary for measuring them.

The option values of a protected area are values derived from the option of using the protected area sometime in the future. These future uses may be either direct or indirect and may include the future value of information derived from the protected area. Future information is often cited as particularly important for biodiversity as untested genes may provide future inputs into agricultural, pharmaceutical or cosmetic products. Non-use values are values which humans hold for a protected area which are in no way linked to the use of the protected area. Two common examples of non-use values are bequest values and existence values. Bequest values relate to the benefit of knowing that others benefit or will benefit from the protected area. Existence values reflect the benefit of knowing that the protected area exists even though one is unlikely to visit it or use it in any other way. Non-use values are particularly difficult to measure.

A Framework for Valuing Protected Areas

Identifying the values which people hold for a protected area may be an interesting intellectual exercise, but without a framework which embeds the values in a broader context, the process is just that – an exercise. A structured assessment process gives purpose and direction to a valuation study and saves time and money in the end. Such a process identifies what the values will be used for, which values are important to measure, and which techniques of valuation are most appropriate. The assessment process proposed in this section involves three basic steps:

1. Define the audience.
2. Determine the scope of the study.
3. Choose the appropriate analytical techniques.

The decisions taken in these steps are interrelated in that the interests of the audience will help to define the scope of the study and the scope will dictate, to some extent, the relevant techniques.

Define the Audience

Before starting a valuation study, the end use and audience for that study need to be determined. Defining the eventual use of the valuation study gives the study a *raison deter*, enables it to be carried out efficiently and effectively, and ensures that the information arrived at is relevant and clear to those who must use it. Valuations can be used to procure support for the continued existence of protected areas. But a valuation study can also inform decisions about the management or financing of the protected area. There are many types of decisions which are made by many different groups. Decisions are made about:

- designing and carrying out projects in or adjacent to protected areas;
- designing and carrying out projects which use protected area goods or services;
- designing and carrying out projects upstream to, or downstream from, protected areas which may impact them;

- establishing and implementing sectoral programmes relating to protected areas;
- establishing and implementing policies for protected area management;
- establishing and implementing policies for protected area financing; and
- designing strategic plans at local, regional, national and international levels.

These decisions are made by protected area managers, community members, government officials, sectoral ministries, private enterprise, donor agencies, NGO's, the international community, and more. A brainstorming session with the economist and relevant stakeholders may help the protected area manager to identify the type of decision to be made and the groups that need to be involved.

The type of decision and the nature of the stakeholder groups help determine which values need to be measured and how those measurements should be expressed. For instance, a decision about carrying out a construction project adjacent to a protected area requires information about a set of values different from those needed for a decision about how much global funding to seek in support of maintaining biodiversity in a protected area. Additionally, a group involved in the public enquiry of the construction project will need the information presented in a manner different from a ministry of finance or the GEF.

The perspectives of the relevant stakeholder groups will also influence what is considered a benefit and what is a cost. Assigning the title of benefit or cost is ultimately a subjective process. One person's costs may be another person's benefits. In some cases it may be necessary for a protected area manager to represent what is a 'cost' to taxpayers (civil service jobs) as a 'benefit' to a particular constituency (local communities). Valuation studies can be expensive and time consuming. But not only is it unlikely to be necessary to measure all the values for a protected area, the values arrived at will not be valid for long. Values which people ascribe to a protected area are like preferences and prices, and thus are likely to change over time. Tailoring the valuation study to suit the particular needs of the decision at hand and the targeted stakeholder groups will make for a more efficient and effective study.

Determine the Scope in Terms of the Time, Data, Resources and Institutional Structure

Having determined what the valuation information will be used for and who will use it, the next step is to determine the appropriate scope for the study. The scope of the study must be defined in geographical, temporal and subject terms.

It is necessary to know what geographical area the valuation study should cover. Protected areas can cover a vast area of land or water, not all of which may be relevant to the decision-making process. For instance, if a local planner needs to know the impact of an infrastructure project proposed for a site on the northeast corner of the protected area then it is probably unnecessary to measure values of unimpacted goods from the southwest corner. On the other hand, an international donor agency which needs information about the protected area's contribution to the global climate change mitigation is likely to need values relating to the carbon sequestration services of the entire protected area, but not the values of viewing its predators by tourists.

Also, for a valuation study to be relevant, there needs to be a clear idea of the timeline involved in the decision-making process. A valuation study that arrives two years after decisions have been taken is irrelevant – no matter how valid the data. Likewise, the decision-makers using the valuation study need to be realistic about time limitations they impose on the study. The time required to conduct a valuation study depends on the types of benefits being measured, the state and relevance of existing data, the level of measurement required, the amount of certainty desired, the capacity to conduct the study, and so forth. Protected area managers must be realistic about their demands – it is unlikely, for example, that a full contingent valuation study can be done in three weeks – and if time is short, then expectations should be realistic.

Finally, it is important to define the scope of the study in subject terms. That is to say, the scoping stage of the study must identify exactly which values are relevant and should be (and can be) measured. As pointed out in Section 2, people ascribe many types of values to protected areas. The first step to determining which values are relevant is to get a broad idea of the benefits attributed to the protected area and the people who value those benefits – or in other words, the people who are stakeholders in the protected area.

The process of conducting this broad scoping exercise is itself a useful tool for internal management and finance decisions. This is because identifying the various values people hold for the protected area and the groups that derive benefits from the protected area highlights opportunities for obtaining revenues, improving services and minimising exposure to threats. Often the actual measurement of all or some of the values is unnecessary.

Of course, not all values identified through this broad scoping process are relevant to every decision. The next task in the scoping process is determining which values are relevant to the end decision. The type of decision will influence the ranking of the values. For instance, a decision about the impact of a development project on the protected area needs information about the values of goods or services affected by the project – therefore measuring these values should be a priority. On the other hand, a decision regarding alternative uses for the protected area needs information about the most important goods and services that would be foregone if an alternative use were chosen.

It is also important to consider the likelihood of being able to measure the values, and the costs of measuring them. As mentioned before, time and money are likely to be constraints on the study and may limit the types of values which can be measured. This is linked to the next stage in the framework – identifying methods of data collection – because the methodologies used will influence the time required and costs involved.

Choose the Analytical Technique

Measuring the direct use values which are traded on commercial markets is likely to be a more straightforward process than measuring the other values attributed to protected areas. This is because the markets have already done the work of eliciting values from the 'customers' of the protected area. The task of measuring these values involves identifying the markets for them, gathering data about prices paid in these markets, and determining the amount of the good or service traded on the market. For instance, the direct use values of tourism could be measured through the direct sales to tourists which may include expenditures on lodging and meals, entrance fees, concessions, rentals, guides and so on. Where prices such as entrance fees are administratively set and not market driven, however, it may also be necessary to estimate the likely market prices. Indicative methods available to protected area managers for capturing these values are given in the right column. These include collecting rents from those regularly using the land, applying user fees through systems such as hunting or camping permits, charging for access to the land or resources and so on.

A study which arrives at a value by tracing the flow of money through the official market is termed a financial analysis. A protected area's contributions to the financial transactions of the economy are its financial values. Values which fall outside of these financial transactions – such as many non-use and indirect use values –would not be included in a financial analysis. As is revealed in the case studies in Part II, these are the very values which often contribute significantly to the overall economic value of protected areas.

As emphasised before, the type of decision which the valuation information will be used for, and the people making the decision, have a significant influence over the nature of the valuation study. In fact, the group making the decision may hold a set of priorities far different from the protected area manager and the study may take on an entirely different perspective because of this. For instance, the Money Generation Model – used by the US National Parks Service to inform local communities of the value of nearby parks – counts jobs and local tax revenues generated by the park among the benefits attributed to it. Treating jobs as benefits can be rational from the perspective of the local community which may indeed see local jobs created by the park and local tax revenues derived from expenditures in the park as direct and indirect benefits attributable to the park. But from the perspective of the park manager who is running the park like a business, jobs and taxes are costs, not benefits. Taxes are, of course, also a cost to the taxpayers.

It is important to know the priorities of the group which will be using the valuation information as this will further affect which values are chosen and how they are presented. For instance, a local community is likely to be more interested in the number of local jobs created by the protected area, rather than the total number of jobs created. On the other hand a national government will be interested in considering employment prospects overall.

Employment may also take on a different significance when the ratio of foreign specialists to local workers is considered. In comparing protected area employment to other uses for which the area could be considered, a preference for work offered to local people may provide added support for the protected area. Alternatively, as is common in many developing economies, emphasis may be placed on the hard currency earnings and this becomes a determining factor.

As this model is specifically addressing a local community decision of whether or not to support the protected area, it may not provide much useful or appropriate information for a Ministry of Finance deciding how much national funding to allocate to the protected area.

Indeed, national government expenditure on the protected area is measured as a benefit in the Money Generation Model rather than as a cost. Nevertheless, such a model offers a simple approach to capturing some of the values of a protected area, for site-specific, local audience situations.

Where markets do not exist, values held by 'customers' must be elicited. An array of methods for eliciting both market and non-market values from people for environmental goods and services have been developed over the last few decades.

Though still a developing field, some of the more common and widely used methods include:

- contingent valuation,
- hedonic pricing,
- travel cost method,
- change in productivity,
- loss (or gain) of earnings,
- opportunity cost, and
- replacement cost.

The Money Generation Model

The Money Generation Model uses protected area-related expenditures from non-local tourists and Governments to determine the neighbouring communities' benefits in terms of jobs and tax revenues. An example from a study of Federal Interest Lands in South Florida done by FAU/FIU Joint Centre for Environmental and Urban Problems is used here to demonstrate the model.

Tourism

A. Sales benefits;
   1. Estimated non-local % of protected area use 90%
   2. Annual recreation visitor day.............................. 398,120
   3. Average daily expenditure.. $119
   4. Direct sales (1) x (2) x (3).. $42,638,652
   5. Indirect and induced sales multiplier 1.95
   6. Sales benefits from tourism (4) x (5)............ $83,145,371

B. Tax revenue benefits from tourism sales;
   1. Sales benefits (A.6)... $83,145,371
   2. Retail sales tax rate (state and local)......................... 6.5%
   3. Sales tax revenue benefits from tourism........ $5,404,449

C. Job benefits from tourism sales;
   1. Sales benefits from tourism (A.6) in millions............83.1
   2. Multiplier for jobs created per million..................41.4
   3. New jobs from tourism sales.................................. 3,440

Federal Government Expenditures 4

A. Sales benefits;
   1. Direct sales... $18,021,448
   2. Indirect and induced sales multiplier1..................... 1.8
   3. Total sales benefits (1) x (2)........................... $32,438,606

B. Tax revenue benefits from government related sales;
   1. Sales benefits (A.3)... $32,438,606
   2. Retail sales tax (state and local)................................ 6.5%
   3. Sales tax revenue benefits (1) x (2)............. $2,108,509

C. Job benefits from government related sales;
   1. Sales benefits (A.3).. $32.4m
   2. Multiplier for jobs per million dollars.................... 41.4
   3. New jobs from government expenditures............. 1,341

1. direct and induced sales multipliers (usually 1.2–2.8 for the US) vary with the complexity of the local community. More isolated areas are likely to have lower multipliers because a larger portion of spending will be conducted outside the area. If this multiplier is small, one option for

the community is to devise ways of providing more services and goods for tourists in the area.

2. The US retail tax system is comprised of state and local taxes. This is unlikely to be the case inmany countries and the level of government collecting retail taxes will affect whether or not they can be considered 'local' benefits.
3. The jobs multiplier will vary from industry to industry and range from 10 to 50 per million dollars in total sales in the US tourism industry. Additionally, rural areas tend to have larger jobs multipliers than towns and cities.
4. The procedures for calculating the job and tax revenue benefits 'non-local' (State) government expenditures in the protected area follow these Federal Government expenditure procedures.

Managers in developing countries may consider including Donor and International Government expenditures in this model. The contingent valuation method (CVM) uses a direct approach to valuing an environmental good or service in that it asks people through surveys or experiments what they are willing to pay for the good or willing to accept for the loss of the good. Contingent valuation is particularly attractive because it can estimate values where markets do not exist or where market substitutes cannot be found. For these reasons, CVM is widely used to measure existence values, option values, indirect use values and non-use values.

Hedonic pricing uses existing markets – such as the housing or labour markets – to determine the value of an environmental good. The assumption is that property values or wages reflect a stream of benefits, some of which are attributable to the environmental good. The analyst's task is to isolate that value which is attributable to the good.

Hedonic pricing can be used to establish some of the more aesthetic values of protected areas as residential property adjoining a protected area is likely to hold a higher value because the protected area is viewed as a benefit. On the other hand, hedonic pricing can be used to value environmental damages, and their effects on property values or wages. Hedonic pricing becomes problematic where alternative markets are distorted or where information about environmental products is not widespread and data are scarce.

Travel cost method also uses existing markets, determining a person's value of an environmental good from what they spend on travelling in terms of time, travel expenditures and entry fees. Travel cost methods are particularly useful for assessing

A Framework for Valuing Protected Areas

Willingness to Pay and Willingness to Accept

People reveal their value for the benefits derived from a protected area through their willingness to pay (WTP) for those benefits. A person's WTP can be elicited through surveys or surrogate markets. People also reveal their value for an environmental benefit through their willingness to accept (WTA) compensation for foregoing the benefit. In the case of environmental loss, people reveal their values through a willingness to pay to prevent the loss and their willingness to accept compensation to tolerate the loss.

These two concepts of benefit, WTP and WTA, should reveal the same values for the protected area. But empirical studies suggest this is not the case. It is generally believed that this is because people value the things they have more than those things they do not have. Therefore WTP is usually smaller than WTA. An additional problem arising from the concept of WTP in practice is that people with high incomes can afford to pay more than those with low incomes. This is particularly problematic when valuing a protected area in a developing country which is used by developed country tourists because the tourists will be able to place a higher value on their use and non-use benefits than the local people. In order to compare two such sets of value it may be necessary to measure the two sets of values as a percentage of income. Such a split may also support segmented pricing for local and foreign tourists as is increasingly common in developing countries. the non-commercial tourism, recreation and leisure values of a protected area. Travel cost methods, however, can be problematic in that they are data intensive, they rely on restrictive assumptions about consumer behaviour (e.g. multifunctional trips), and they are highly sensitive to the statistical methods used.

Change in productivity methods value the goods and services of a protected area by estimating the change in the value of production of a good or service that occurs as a result of the change in land of the protected area. Measuring the change in productivity is particularly useful when trying to discover the ecological values of a protected area. To take an example, a forested protected area is being considered for a clear-cutting operation. As it stands, the forest provides a service to farmers downstream by keeping the river from silting up. The change in productivity method would measure the current level of productivity and estimate its level after the clear-cutting, and calculate the difference between these levels to derive the loss in productivity. This loss is then a value of the protected area as it correctly stands.

Loss (or gain) of earnings methods evaluate the change in productivity of humans resulting from environmental deterioration (or improvement). Such methods may be useful in determining some of the more concrete effects of a change in the regulatory functions of protected areas. These regulatory functions include watershed protection, storage and recycling of organic matter, nutrients, and human waste, and climate regulation. For example, if water quality improvements reduce the levels of disease resulting from poor water quality, then the loss-of-earnings approach can be used to estimate benefits of clean water.

The opportunity cost approach provides an estimate of the value of a protected area based on the foregone income of the best alternative use of the area. Measuring the opportunity cost of the protected area can give the manager an idea of the competitive threats to the area. In the case of potential threats from people living adjacent to a protected area, the relevant opportunity costs will be the value of alternative land uses they may prefer, such as farming or ranching. Other interest in the area may come from pressures for industrial or urban development, mining or intensely modified recreation uses.

The replacement cost approach can be used to measure the cost of damage done to the protected area by looking at how much it would cost to replace the assets that are damaged. For example, the cost of restoring a protected area could be used as an estimate of the cost of environmental damage to the protected area. These costs are then compared to the costs of preventing the damage in the first place. If the replacement costs exceed the prevention costs then the damage should be avoided.

Case studies in Part II use these and other related methods to determine protected area value. As is evident from the cases, the methods used for a valuation study largely depend on the specific situation of that study and will likely be adapted for the study's specific needs.

The methodology for valuing environmental goods and services is continually developing. New methods are devised and old ones amended with every study that is conducted. Deciding on the methods which suit the needs of the study requires imagination and ingenuity. Those described in this section should not be seen as all inclusive, but as an introduction to the possible approaches to valuing protected areas.

Monitoring Tourism in Protected Areas

Sustainable Nature Tourism in Protected Areas

Many of Finland's protected areas are significant tourist attractions. Although the main purpose of protected areas is to protect natural features, they are also beneficially used for scientific research, amateur nature studies and outdoor recreation. The recreational use of protected areas can usually also be described as nature tourism.

Metsahallitus manages almost all of Finland's national parks and other protected areas in areas owned by the state. To help improve nature tourism and the related facilities, Metsahallitus nas drafted a special set of principles for sustainable nature tourism in protected areas, wilderness areas and sites in special conservation programmes.

Sustainable nature tourism is promoted in cooperation with local residents, the local authorities, firms offering tourist services, and other organisations. These principles for sustainable nature tourism are not simply a list of "dos and don'ts", but rather represent jointly agreed practical guidelines that will help to promote sustainability. These guidelines may be followed in different ways by different organisations, according to local conditions.

Principles for Sustainable Nature Tourism

The following nine principles are intended to guide the operations in protected areas. Explanations and examples are given to illustrate how these principles are put into practice. In protected areas, wilderness areas, and sites in special conservation programmes that are managed by Metsahallitus, sustainable nature tourism is practised according to the following principles:

1. Natural values are preserved and all activities promote nature conservation.
   - Nature is an important reason for visits.
   - Visitors can learn about nature and conservation.
   - Tourism does not disturb nature; not all areas are suited to tourism.
   - Groups are small, and use marked trails wherever possible.
   - Tourism is channelled into areas with suitable facilities.
   - Facilities are designed to fit in with the surroundings; the most beautiful natural areas are left undeveloped.
   - Erosion and other impacts are monitored, with corrective measures taken as needed.
2. The environment is subjected to as little pressure as possible.
   - Nature comes first; every effort is taken to avoid damage or disturbance.
   - Visitors leave no trace behind them.
   - Firewood is used sparingly.
   - Emissions of all kinds are minimised, and renewable energy sources preferred.
   - Metsahallitus and other organisations set good examples on environmental protection.
3. Local traditions and cultures are respected.
   - Visitors are encouraged to learn about local cultures.
   - Local cultures are suitably considered in the provision of information and activities.
   - Guides are familiar with local conditions.
4. Visitors increase their understanding and appreciation of nature and cultures.
   - Information is available for visitors before they come.
   - Information is easily available and attractively presented.
   - Visitors can contribute to the management of the area.
   - Guides are well trained.
5. Improved recreational facilities are provided for visitors.

- The needs of all visitors are considered.
- Facilities suit local demand and conditions.
- Visitors can enjoy peace and quiet, as well as guided activities.
- Facilities and services are developed in cooperation with local firms.

6. Visitors are encouraged to enjoy both mental and physical recreation.
   - Visitors are encouraged to move under their own steam.
   - Facilities are provided for hikers and other visitors.
   - Easy and demanding routes are available.
   - Opportunities exist for a variety of activities in natural surroundings.
   - All trails and other facilities are safe.
7. Local economies and employment are promoted.
   - Local firms' products and services are used where possible.
   - Employment is given to local people where possible, although outsiders may also contribute valuable ideas to help promote local development.
8. Publicity materials are produced responsibly and carefully.
   - Information is reliable and up-to-date.
   - Publicity work is conducted openly and interactively.
   - Publicity does not work against nature conservation.
9. Activities are planned and organised co-operatively.
   - Visitors' opinions are very important.
   - Training is organised together with local firms.
   - All interested parties may participate in planning.
   - In cooperation work, preference is given to organisations committed to these principles of sustainable nature tourism.

What is Sustainable Nature Tourism?

The goal of sustainable nature tourism is to provide visitors with valuable experiences in natural surroundings in fully sustainable ways. The above principles for sustainable nature tourism in protected areas relate to the various ecological, social, cultural and economic aspects of sustainability. Ecological sustainability involves respecting natural values. Not all areas are suited to nature tourism. Social, economic and cultural sustainability depend on the impacts of nature tourism on local residents and communities, and also the experiences of visitors. Nature tourism has the potential to improve both economic and spiritual well-being, but poorly planned or badly organised tourism can endanger natural features and local cultures, and also disturb other people using natural areas.

Measuring Sustainability

Metsahallitus is currently developing indicators to evaluate the sustainability of nature tourism. These indicators will be used to monitor the ecological, social and economic impacts of nature tourism in specific areas. Such indicators will also be used in the planning of the use and management of protected areas.

Sustainability through Cooperation

The increasing use of protected areas for nature tourism means that clear rules must be jointly agreed by everyone concerned. Written agreements are made between Metsahallitus Natural Heritage Services and local firms, to define acceptable and sustainable practices. In addition to the contracts entitling firms to organise activities in protected areas, even more detailed cooperation may be established through cooperation and partnership agreements. Sustainability can only be achieved through cooperation.

Visitor Management, A Tool for Sustainable Tourism Development in Protected Areas

Tourism is one of the world's fastest growing industries and its global impacts are immense and highly complex. Given that a high percentage of tourism involves visits to naturally and culturally distinguished sites, there are clearly major opportunities for investing in the maintenance of biological resources.

Tourism can help the sustainable management of protected areas, as a market-based alternative catering to the growing number of discriminating travellers trying to find, understand and enjoy a natural environment.

Tourism can help the sustainable management of protected

areas, as a market-based alternative catering to the growing number of discriminating travellers trying to find, understand and enjoy a natural environment. Tourism can support the protection of natural resources, as local residents realize the value of their asset and want to preserve it.

At the same time, our global heritage of living species is threatened as never before, as the protected areas that harbor so much of our biodiversity are exposed to the pressures of unsustainable development. The precautionary approach urges us to be especially concerned about tourism in protected areas, given the risk of damage and destruction to this unique natural resource.

Tourism is a major management issue for many protected areas as the presence and actions of visitors can present serious problems for biodiversity conservation.

Therefore tourism has to be managed with care and site managers must assess and balance the costs and benefits of tourism in protected areas. It is also important to find ways for local people and communities to benefit from tourism linked to conservation, as this helps to demonstrate the economic value of the natural resources being conserved.

Sustainable Tourism Development in Protected Areas

According to the World Tourism Organization sustainable tourism should:

1) Make optimal use of environmental resources that constitute a key element in tourism development, maintaining essential ecological processes and helping to conserve natural heritage and biodiversity.
2) Respect the socio-cultural authenticity of host communities, conserve their built and living cultural heritage and traditional values, and contribute to inter-cultural understanding and tolerance.
3) Ensure viable, long-term economic operations, providing socioeconomic benefits to all stakeholders that are fairly distributed, including stable employment and income-earning opportunities and social services to host communities, and contributing to poverty alleviation.

Sustainable tourism development guidelines and management practices are applicable to all forms of tourism in all types of destinations, including mass tourism and the various niche tourism segments. Sustainability principles refer to the environmental, economic and sociocultural aspects of tourism development, and a suitable balance must be established between these three dimensions to guarantee its long-term sustainability.

Sustainable tourism development requires the informed participation of all relevant stakeholders, as well as strong political leadership to ensure wide participation and consensus building. Achieving sustainable tourism is a continuous process and it requires constant monitoring of impacts, introducing the necessary preventive and/or corrective measures whenever necessary. Sustainable tourism should also maintain a high level of tourist satisfaction and ensure a meaningful experience to the tourists, raising their awareness about sustainability issues and promoting sustainable tourism practices amongst them.

Although the relationship between tourism and protected areas is complex and sometimes adversarial, tourism is always a critical component to consider in the establishment and management of protected areas. The definition of a protected area adopted by The International Union for the Conservation of Nature (IUCN) is: "An area of land and/or sea especially dedicated to the protection and maintenance of biological diversity, and of natural and associated cultural resources, and managed through legal or other effective means". Tourism can degrade natural areas, but can also be a reason to protect nature and culture. It can fund nature management and give nature a direct economic value, providing an incentive for local inhabitants and governments to protect nature.

Planning guidelines applicable to government and managers of protected areas include:

- Develop and implement effective land use planning measures that maximize the potential environmental and economic benefits of travel and tourism while minimizing potential environmental or cultural damage.
- Tourism activities should be planned at the appropriate level with a view to integrate socioeconomic, cultural and environmental considerations at all levels.
- Planning for tourism development must be integrated with other planning efforts at the site, regional and national levels, applying tools such as strategic environmental assessment and integrated resource management.

Poor planning and management of tourism development in and around protected areas can have devastating, longlasting and sometimes irreversible effects. Non-sustainable tourism is negative for conservation goals, for local communities and for societies in general.

Visitor Management in Protected Areas

Managing tourism in a sustainable way however requires both a long-term perspective and careful consideration of the many ways in which tourist activities and environment interrelate. What is needed is a systematic approach and a tool kit for planning in order to provide the necessary resources for visitor management. Therefore it is important to provide standardized data and collect them as early as possible.

Increasing recreational use of national parks and protected areas can impact natural and cultural resources and the quality of the visitor experience. Determining how much recreational use can ultimately be accommodated in a park or protected area is often addressed through the concept of carrying capacity.

From a management perspective, visitor impacts are significant because they directly reflect management success in meeting two primary mandates: resource protection and recreation provision. In this respect visitor impacts need to be managed since:

1. Visitor use can negatively affect vegetation, soil, water and wildlife resources as well as the quality of visitor experiences.
2. Visitor crowing and conflict can reduce the quality of visitor experiences.
3. Environmental attributes such as vegetation and soil resistance and resiliency, influence the type and severity of visitor resource impacts.
4. The use/impact relationship limits the effectiveness of visitor use reduction and dispersal strategies.
5. Decision-making frameworks can provide an explicit and flexible means of managing visitor impacts.
6. Indirect management strategies are often less costly to implement and are preferred by visitors.

Visitor management is an administrative action oriented towards maintaining the quality of park resources and visitor experiences. In many but not all situations management tends to focus on the negative impacts resulting from unrestrained visitor activity.

In other situations management acts assertively to create and maintain opportunities for visitors to view, experience, learn about and appreciate their natural and cultural heritage.

Broadly speaking there are four strategic approaches which can be used to reduce the negative impacts of visitors on protected areas:

1. *Managing the supply* of tourism or visitor opportunities, e.g. by increasing the space available or the time available to accommodate more use;
2. *Managing the demand* for visitation, e.g. through restrictions of length of stay, the total numbers, or type of use;
3. *Managing the resource* capabilities to handle use, e.g. through hardening the site or specific locations, or developing facilities; and
4. *Managing the impact* of use, e.g. reducing the negative impact of use by modifying the type of use, or dispersing or concentrating use.

The visitor management techniques available to managers of natural resources include:

- Regulating access by area (zoning);
- Regulating visitation by visitor type (through pricing)
- Implementing entry or user fees;
- Providing interpretation programmes and facilities;
- Regulating visitor behavior (codes of conduct);
- Concentrating on allowing accredited organizations to bring visitors to the site.

Sustainable tourism practice within protected areas is a long-term commitment.

But while it is important to think longterm, it is also necessary to set realistic short and midterm goals. Individuals, businesses and organizations must be aware that benefits are long-term, and should not expect to experience them immediately after sustainable practices are implemented. In practice, only a small portion of benefits will arise quickly; most will depend upon many years of continued effort.

Sustainable Tourism in the New Century

The nineteenth and twentieth centuries appear at first glance to have been a golden age when technology began to conquer all. Again Fukuyama says it clearly: "technology makes possible the limitless accumulation of wealth, and thus the satisfaction of an ever expanding human set of desires". That science backed scenario was backed by the philosophers Hegel and Marx in the past, and lives on at the UN, at the World Bank, and in the minds of most people in the developed world. But it is interpreted too simplistically by too many.

Since then progress through technology has been made but in a fashion that has brought new problems of pollution, resource pressures, global terror and war, and fast changing industrial and societal uncertainties. Sail gave way to steam, and then to electricity and now to electronics. Empires have grown and collapsed. Linear change, especially inevitable linear change, has been challenged by chaos and other change theories. The issue of limits to growth – a simple concept – perhaps too simplistic-has become an intense pre-occupation. The success of technology, in raising living standards, in raising expectations and in bringing more people into the developed world, has probably exceeded the earth's carrying capacity. And so-put simply – the ways that we manage the world may have to be changed, moving from unsustainable development to new forms of sustainable development. That change will involve new technologies. It will also involve new management techniques, and *above all* it will involve a very difficult process called behavioural change.

Sustainable Development

Sustainable Development is an old concept. In the agricultural terminology of the past it was called good husbandry or stewardship. It re-emerged in the 1960s, as global economic growth gathered speed after World War 2. A major milestone was reached by the founding of the international Club of Rome in 1968.

In 1980 the International Union for the Conservation of Nature (IUCN) based in Geneva, issued the *World Conservation Strategy*: it brought the cautious and sometimes negative thinking of the conservationist together with the positive but sometimes heedless world of the developer. It set the stage for the publication of the *Brundtland Report* of 1987, a work created by the World Commission on Environment and Development, and the work from which most of the current thinking on Sustainable Development stems.

According to Bruntland, sustainable development is:

"development that meets the needs of the present without compromising the ability of future generations to meet their own needs".

In 1992, at the Earth Summit in Rio de Janeiro, sustainable development became a goal agreed upon by the nations of the world.

Sustainable Development Principles

Four basic principles are crucial to the concept of sustainability:

(1) The idea of holistic planning, cross-sectoral planning and strategy making
(2) The importance of preserving essential ecological processes
(3) The need to protect both human heritage and biodiversity
(4) The requirement that development should be carried out so that productivity does not deplete resources for the long term and future generations

Business watchers will recognise in the above points the making of the case for a new Triple Bottom Line – replacing company and national bottom lines that were concerned with cash alone. The triple bottom line accounting concept requires accounting for financial, social and environmental outcomes. As we shall discuss later, that triple bottom line accounting may be about to give way to Quadruple Bottom Line accounting – with the need to assess climate change responsiveness.

The key words throughout Brundtland are balance and thought-thought about consequences before precipitate action. In addition to all the above Brundtland introduced to the debate the issues of fairness-of intergenerational equity, and also of international equity-requiring a greater convergence between rich and poor nations if the global system was to remain stable. And linked closely to the whole sustainable development discussion are two teasingly difficult areas-the Precautionary Principle and the need for a holistic approach.

Reaction in the USA

Early interest in the concepts of sustainable development was centred on Europe, although there were many thinkers and writers on sustainable development in the USA. Key US developments included the publication by the American Planning Association's Planning Advisory Service of the *Planners Guide to Sustainable Development* (PAS 467), and the work of the Presidents Council on Sustainable Development which worked between 1996 and 1999. Its final report, *Towards a Sustainable America: Advancing Prosperity, Opportunity and a Healthy Environment for the 21st Century,* put forward 140 ways forward to achieve a more sustainable agenda.

Shades of Green

Within the discussion of sustainable development there are two contrasting approaches, the so-called Deep Greens, and the so-called Shallow Greens (these groups are also sometimes called Deep Ecologists and Shallow Ecologists). Deep Greens evolved from the work of the Norwegian philosopher Arne Næss, basing his work on the idea that man is but a part of nature and that the whole environment has a right to live and flourish: all forms of life have intrinsic value. Deep Greens support traditional land use systems and technologies. They have close links to the Gaia movement.

Shallow Greens, while supporting sustainable development, are more pragmatic, and at the far end of the shallow green spectrum they are linked to the Wise Use movement in the US. Shallow Greens support and believe in the use of new technologies as a key way to create more sustainable development.

Within the world of sustainable development, there have been changes in polarisation as the threats to the environment created by the acceptance of the existence of climate change have been popularly recognised. But polarity of thinking lives on in many forms: a classic case is the European debate over the sustainability, and even the morality, of short haul air travel.

Overall, however, after 40 years of debate and discussion, the need for more sustainable forms of development is now established and accepted. The problems lie in understanding its *implications,* and in *implementing the ideas* within the paradigm.

Sustainable Tourism

Sustainable tourism was being discussed long before Mrs. Brundtland's commission delivered its verdict on the general economic development process. It emerged as a theoretical concept in the European Alps and around the Mediterranean Sea in the late 1970s. But theory was long in discussion before it became practice-that had to wait until the late 1980s, and until recently the concept was slow to find widespread implementation.

Tourism has had a long history. Some commentators place its origins in mediaeval pilgrimages, some in the Grand Tours of the eighteenth and nineteenth century, and others in the railway age world of the spa, mountain and seaside resort. But the real rise of tourism as a major pursuit and as a major industry begins in the post war period. UN World Tourism Organization statistics begin in 1950, when 25 million international travellers were recorded. Then the meteoric rise of the tourism industry began, with average year on year growth rates of 6.5% over the period 1950-2007. The year 2007 saw 903 million international arrivals world wide. UNWTO looks forward to 1.6 billion international arrivals by 2020. And far greater numbers holiday in their own countries: it is much easier however to count international arrivals. After 50 plus years of growth, no one working in the industry today can personally recall the pre-growth era. Growth – in numbers – in geographical impacts – in product terms – is regarded as an ongoing and given norm.

But tourism growth can have serious impacts on the environment and the world's peoples:

- It can have powerful physical impacts on places visited-farm and forest land swept away for airport and road construction, hotels and golf courses-often in scenic regions. Physical impacts can be complex and far-reaching-ski run development clearing trees can open the way to soil erosion, leading to landslides and potential major disasters. Heavily used areas can suffer erosion from sheer numbers of visitors-mountain erosion in the Alps, and Himalayas are classic examples. Whole ecosystems can be damaged.
- It can have serious cultural impacts. Tourists are wealthy and demanding guests. They can dismiss local customs, turn land values and labour markets upside down, make local languages redundant, and shift the balance of political power in favour of distant multi-nationals. In some scenarios tourism can bring vice and crime.
- More subtly, tourism can destroy the future it promises by rendering the destination dependent on its dollars,

then declaring a spoilt destination unfashionable and redundant. This, the operation of the tourism cycle, can effect both large resorts and rural retreats, rich and poor countries alike. Tourism is a volatile, fashion industry: it needs to be understood and well managed.

- In recent years, the impacts of the transport systems that are fundamental to modern tourism growth have been increasingly recognised. They burn large quantities of fuel in a fuel hungry world; they produce large quantities of emissions in a world beset by climate change issues. Climate Change and Transport Issues are major issues that loom over the world of tourism and sustainable tourism.

Sustainable tourism was designed not to stop tourism but to manage it in the interests of all three parties involved-the host habitats and communities, the tourists and the industry itself. It seeks a balance between development and conservation. It seeks to find the best form of tourism for an area taking into account its ecology and its culture. It may mean limits to growth, or in some cases no growth at all. The precautionary principle is important here.

Sustainable tourism seeks not just to plan for tourism, but to integrate tourism into a balanced relationship with broader economic development. That is the way in which sustainable tourism fulfils its requirement to think holistically, and one of its approaches to responsibility in business, the triple bottom line. In many rural areas the watchword is that tourism should be a tool for rural conservation, service retention and diverse development-not just a business for its own sake. In many urban areas, tourism can also work with heritage conservation by using redundant historic buildings for tourism purposes, by injecting tourism expenditures into areas needing urban regeneration, and by bringing jobs and re-training to areas with unemployment/social problems. But there is a key caveat. Sustainable development cannot be created by planning alone: it needs to work with the market and it needs to work with businesses great and small.

Progress and Problems

Sustainable tourism began as a purely reactive concept to the above issues, trying to stop negative change. Early outlines simply listed the negative impacts down the left side of the page and then had a wish list of their opposites, presumed to be positive outcomes, down the right side of the page. To be fair to their authors, there were no research findings or exemplars of successful sustainable tourism to draw on. Only gradually did sustainable tourism become pro-active, trying to create positive change. Many commentators – professional as well as amateur – enjoy criticising tourism. The key to achieving sustainable tourism is, however, to carry out analytical review and criticism, then implement effective management techniques, and then carry on a rolling review, criticism and management process.

What has been Achieved so Far?

Progress in sustainable tourism to date has concentrated on:

- Discussions and definitions, and devising basic assessment/evaluation programmes for small scale sites.
- Testing a range of individual management techniques, notably a range of visitor management programmes, especially those for protected areas, more sustainable accommodation provision, transport centred research and the creation of partnership programmes.
- Local and individual projects, often innovative, many very short term.
- Local Sustainable Tourism Strategies, usually written by or for local governments.
- A number of certification programmes of varying types and varying quality, largely voluntary membership programmes with all the inherent problems that membership programmes bring with them: such programmes are essentially prisoners of their members, succeeding with the success of their members, failing if their members either dilute their aims or leave the programmes.
- Discussion and trialling of a range of indicators designed to show progress (or lack of progress) in implementing sustainable tourism.
- The thinking through of the ethics and key concepts of the "subject" – one of the most important examples of this has been work by authors such as Bob McKercher, Bryan Farrell, Louise Twining Ward, and John Shultis, which

introduced uncertainty, risk, chaos and organic change into the previously linear, inevitable progression development scenario.

- Research and case study work: a wealth of knowledge now exists on some issues. We understand, for example, much more about the role of information provision and interpretation in implementing sustainable tourism. Much research remains to be done, even more remains to be implemented.
- The emergence of a "first generation" of academics who have worked on sustainable tourism. Many members of that first generation are now beginning to reach retirement or to take senior posts that make active research and authorship difficult.
- The peer reviewed international *Journal of Sustainable Tourism* was founded, publishing its first issue in 1993. It is now into Volume 16, with 768 pages each year. It is ranked 4th out of nearly 100 peer reviewed tourism journals in the world. It is one of the few tourism journals on the Thomson Social Science Citation Index. Over 1,000 papers have been submitted to it over the last 16 years: not all have been accepted.

Despite the list above, real progress in sustainable tourism – especially in implementation-has been remarkably slow until recently. Why?

- The tourism industry has not been driven, either by government or market forces, to achieve a more sustainable form of tourism. The industry has successfully opposed attempts to regulate its impacts, often by invoking the idea of self regulation as being the best way forward. The market for tourism remains strongly driven by price and fashion factors, and both the market and the industry remain conservative. Until recently there has been no powerful political, market based, moral or financial case for the industry to change. Denial has been a common approach
- Ecotourism became a development trap for some sustainable tourism advocates. Ecotourism is a subset of sustainable tourism, dealing with rural nature based activities. It was relatively easy to develop and assess

small scale sustainable tourism projects in rural areas. These projects appealed to the "small is beautiful" beliefs common amongst many and avcided the problems of contact with the mainstream tourist industry. Many people even assumed, wrongly, that it would be impossible to make "mass" tourism sustainable. It is not impossible: it is a must.

- Governments have been shy to encourage or require change in the tourism sector beyond basic safety regulations. Governments have traditionally practised boosterism towards tourism. In the new privatism that dominates governance, regulation is not welcome. The obvious places to try out regulatory systems, the urban and rural protected areas, are typically weak in tourism management skills, funds, political support and the new ethos required by the sustainable tourism approach.
- Society generally, the wider community, has not understood the need for sustainable development of most kinds. Sustainable development requires thought, change and investment: all are difficult to achieve. Sustainable living needs behavioural change by all stakeholders. Behavioural change is very hard to bring about. It is seen by many as unnecessary and painful.
- The Nature of Holiday Making. Many years ago (1990), the author was asked to address the main board of Thomson Travel about Sustainable Tourism. Thompson was, at that time, the largest tour operator in the UK, with a market share of the outbound holiday market in excess of 40%. The request was one that could not be refused – a major challengc. The address was made. The Board's reply can be summarised as: "nice idea, but the future is bright, the future is Euro-Disney, and we do not need a more sustainable product". A discussion ensued, followed by lunch. I was taken aside by a wise and experienced member of the board, who said, very gently but firmly, that I had to understand that holidays were the 2 weeks of the year when selfishness and thoughtless consumption were possible for everyone, when caution could be relaxed. She was the Director of Marketing. She was, in the real world of that time, correct.

- The academic research community also has to shoulder blame. Very few academic researchers have worked inside the tourism industry, and they remain outsiders, not understanding the pressures and the drivers within the industry, nor how to work with the industry. Equally, the industry has not been keen to work with academics because of the industry's essentially utilitarian, typically short term approach. There is an ongoing tension here.

Why has Sustainable Tourism Moved up the Public Agenda Now?

The fundamental reason is the recognition that climate change is happening, that its consequences could be seriously damaging, and that a series of changes are required in our existing life styles. Those changes could affect us all. And they could impact very strongly upon tourism and its growth. For the first time since 1950 tourism's growth rates are being threatened; for some regions the very existence of the tourism industry is threatened. The media is displaying new interest in green issues, and new anti-travel, anti-tourism pressure groups have developed. Air travel is being scapegoated. It must also be recognised that wider pro-nature, pro-heritage interests are growing in many (but not all) societies and parts of society, with strong implications for non-sustainable tourism. And it must also be said that long distance travel is becoming much more expensive.

New life has been breathed into the concept of sustainable tourism. Suddenly governments, regulators, the media, the industry and even a few travellers are questioning the survival of the status quo. They are less scornful of sustainable development. A powerful driver has emerged. Greed has, to a small extent, been replaced by fear. Sustainable Tourism is reacting to the new challenges by developing new approaches, including Slow Travel and the idea of Carbon-Free Destinations (Gosling 2009).

The concept of the triple bottom line is moving towards the concept of the Quadruple Bottom Line. The Fourth Line, is that of climate responsiveness. This idea was floated by the UN World Tourism Organization at Davos in 2007. (Becken, 2008) North Carolina could be the first state in the US to work on that idea: it has a special interest in railways and a remarkably intact rail net, if only for freight.

Whole new fields of research are developing within sustainable tourism- including behaviour change, market linked interpretation, eco-museum landscapes, social marketing, rail tourism, pluri-activity and life-style entrepreneurialism and new forms of food, beverage and hospitality linkages. They are especially remarkable within the University sector, because so many are multi and cross disciplinary in character.

And coupled with the fear created by climate change is the fear and uncertainty of now, of recession and financial issues. That could, paradoxically, be a powerful if unpleasant tool for behavioural change.

The Planning Process at International & National Scales

Sustainable tourism attracted interest at international level long ago. The United Nation's Environmental Programme (UNEP) published a review of voluntary codes of conduct for tourism in 1993 (Genot, 1995). The World Travel and Tourism Council (WTTC) launched its voluntary Green Globe triple bottom line certification programme in 1994. UN's World Tourism Organization produced a number of advisory publications from 1998 onwards. But few long lasting implementation examples can be directly linked to these activities. At national level the position was also weak, until recently. The UK's English Tourist Board published its plan, *The Green Light: A Guide to Sustainable Tourism*, in 1992, but it was little more than a short wish list. Other nations, such as Spain, have produced similar slight volumes. But in recent years national level progress has gathered speed. Australia has developed its powerful national Sustainable Tourism Cooperative Research Centre (STCRC), the industry backed Australian government initiative to carry out research using University research skills. Work on national sustainable tourism strategies has recently produced useful documents in, for example, Scotland and Norway. In Norway a totally new sustainable tourism strategy, aiming to make Norway into a carbon neutral destination, is being produced at this moment (2008) for implantation in 2010 – aiming to have carbon neutral status by 2025 (Gosling, 2009).

Regional and Local Implementation

It is at the regional and local level that much more tangible progress has been made, and where strongest links have been made with the business and community sectors.

Accommodation Provision

Accommodation is central to tourism. It is also central to sustainable tourism, setting the tone of provision for the visitor, and providing, if successful, employment directly and indirectly for the local area. It is also claimed that aspects of sustainable life styles seen and used on holiday are likely to be taken up by visitors in everyday life.

The Hotel Ucliva, Waltensburg, Graubunden, Switzerland

This is an innovative hotel development in a village far from the main tourism areas in Switzerland. The venture began in 1983, following the decision of a group of villagers to build a new hotel to help retain and expand employment and services in their declining rural area. It is a classic example of the holistic approach that sustainable tourism can develop: it uses tourism as an environmentally/community friendly development tool.

The hotel now has 72 beds and concentrates on family holidays and conference/course work. It uses traditional construction, with components made locally to ensure local jobs and income. Chemically based finishes and plastic were avoided: natural materials were used. It has high levels of energy efficiency and uses local wood and solar energy. Full kitchen and restaurant facilities serve locally sourced and locally processed foods. Farmers in the area were trained to supply the hotel's organic and semi-organic requirements. Ownership and control are local, a status obtained by innovative capital structures.

The hotel was planned and developed with input from University architecture and hospitality department staff as a demonstration project. From the outset the strong ecological design of the hotel and its many special features gave it a unique selling point, which was exploited by skilled PR and marketing, leading to it winning a series of prizes and awards. While collectively owned it has been operated on strict business principles but employing a triple bottom line accounting approach. When, in 1995, the hotel suffered falling customer numbers and revenue, rapid action was taken to replace the manager and introduce new marketing techniques and other improvements.

There have been 18 full time and 18 part time jobs created directly in the hotel, together with more jobs in the area as a result of the multiplier effect, especially in agriculture. Total cash flow to the area is calculated to be well over $4 million per year. Waltensburg's population has risen from 311 in 1984 to 400 in 2002.

The Talbot Inn at Knightwick, Worcestershire, England

In contrast to the Hotel Ucliva, the Talbot Inn is old and is privately owned. The inn has existed since the 14th Century, although it must be stressed that it is very largely a much later building. It is located in a rural area, and like many rural Inns, suffered from falling revenue, conservative management, and little innovation.

It was saved by the arrival home, in 1999, of the two daughters of the owners. While working in other areas of the UK they had begun to understand the principles of sustainable tourism, and notably the importance of *innovation to reintroduce tradition,* the ability to attract market share by offering a sustainable product, and the use of the triple bottom line as an asset rather than a burden. Under their guidance the hotel has been transformed from decline to award winning success, created local employment and income, and helped save the local farming economy.

Key innovations have included:

- Improvements to bedrooms to cut energy consumption, improve comfort, stress heritage links, and raise prices.
- Dramatic changes to restaurant provision to use local produce, grow some produce on site, use free range/ organic produce where necessary, update menus and work on heritage as well as modern dishes. The local farm economy has been boosted. Links have been made to the Slow Food movement.
- The building of a micro brewery on site to attract niche markets, use local barely and hops, save the local hop growers from low cost eastern European competition and create jobs.
- Development and hosting of regular farmers markets, to both boost Saturday daytime trade, market the Inn as a place to visit and help local producers.
- Development of a web site that links to other businesses and communities in the area.
- An effective marketing policy developed, and used to market the area as well as the business itself.

Transport Development

The role of public transport in sustainable tourism is an especially important one in Europe, where a dense bus and rail public transport network is slowly dying because of competition from airlines over long distances and cars over short distances, and because of unimaginative management, unaware of customer needs. Public transport is important to retain for older people, those without cars, or access to cars, to maintain employment, cut emissions and fuel use, and to engender long term behavioural change.

The examples below focus on the work of two UK Universities, Bristol and Plymouth, to encourage private railway companies to develop their slow local train services in rural areas for visitor use, boosting user numbers by over 25% within 4 years, and thus retaining the services for local people

The key to success in both cases lay in unlocking access to additional funding, developing partnership working to aid marketing, understanding market needs, and creating new products that built on the natural advantages of the local train and often indirectly developed additional more sustainable forms of tourism. The role of the Universities lay in their access to innovatory ideas, their market research skills, their knowledge of partnership management, their honest broker role and their ability to understand the ways to access public sector project funds.

Key developments included:

- The creation of short self guided walks from stations along the lines, carefully routed to pass interpreted points of interest, inns and cafes. Similar provision has been introduced for cycling.
- The introduction of line by line web site provision
- Linkages of rail travel to local food and drink providers – a classic on both lines has been the creation of Rail Ale Trails.
- Researching community and visitor needs to help develop better timetabling and ticketing.
- Motivating customer care amongst front line rail staff.
- Drawing into a meaningful partnership local councils, and/or the community to promote rail services.

- Obtaining funding from national and EU sources by stressing the triple bottom line approach, tapping into environmental and community support funds.
- Making rail services easy to use, by producing understandable and informative timetables.
- Making a rail trip an experience rather than a way of travelling from A to B.

Non-motorised Transport Provision

The development of cycle holiday companies is in some ways the ultimate form of transport for sustainable tourism. CountryLanes is a good example of this sort of private venture which has achieved triple bottom line success, making money, conserving the environment and helping local communities and other local business.. This company offers cycle hire and cycle holidays at several destinations across rural England, using skilled web site marketing, working closely with the media, local councils, communities and businesses and injecting large amounts of revenue into often remote areas. The business has been revamped several times over the last 15 years as markets and competition has changed.

Heritage Conservation

Heritage sites: Sustainable Tourism management techniques have been applied to a range of heritage sites in the UK to re-invigorate markets and product offer, cut emissions and work with and maintain local communities and businesses. Two good examples include:

- Hadrian's Wall, (a major Roman legacy) An important factor here has been the creation by a partnership of agencies of a private sector company, Hadrian's Wall Ltd. to deliver a sustainable tourism plan against a set of economic and environmental targets.
- The Blaenavon World Heritage Site in Wales, where a new Visitor Experience Plan and related Interpretation Plan will boost off peak visitor numbers, steer visitors into underused areas, avoid fragile environments, introduce new bus services and help regenerate the community and its businesses while increasing visitor satisfaction.

Landscape and Farm Conservation: Unmanaged tourism into heritage landscapes and farming areas can be a problem. The application of sustainable tourism marketing, management and monitoring techniques can give valuable triple bottom line benefits to such areas. Food trails have been especially valuable in remote mountainous parts of northern England, in helping farms recover from the disaster of the 2001 Foot and Mouth disease. The success of this trail has allowed traditional high cost farming to survive and the landscape patterns and associated ecologies to be conserved by targeted marketing and diversification in managed tourism. Some protected areas in the UK now use the vehicle of sustainable tourism to come to terms with visitor management and the private sector businesses. And others have used the concept of Food Heroes to market traditional food and farming.

Sustainable Tourism Strategy Planning

Over much of the developed world, the creation of regional, district and local sustainable tourism strategy plans has enabled business, community and environmental interests to come together to learn, discuss and develop viable sustainable tourism strategy plans, to guide and inform investment by the private sector, non-profits and public sector interests. The creation of the West Oxfordshire Sustainable Tourism Strategy in the UK was an example of the success of this technique. It used carefully mediated stakeholder involvement to understand the needs of business, environmental and community interests. It assessed by market survey and asset review the optimum way forward for each part of the district, a total area of 276 square miles. It used visitor management techniques to channel visitors into key areas. And it helped create partnerships between businesses to market and manage the strategy.

Similar techniques have been very successful in other areas. They require an effective knowledge of sustainable tourism management techniques, of partnership creation and business advice services.

But what could be done in North or East Carolina?

The success of the schemes described above can be related to a number of factors, many of which could be replicated in North or East Carolina. These include:

1) The ability of University staff to provide a lead into this new and complex area, by providing technical assistance, information, awareness raising, training and leadership.

2) The willingness of public sector and non-profits to work with business interests and to understand the economic realities of business.
3) A knowledge of, and the ability to implement, partnership working.
4) Accurate and targeted market knowledge and the skills to access those markets.
5) Knowledge and understanding of success stories in sustainable tourism, and the ability to adapt – not copy – those stories to the North/East Carolina situation.
6) Finding and supporting informed risk takers from, and risk taking by, all sectors.
7) Leadership – coming from all sectors.
8) Determination and Flexibility – in business there is little time for conflicts between deep and shallow ecology.

Taking that background into account, what tangible measures could be taken on the ground to make North/East Carolina a leader in sustainable tourism within the USA?

Political support is essential – to provide a platform for persuasion, to convince local officials and elected members, to supply start up funding for new infrastructure and marketing projects. The University has an important advice and lobbying role here.

Jealousy and example are also key, if surprising, factors. Potential stakeholders are best convinced by example; successful example engenders jealousy amongst others to achieve or exceed the outcome of those examples. In practice the use of the jealousy factor requires pilot projects to be created to demonstrate good and bad practice. The choice of pilot projects is central to success – they must be areas or businesses likely to succeed – through both the drive and skills of the individuals involved or the suitability of the assets that areas and people have.

Media support is also essential – to obtain broader support for initiatives across the region, and maintain political support.

Marketing skill – to sell the concept to communities, to business and to tourists. And here recent research has confirmed something many have long suspected. Marketing appeals to save the earth are ineffective. The adoption of behavioural change requires people to believe that they personally will gain, often in a tangible way, from change. They will gain financially, or increase their comfort, prestige or choices. Going green is just not enough for the great majority.

Financial support will also be important to provide incentives and advice – that support could come from agencies, from environmental or community support funds, from state tourism marketing agencies, from large companies with non tourism related triple bottom lines, from foundations or from the regions private investors.

Technical expertise and technical contacts worldwide are also important – and the University of East Carolina is well placed to supply that role.

A start list might be:

1) Create a university/private sector/public sector/non profit group to steer Project East Carolina Sustainable Tourism 2020. The choice of its members is critical – no passengers can be taken.
2) Work out a practical manifesto and action plan for that Project. That Manifesto must be plausible, inspiring, link all sectors, and aim high enough to gain potential national recognition. It must however be achievable. It must contain sure fire winners. Nothing succeeds like success.
3) Hold one or more stakeholder meetings to get public support for the Manifesto.
4) Start a series of local projects of various kinds including farm related, community regenerating related, heritage related and others. Pay special attention to media coverage, and ensure that the products and marketing work. Try the Food Heroes concept; Find a Trial Area where a sustainable tourism strategy can be tested; Work with the North Carolina Train Host Association, with its over 100 volunteers serving as North Carolina's goodwill ambassadors on board the *Piedmont* and *Carolinian; set up the Heritage Region concept in one or more key areas, following Canada's experience; try to create your own group of "Sustainable Hotels" following the example of the Talbot Inn, and the Hotel Ucliva. It may even be possible to test Austria's Soft Mobility project at a selected location.*

5) The Austrian Ambassador would be happy to personally declare that project open !
6) Produce an East Carolina Sustainable Tourism Strategy – and remember that your aim is as much the adaptation of existing businesses and assets as it is the creation of new businesses and assets. Take heed of market requirements. Understand the key measures for changing visitor behaviour with particular reference to social marketing, targeted information provision, targeted heritage interpretation, and the value of personalities. Above all – remember that tourism is a fashion business, visitor experiences must be enjoyable and rewarding – but greenwash is soon exposed.

Remember, sustainable tourism is not just a planning technique, or a marketing device, or an unreachable aim, it is an adventure with rewards. Those rewards could be especially strong here. North Carolina is a train trip away for millions of people, no airline is necessary; even a car trip – with 2 or more people – is more sustainable, given an eco-friendly car. it is a remarkable opportunity for business and Universities and non-profits and the public sector to work together, first in learning networks, leading to effective action partnerships.

Problems of Sustainable Tourism

While authorities want to stop the access to forest lands and natural resources of village people, another group of people-namely tourism developers and tourists with lots of money to spend-are set to gain access to the area. While authorities believe that local people, who have often lived in the area for generations, are not capable of managing and conserving their land and natural resources-under a community forestry scheme for example-they believe they themselves in cooperation with the tourist industry can properly manage and conserve 'nature' under a national ecotourism plan. Taking the above quote seriously, cynics may be tempted to say there is obviously a gap between 'human rights' and 'animal rights'.

How is this story linked to globalization? First of all, that humans cannot live in the forest is-of course-not a Thai concept. It is a notion of Western conservation ideology-an outcome of the globalization of ideas and perceptions. Likewise, that ecotourism under a 'good management' system is beneficial to local people and nature is also a Western concept that is being globalised. In fact, Thailand's forestry chief thinks globally and acts locally. A lesson that can be learned from this is that the slogan 'Think Globally, Act Locally' that the environmental movements have promoted all the years, has not necessarily served to preserve the environment and safeguard local communities' rights, but has been co-opted and distorted by official agencies and private industries for profit-making purposes. The tourism industry is demonstrating this all too well.

Many developing countries, facing debt burdens and worsening trade terms, have turned to tourism promotion in the hope that it brings foreign exchange and investment. Simultaneously, leading international agencies such as the World Bank, United Nations agencies and business organisations like the World Travel & Tourism Council (WTTC) have been substantially involved to make tourism a truly global industry.

However, tourism in developing countries is often viewed by critics as an extension of former colonial conditions because from the very beginning, it has benefited from international economic relationships that structurally favour the advanced capitalist countries in the North. Unequal trading relationships, dependence on foreign interests, and the division of labour have relegated poor countries in the South to becoming tourism recipients and affluent countries in the North to the position of tourism generators, with the latter enjoying the freedom from having to pay the price for the meanwhile well-known negative impacts in destinations.

Transnational Corporations

Travel and tourism has emerged as one of the world's most centralised and competitive industries, and hardly any other economic sector illustrates so clearly the global reach of transnational corporations (TNCs). Over recent years, the industry has increasingly pressured governments around the world to liberalise trade and investment in services and is likely to benefit tremendously from the General Agreement on Trade in Services-a multilateral agreement under the World Trade Organisation (WTO).

GATS aims to abolish restrictions on foreign ownership and other measures which have so far protected the services sector in individual countries. For the hotel sector, for example, GATS facilitates franchising, management contracts and licensing. Moreover, foreign tourism companies will be entitled to the same benefits as local companies in addition to being allowed to move staff across borders as they wish, open branch offices in foreign countries, and make international payments without restrictive regulations.

Foreign investment will also be increasingly deregulated under the GATT/WTO system. According to the Agreement on Trade-Related Investment Measures (TRIMs), foreign companies will no longer be obliged to use local input. The Multilateral Agreement on Investment (MAI) proposed by Organisation for Economic Cooperation and Development (OECD) countries goes even further, calling for unrestricted entry and establishment of foreign firms, national treatment, repatriation of profits, technology transfer, etc.

Accordingly, the WTTC has recently presented its 'Millennium Vision' on travel and tourism, including the following key areas:

- Get governments to accept travel and tourism as a strategic economic development and employment priority;
- Move towards open and competitive markets by supporting the implementation of GATS, liberalise air transport and deregulate telecommunications in international markets;
- Eliminate barriers to tourism growth, which involves the expansion and improvement of infrastructure-e.g. the increase of airport capacity, construction and modernisation of airports, roads and tourist facilities.

On a tour through South-East Asian countries in February 1998, WTTC president Geoffrey Lipman also strongly supported the privatisation of state enterprises, particularly airlines and airports. His visit in Thailand, for example, coincided with the announcement of British Airways-a prominent member of the WTTC-that it was interested in taking over 25% of Thai Airways International. And the British Airport Authority promptly followed up by proposing to buy a major equity share in the provincial airports of Chiang Mai, Phuket and Hat Yai, which are all located at popular tourist spots. However, the selling out of state companies to foreigners has been facing growing public opposition in Thailand so that privatisation is not progressing as planned.

Meanwhile, even the voices of the tourism industry in Asia are urging a cautious approach towards globalization. Imtiaz Muqbil, a renowned tourism analyst based in Bangkok, warned: 'The independence of thousands of small and medium size enterprises, including hotels and tour operators, is at risk.' This is because most local enterprises will hardly be able to compete with foreign companies. Moreover, Muqbil suggested that as an outcome of globalization, Asian countries may face 'the prospects of huge growth in leakage of foreign exchange earnings.' In conclusion, he said, 'The radical restructuring of travel and tourism... could strike at the heart of national economies.'

It is already a well-established fact that in some developing countries, more than two-thirds of the revenue from international tourism never reaches the local economy because of the high foreign exchange leakages. Now, as the new free trade and investment policies are being implemented, their balance sheets may even worsen because the profits and other income repatriated by foreign companies is likely to grow larger than the inflow of capital. That means, the claims that globalization and liberalisation of tourism will bring wealth, progress, social achievements and improved environmental standards to developing countries need to be seriously questioned.

A recently published document by the UN Conference on Trade and Development (UNCTAD) states that Asia-Pacific countries urgently need to bolster their bargaining positions in the field of tourism services and negotiate better terms in exchange for opening their markets. However, governments have barely had time to examine the potential impacts of globalization, and many local tourism-related companies are already in financial trouble due to the economic crisis. So it is very unlikely that they can strengthen their negotiating power. Even major Asian airlines can hardly survive in this crisis-hit business environment; the recent temporary closure of Philippine Airlines is an illustrative example.

Economic globalization has also generated considerable criticism because it comes along with the erosion of power of governments. Opponents argue that local and national institutions will no longer be able to properly fulfil their responsibilities such as providing social services, preserving the environment, and implementing sustainable development programmes.

Indeed, the multilateral agreements facilitating globalization have shown little, if any, concern for social and ecological issues. On the environment front, the WTO has discussed proposals to introduce 'environmental standards' and 'eco-labels' developed by international setting bodies.

Critics say this move is likely to be dominated by TNC interests, which attempt to appropriate the environmental agenda and push for self-regulation. Meanwhile, existing national environmental policies and laws adopted by democratically elected governments will be undermined.

The WTTC, for example, vows to 'promote sustainability in travel and tourism' through its Green Globe programme, but-as its 'Millennium Vision' document states-'strongly believes that the environmental policy agenda should focus on (the industry's) self-improvement, incentives, and light-handed regulation as the preferred approach'.

Concerns

The increasing influence of private sector interests on international forums negotiating the environmental agenda has reinforced concerns that genuine efforts to set up a more stringent framework for the tourism industry may be jeopardised. In this context it is important to note that the seventh session of the UN Commission on Sustainable Development (CSD) this year will include important discussions on the issues of sustainable tourism.

So far, the UN General Assembly has adopted a resolution on 'Sustainable Tourism' as part of its 'Programme for the further implementation of Agenda 21', the action programme adopted at the Rio Earth Summit. This resolution acknowledges the need to consider further the importance of tourism in the context of Agenda 21. Among other things, it states: 'For sustainable patterns of consumption and production in the tourism sector, it is essential to strengthen national policy development and enhance capacity in the areas of physical planning, impact assessment, and the use of economic and regulatory instruments, as well as in the areas of information, education and marketing.'

Furthermore, the resolution calls for participation of all concerned parties in policy development and implementation of sustainable tourism programmes.

What is important to keep in mind is that this UN resolution stresses the need for a democratic regulation of tourism development, which is in stark contradiction to the lobbying efforts by the agents of tourism globalization towards deregulation and an industry-led and self-regulated scenario.

This conflict featured prominently at the fourth Conference of Parties to the UN Convention on Biological Diversity (COP4) in Bratislava, Slovakia, last May, which included discussions on the integration of biodiversity into sectoral activities such as tourism.

Many government delegates there resisted attempts by the German government to get approval from the Ministerial Roundtable at COP4 for a programme to develop global guidelines on biodiversity and sustainable tourism. Observers noted that the increased promotion of interests of the powerful German tourism industry at the UN level by the German government has been conspicuous over recent years.

Official and NGO representatives were surprised by the insistence of the Germans to work on global guidelines and to seek endorsement for this programme from the CSD. The delegate from Samoa, for example, reiterated that sustainable tourism is a complicated issue that will be dealt with by the CSD next year and complained: 'We are not in favour of some of the top-down approaches we have seen here (at COP4).' Other delegates expressed concern over the relevance, objectives and funding of the proposed programme.

Significantly, critical observers warned that an ill-advised proposal on global guidelines under the Convention could have devastating consequences for local and indigenous communities-socially, culturally and ecologically. 'The tourism industry's propensity towards unrestricted growth and its commoditisation of indigenous cultures must be recognised as clearly unsustainable,' commented an NGO representative during the Bratislava Conference.

Meanwhile, there are justifiable fears that under the new economic globalization schemes, sustainable and ecotourism activities will even further enable TNCs to gain commercial access to ecologically sensitive areas and biological resources and accelerate the privatisation of biodiversity, all to the detriment of local communities' land and resource rights and the natural environment. As the Austrian environment minister told delegates at COP4, 'Sustainable tourism offers new market opportunities.'

Vague, with Buzzwords

Indeed, the debate on tourism principles and guidelines is a tricky one-not only because it is heavily overshadowed by politics of global players. Another point of concern is that guidelines and programmes, as discussed and adopted by advocates of sustainable tourism at the international level, naturally remain very vague. Usually, they are also overly euphemistic, with buzzwords abounding: e.g. empowerment of local communities; local participation and control; equitable income distribution; benefits to nature conservation and biodiversity protection; etc.

A tourism researcher from the University of British Columbia, Nick Kontogeorgopoulos, suggested that attempts to implement tourism projects based on such guidelines are bound to fail altogether because it is simply impossible to apply them to highly disparate and heterogeneous destinations. He says, 'While these altruistic principles are laudable in theory, the absence of place-specific context strips them of empirical evidence.' In conclusion: Not the global game, but local circumstances and conditions represent the essential determinant of success for sustainable development.

In Asia, social and environmental activists argue that the inflationary tourism policies in the context of globalization have greatly contributed to the present economic crisis. During the era of the so-called bubble economy, indiscriminate and unsustainable investments led to the rapid conversion of lands into massive tourism complexes, including luxury hotels, golf courses and casinos, and related infrastructure such as airports, highways, and dams to generate electricity. With economic liberalisation, the tourism, real estate and construction industries boomed, backed by local banks and global speculative capital. An essay written by renowned tourism critic and media activist Ing. K. reflects the anger of many Thais about the developments that have led to the country's bankruptcy. She presents the hard facts as follows:

'Land speculation became a national pastime, permeating every beautiful village, however remote. Land prices skyrocketed. Villagers sold agriculturally productive land to speculators. Practically overnight, fertile land became construction sites. The plague kept spreading; corruption got out of control. National parks and forest reserves were encroached upon by golf courses and resorts...

'Many instant millionaires were made, but much of this new rich money was not wisely invested in productive ventures. Instead, most of it was spent on luxury "dream" products and services, in pursuit of the consumer lifestyle.

'Many of these people were merely imitating tourists and were influenced by the prevailing free-spending frenzy. Greed and consumerism devastated whole communities all over Thailand, raising the temperature even higher, on every level of society...

'In the end, we have nothing to show for it but whole graveyards of unsold high-rise condominiums, shophouses, golf course and resort developments and housing estates.'

Now, all discussions and work programmes relating to the implementation of global and local Agendas 21 and sustainable development appear-more than ever-removed from reality in view of the unfolding Asian crisis-a human disaster with millions of unemployed and landless people falling below the poverty line. According to the latest figures from UN agencies, more than 100 million people in the region are newly impoverished. And there are growing fears that the machinations of unregulated global speculative capital now threaten to ruin not only Asian economies but the rest of the world as well.

A major question that needs to be addressed in this context: Where will all the money come from for sustainable development and tourism projects? In Thailand, for example, the World Bank and the Japanese OECF have agreed to provide loans to improve and expand tourism as part of a social investment programme (SIP) aimed at tackling the problems of unemployment and loss of income arising from the economic crisis. It has been stressed that tourism development is crucial for the country's economic recovery, and 'community participation' and 'sustainability' are mentioned as major components in projects. But critics have warned that firstly, tourism is not a quick commodity that can pull the country out of its economic pains. And secondly, much of the borrowed money will be used for new developments in national parks and biodiversity-rich areas in the drive to promote 'ecotourism'.

Let me confront you with a provocative idea now. It is not the longstanding efforts by the many experts promoting and working on the implementation of global and local Agendas that bring us closer to sustainable tourism. Ironically, it is rather the current all-embracing crisis which may eventually make tourism more sustainable-at least in environmental terms. Why?

First of all, a basic problem of sustainable tourism has been the rapidly expanding numbers of travellers. But as a result of the crisis, tourism growth has come to a standstill. Due to currency devaluation, increasing unemployment, declining income and deflation, Asian markets are collapsing. Even the numbers of Japanese going abroad for holidays are now declining for the first time in 18 years. European and American holidaymakers have also shunned South-East Asian countries because of 1997's smog disaster, caused by forest fires in Indonesia, and political turmoil in the region-e.g. in Burma, Cambodia and-more recently-Indonesia.

As the economic contagion is spreading, the travel fever that had gripped Russia and other East European countries after the fall of the Soviet Union is also on the wane, as the Russian currency, the rouble, has plummeted dramatically and the economy slumps. Moreover, amid the decline of business activities in Asia, stockmarket slumps and fears of a global recession, nervous companies around the world are limiting corporate travel spending. The WTTC, which had earlier in 1998 forecast growth averaging 7% a year throughout 2008, now expects the global tourism market to remain flat in the next years. This may be bad in terms of economics but, unquestionably, the environment will benefit from stagnating or even decreasing tourist numbers.

For instance, the air travel industry has been identified as one of the biggest environmental villains in tourism. With fewer people travelling, however, the Asia-Pacific aviation industry is now flying into a deep recession. Airlines are fighting for survival by closing or cutting unprofitable routes, selling aircraft and cancelling orders for new aircraft. Governments are forced to cut budgets for airport expansion and construction. Ultimately, that means less pollution and less environmentally damaging developments.

The real estate and construction industries, which are both inextricably linked to the tourism industry, were the first industries that crash-landed when the Asian bubble economy burst. As a result, many speculative and unsustainable hotel and resort development projects have been abandoned, and new construction is down to a trickle. An excellent example is golf, which became a symbol of globalised leisure and tourist lifestyle in Asian tiger societies. But as the frenzy to build luxurious golf course complexes-including hotels, housing estates and shopping centres-has almost stopped completely, and middle-class people affected by the crisis are turning away from the expensive sport of golf, environmentalists can be relieved: The malaise of rampant land grabs, national park encroachments, deforestation, etc. related to golf courses is no longer as threatening as it was a few years ago.

On the other hand, while many tourism-related companies may have scrapped or postponed potentially harmful projects, one needs to acknowledge that because of the financial crunch, public and private investments in environmental protection are also being cut. Moreover, there have been warnings that the crisis has resulted in an upsurge of crime, prostitution, drug abuse and other social vices related to tourism.

Failed

But most importantly, Asian societies are beginning to realise that the current global economic capitalist system has utterly failed to bring achievements in all terms. Now burdened with having to pay for the activities of unscrupulous speculators and additionally suffering from free-market-oriented structural adjustment programmes imposed by the International Monetary Fund (IMF), people are losing faith in a globalised economy. Some experts even go so far as to say that free trade and investment liberalisation is 'yesterday's story'. Malaysia in particular has recently taken decisive steps to shut itself off from global markets by strictly controlling foreign capital flows.

Asian governments are now likely to move towards greater self-reliance as they are pressured by people of all walks of life to look into economic strategies that are chiefly based on domestic financial resources and the domestic market. This involves the strengthening of the agricultural sector and local industries to protect people's livelihoods in the first place. Forces still seeking to further prop up economically risky service industries such as tourism are likely to be weakened. Moreover, the crisis has also created considerable public debate about the impacts of global culture and lifestyle, including the issues of consumerism and the wasteful and unproductive use of resources. In several Asian countries-such as Korea, Thailand and Malaysia-outbound tourism is now being discouraged as it is seen as conspicuous consumption that has contributed to the negative balance of payments.

The issues of democracy and human rights are also gaining momentum in the region. As never before, people are making use of their civil rights and call for transparency and democratic procedures to phase out corruption and harmful government policies and development plans. The growing opposition of Thai environmentalists and villagers to the move of the government to open up protected areas for 'mass ecotourism' is just one example.

All in all, I believe, the current Asian crisis, which is likely to become a global crisis, poses a fundamental challenge-and an important opportunity-to re-evaluate the issues of globalization, sustainable development and tourism. As Asian societies begin to acknowledge that rapid economic growth under global regimes has devastating effects on people's lives and the environment, we may find that a stringent regulation of tourism, which involves a stricter limitation of tourist numbers and a halt to the unlimited spatial expansion of tourism, is better than further promoting tourism growth and hoping that this growth can be handled with 'good management', education of tourists, etc. What the current crisis really appears to confirm is-what many tourism critics have been saying all along-the global tourism industry just cannot be propelled towards sustainability under the conventional economic and political structures. That means, efforts to implement social and environmental agendas and sustainable tourism are unlikely to progress unless profound structural changes take place in the global system.

Understanding the Market for Tourism

Understanding tourism marketing has become essential in professional scenario of today. As the market is consolidating, the role of marketing as a driving force in a business endeavor is also being recognized. With growing competition, organisations in tourism business have no option but to engage in organised marketing. A professional approach to marketing always helps, whether it is on the tour operators' end or at destinations. Guides, escorts, restaurants, hotels, transporters, shops etc. closely compete and have to out-market one another to stay ahead. A proper tourism marketing strategy at national level needs close cooperation between the government, tourism industry and the local population.

Evolution of Marketing

Marketing as a concept has evolved in the last 30 years. Development of marketing and modern business practices has three stages: Production Era, Sales Era and Marketing Era. Marketing era arrived when organisations began to produce what they could sell rather than trying to sell what they produced. While planning and designing a product, consumers' needs, tastes and satisfaction are considered. Growth of competition prompted organisations to frame new marketing techniques.

Changing tourism trends also demanded a new approach. The emergence of long haul tourist created the need for marketing research which took into account market trends, consumer behavior and ascertained procedure to make products which satisfied the users of tourism products. Gradual social and economic development culminated in segmentation of mass market into specialized target markets. Tackling these markets needed new approach and understanding of tourism marketing.

Selling and Marketing

Selling and Marketing are two different concepts. Selling concentrates on the needs of the seller while marketing concentrates on the requirements of the buyer. A marketing oriented organisation focuses on customer needs and earns profits through customer satisfaction. Many organizations in tourism sector are product oriented. They stress on the available services of products but ignore consumers' needs or attitudes. A marketing oriented tourist organisation takes totally different approach.

Business Philosophy

A marketing oriented business philosophy keeps consumer needs at centre-stage of all activities. An organisation could offer quality tourism products but if it lacks supporting infrastructure, it would have no takers. A tourist organisation needs to look after the needs like accessibility, accommodation, leisure and entertainment facilities. Tourists have their own needs, preferences and tastes, and these have to be taken into account while developing a product for them.

Marketing and Research-know Your Markets

To succeed in a competitive environment, it is important to tailor your business to the wants and needs of your customer.

Marketing is about matching every part of your business with your customers so that:

- You meet their needs.
- They are aware that you meet their needs.
- They are motivated to buy from you.
- They are motivated to keep buying from you.

Market research is an essential tool in assisting you to do this.

Undertaking market research will allow you to:

- define the essence of your business so you know what you are offering visitors;
- determine who your potential visitor markets are; and
- Establish their needs and how you will go about meeting those needs.

Define Your Business

- Your product or service;
- Your geographic marketing area—neighbourhood, regional or national;
- Your competition;
- How you differ from the competition—what makes you special;
- Your price;
- The competition's promotion methods;
- Your promotion methods;
- Your distribution methods or business location

Define Your Customers

- Your current customer base: age, sex, income, neighborhood;
- How your customers learn about your product or service-advertising; direct mail, word of mouth, Yellow Pages;
- Patterns or habits your customers and potential customers share e.g. what they read, watch, listen to;

- Qualities your customers value most about your product or service-selection, convenience, service, reliability, availability, affordability;
- Qualities your customers like least about your product or service-can they be adjusted to serve your customers better?
- Prospective customers like least about your product or service but whom you aren't currently reaching.

Tourism Queensland provides research on a number of areas of the tourism industry and access to regionally specific research and information. This includes:

- International market research
- Domestic and International aviation research
- Destinations-including a regional update, regional snapshot, visitor surveys, aviation information and fact sheets.

Owners of the Heritage Tea Rooms, Allan and Michelle Sharpe discuss the importance of market research in being able to foresee changes in the market, and adapting to those changes.

Create a Marketing Plan

With knowledge backed by research about your customers, a marketing plan brings together the planned activities and opportunities to promote your product or service. The key sections in developing a marketing plan are outlined below.

Background

- Overview of your business, your industry and the current state of the market place.
- Mission.
- Goals.
- Competitive advantage-what is special about your business.

Situation analysis:

- External and internal factors affecting your business success.
- Strengths Weaknesses Opportunities Threats (SWOT) analysis.
- Competition analysis.

Market identification:

- Target markets-who are they, how do they behave?
- Segmentation-how can you split your market up for the purposes of targeting them?

Marketing mix:

- Product (or services)-e.g. tours, accommodation, camping, souvenirs, restaurant, bush tucker etc.
- Packaging-how do you 'wrap up' your tourism product to market it? e.g. 2 night camping package with a bush tucker tour and breakfast included.
- Place-where will you promote yourself, and how will you achieve this e.g. in Europe through inbound travel agents, in my nearest town through tour desks etc.
- Price.
- Promotion.

Action Plan:

- Who is going to do what, and by when?

Budget:

- How much have you got to spend or how much will you need to spend to be effective?

Monitoring and Evaluation:

- How will you track which strategies have converted into bookings?
- What is the yield of the visitors you are attracting?

Packaging

Visitors are seeking experiences more so than specific products and services when they visit destinations. This requires the seamless provision of a coordinated range of products and services that collectively offer particular experiences desired by visitors.

The definition of packaging is the combining of two or more facilities/services/attractions as a single unit for sale to visitors to an area. The overall aim of any packaging is to produce an integrated, interesting product to encourage visitors to increase their stay within the region.

Working together with other tourism operators to provide packages also helps you to achieve economies of scale in relation to marketing costs and provides further opportunities to raise the profile of your tourism business. Not only does each individual operator benefit by such arrangements, but the region in general benefits by greater visitor numbers and increased expenditure.

In turn visitors benefit from new, innovative and interesting experiences reflecting a particular region's attributes.

Distribution

Distribution is making sure that your product or service information reaches the visitor. There are three distinct groups that you can work with to distribute your product or service:

- consumers
- trade including travel agents, wholesalers
- other industry and sector associations or professionals including RTOs, VICs, media, industry suppliers

From these three groups there are many different types of distribution channels available:

- Cooperative marketing initiatives
- Regional tourism brochures or travel planners
- Visitor Information Centres
- Australian Tourism Data Warehouse
- Online-regional websites, online booking systems
- Direct to the consumer-via brochure or website
- Retailers, travel agents or booking agents
- Wholesalers.

Visitor Information Centres

There has been increased recognition of the role of visitor information centres and their importance in providing high quality tourist information. In Queensland, accredited visitor information centres provide, local, regional and state wide information to visitors. They are recognisable by the italicised yellow on blue *'i'* sign. Visitor Information Centres that are accredited in Queensland provide a high quality level of service and facilities.

Online distribution

Traditional and emerging online distribution channels are converging. Technology is rapidly evolving and is one of the most significant factors affecting the tourism sector. Emerging online technologies can effectively facilitate information flows and transactions, and improve efficiencies within the tourism distribution chain. Travellers look for information before going on a trip to help them plan and choose between options. They also need more information during their trip as the trend towards more independent travel increases.

The use of employing Internet distribution channels is one way to meet these needs. Some of these include:

- Online booking systems
- Online travel planners
- State and regional websites
- Search engines such as Yahoo, ninemsn travel services.

Online Presence

The Internet has become one of the most significant communication tools for businesses and individuals all over the world. Users turn to the Internet to search for information and interact with other users such as friends, peers and communities.

It comes as no surprise that travellers use the "net" extensively to plan and organise their trip, more than 80% of travellers do so according to international research.

The increased accessibility of markets and speed of communication facilitated by the Internet is a double-edged sword. Tourism industry suppliers and operators need to be increasingly flexible and responsible to changing consumer needs, trends and preferences.

Why Should I be Online?

The Internet is the quickest and cheapest way of reaching potential travellers anywhere in the world. It will allow you to be connected with your customers, suppliers, partners and competitors to access an enormous amount of information.

The Internet provides new ways for you to deliver the information and services to customers and suppliers, with the benefits including:

- more effective marketing and the identification and development of new markets;
- improved customer service and relations;
- cost savings in communications, accounting, banking, financial

- management and purchasing; and
- efficiencies in linking 'back office' systems with external requirements etc.

Owners of Hidden Valley Cabins express the positive affect the Internet has had on increasing the number and frequency of visitors to their business. By creating a mechanism by which visitors can book online, Hidden Valley Cabins were able to increase the number of both and domestic and international visitors.

Starting your online presence

As a tourism operator it is essential that you consider what the Internet can do for you and your business, as well as the possible consequences to your business development if you do not take advantage of the Internet and its services. The following issues need to be taken into account:

- Your future communication needs
- Your business' growth expectations
- How you will conduct business in the future and with whom
- How much value Internet connection will add to your competitiveness
- Staff training and motivation to embrace the changes required.

It is important to consider when you're thinking about going online, the commitment of management and staff to dealing positively with the change. Success on the Internet requires rethinking how business is done, communicating with customers to staff training and motivation, and to how different sections of the organisation work together.

Improving Your Online Presence

Get smarter about e-marketing knowledge through step-by-step lessons. The Tourism E-kit is a complete suite of tutorials that covers everything from the basics of developing a good web site to the more complex issues of Google ad words, search engine marketing and online product distribution.

Trade Distribution

Wholesalers are the vital link between the originating manufacturers and businesses at the point of sale. Wholesalers package tour programs including travel, accommodation, and tours that are sold to the public via retail travel agents. Wholesalers do not sell directly to customers. Wholesalers link individual tourism operators with retailers. They consider what type of tour program would appeal to a particular market and package the program accordingly. They offer goods in large quantities at a trade price to those who are seeking to resell the products for retail purposes rather than personal use. Wholesalers-what is their commitment to your product?

- Product development
  - sourcing
  - negotiating special rates from participating products and services
  - creating packages
- Producing a brochure which is the major sales tool for travel agents to use and recommend your business
- Distribution of brochure to consumers through travel agents
- Advertising to visitors and travel agents
- Travel agents training on products and services offered
- At point of sale (e.g. travel agency), in-store merchandising, and window displays.

Retail travel agents sell travel services direct to customers and act on their behalf to book and purchase holiday packages, travel, accommodation, tours and so on.

Wholesalers package tour programs including travel, accommodation, and tours that are sold to the public via retail travel agents. Wholesalers do not sell directly to customers.

Inbound tour operators act on behalf of national and international tour wholesalers to organise the 'land/ground' content of a tour program. Inbound tour operators act as intermediaries between wholesalers and tourism operators. They are usually able to negotiate better rates due to the volume and regular use of the tourism products they book.

International Marketing

Have you considered whether your product is suitable for the international market? A number of issues need to be considered when promoting your product internationally.

Ask yourself the following questions:

Accessibility-is your product close to a regular air/bus/train service?

Usually overseas visitors are limited in the amount of time they can spend in any particular location; therefore access to your product is vital. In certain circumstances investment in a transfer facility should be a major consideration.

Service-does your establishment or product reflect high levels of service expected by international visitors? High service standards have become synonymous with the tourist industry in Australia and constant reviewing and training is essential to maintain these levels.

Distinctive-does your product reflect an Australian experience to the customer?

Visitors to Australia want to experience our way of life. Ensure that there is as much "Australiana" as possible in your product. However, you must differentiate between "Australiana" and "Ocker".

Credibility-is your product already established in the Australian domestic market? It is important that you already have a customer base, which illustrates your product's credibility. Remember, not all tourism products are suitable for marketing overseas on an individual basis. It is important to arrange your product as part of a package of attractions, then contact Inbound Tour Operators and sell them your product or package.

Have you selected a specific target market?

Don't try to enter every market at once, for it is far more important to select your market carefully. An overview of the international markets is included in this publication.

Are you a member of the local Regional Tourist Organisation?

Your local Regional Tourist Organisation can assist you in promoting your product and keep you abreast of invaluable opportunities as they occur. They are also an excellent source of information and advice.

Is your current domestic brochure adaptable to the overseas marketplace?

Make sure that when producing a brochure you are aware of the experiences or key selling points of your product for both your domestic and international markets and produce a brochure accordingly. Experiences in the domestic market may not be appropriate for the International market and while it is important to retain the Australian flavour in your prose.

Ensure that your property, attraction or service is well presented. The overseas traveller is accustomed to seeing informative, well-conceived and attractively produced material whereby decisions are often made.

If you are planning to distribute your brochure to both the trade and consumer, the following information is essential in brochure design:

- A concise description of the product
- Where it is located (include a map with Australia, Queensland and the Region)
- When it operates (use months, as seasons are reversed)
- How to get there (use both miles and kilometres)
- How to book (your full address, telephone, fax numbers (with area codes), email address and web address)
- How much it costs (use Australian dollars and approximate local currency equivalent or exchange rate at time of printing).
- Allow space for the travel agent's stamp and sticker-usually on the back of the brochure.
- Ensure your brochure conforms to appropriate envelope sizes (this can bring down your costs considerably).

If you plan to distribute your product through wholesalers, it is not compulsory to have your prices in local currency. Your product may be featured as a component in the wholesalers' brochures.

Is your product readily available?

You must ensure that your product can be booked quickly and efficiently in the overseas market, as travel agents and consumers will usually not contact

Australia for bookings or information.

Have you considered a sales visit to meet the major wholesalers and agents in the relevant markets?

Maintaining regular contact with your distribution system and providing them with updated information on your product is very important. There are several do's and don'ts when conducting business with international wholesalers:

Dos:

- Source information about the market you wish to target and the type of product that is saleable in your target market
- Do your research and have your prices fully prepared for negotiation
- Expect to negotiate-buyers invariably have a choice of product
- Take advantage of the opportunity to meet buyers at the annual trade shows held in Australia, such as the Australian Tourism Exchange (Adelaide, 2006)
- Pre-schedule all appointments (well in advance) and reconfirm the visit a day or two beforehand
- Make your presentation brief and to the point

Don'ts

- Don't visit during the public holiday periods, including Christmas and New Year
- Also avoid visiting when large major travel shows are being held elsewhere in the world
- Don't arrive unannounced
- Don't play one operator off against another
- Don't commit to rates or services without keeping written records
- Do not pay brochure support. Your inclusion in a wholesale operator's brochure will not necessarily guarantee that an operator will sell your product.

You will have to allow for levels of between 20-30% to cover an Inbound Tour Operator, an overseas Wholesaler and Retailer to deliver and sell your product internationally. You must also be prepared to quote firm prices well in advance-up to 18 months ahead and ensure it is fully understood that your rate is gross or net. Be careful that your international pricing is not higher than your domestic rate and be flexible but realistic when setting your price levels.

6

Tourism on the Prairies

Tourism and recreation both affect and are affected by the natural and economic environment and changes to it. Many prairie communities, being faced with changes in their economy due to the loss of subsidies and the concomitant effect on agriculture, are looking to tourism as an alternative source of income and a way to bolster their economies. This is a response to a changing economic environment but what of a changing natural environment? What are the implications of climate variability and possibly change for this economic choice? While many factors such as culture, age, level of disposable income, available leisure time, and climatic conditions play a role in people's tourism and recreational choices, the focus of this paper is the effect that changing weather and climate have on the tourism and recreation sector.

The natural resource base is a necessary part of outdoor recreation, be it water for sailing, swimming, fishing etc.; or snow for skiing, snow shoeing or tobogganing; or wildlife for viewing or hunting. Climate change and variability are expected to affect ecological zones pushing the prairie region north. As ecozones and the resource base adjust, recreational activities will adjust with them. Weather patterns (temperature, rainfall, wind, snow conditions etc.), on the other hand, influence when recreational activities take place. Hence, this paper looks at how the resource base could change in the light of climate variability and change along with a change in weather conditions, and how they will affect the mix of activities that people engage in for recreation. The socioeconomic consequences of a changing mix of recreational activities are also reviewed in order to gain a holistic picture of the kind of impacts that can be expected and that the tourists in the prairie region will have to adapt to. Following this, some recommendations will be made for further research relating to this topic.

This paper is based on a literature review of articles and papers relating to climate change and recreation on the Canadian prairies. Very limited literature was found on this topic specifically. Most of the literature found related to Saskatchewan, with one paper from Alberta. For this reason, the scope of this review is fairly limited. Its usefulness, however, lies in the knowledge gaps that are revealed. These gaps that are identified form the basis for recommendations for further study.

Recreation and Tourism

Recreation and tourism can be defined in a variety of ways. The first is to make a distinction between recreationçfor the purpose of this paper, the pursuit of outdoor activities by residents of the three prairie provinces or visitorsçand tourism. Tourism refers to trips taken that exceed being away from home for longer than one night and that do not have work or commuting as their purpose. It often includes the pursuit of recreation. Tourism can also be categorized by who is doing the traveling. So it becomes possible to talk about domestic and international travel, which refers to people crossing the Canadian border (Wittrock et al., 1992).

Recreation can be broken down according to the season and the type of activity. Thus, Masterton et al. (in More, 1988) refer to winter season (the period between the first and last dates of snow cover of 2.5cm) and summer season (the period starting two weeks after the last date of snow cover) recreation. Outdoor recreational pursuits are then classified by the type of resource base that is required for the activity: dry-terrain (e.g., golfing, picnicking, walking, camping); water-based (e.g., sunbathing, swimming, bathing, fishing); and snow-and/or ice-based (e.g. nordic skiing, alpine skiing, snowshoeing, snowmobiling, tobogganing, ice fishing, skating). It is obvious from the above examples that outdoor recreation is extremely dependent on the resource base and on the weather. Weather will influence the way people use outdoor recreational facilities as well as their demand for outdoor experiences. It is important to realise, however, that what recreation and how much takes place is not only affected by the weather but also by socioeconomic factors such as cultural norms, levels of disposable incomes, school/other holidays, the attractions present and attractions offered elsewhere. An example is the shift in people's preferences from consumptive recreation (e.g. hunting) to appreciative recreation (e.g. hiking) which increases the demand for pristine environments and parks.

Impact of Climate on the Mix of Recreation Activities

Climate Change Scenarios for the Prairies

Prairie climatic conditions have always been varied and to a degree unpredictable. The prairie climate is characterized by droughts and dry spells, early and late frosts, cold spells, excessive moisture and flooding. It is a climate of extremes with minimum temperatures dropping below-400C in January and rising to a maximum of between 350C and 400C in July. Annual precipitation is between 250 and 450mm, with more than two thirds occurring during summer (May to August) months. Passages of cold fronts, depressions, and numerous storms generate strong winds throughout the year. Dust storms are frequent during drought years but have also been found to occur during relatively short-lived dry conditions.

Various General Circulation Models have been used to project climate change scenarios if a doubling of the concentration of carbon dioxide in the atmosphere were to occur. Most models predict that temperatures will increase for both summer and winter, and that the variability observed in the current climate will continue under climate change. There is less agreement about whether precipitation (in the form of both rain and snow) will increase or decrease but there is agreement that the availability of water will diminish due to high temperatures and evapotranspiration.

These conditions are expected to have significant effects on the water resources available to inhabitants of the prairies, the vegetation and wildlife populations. What follows is a brief assessment of how these resources are expected to be affected increased climatic variability and change.

Water Resources

Many of the surface waterbodies (lakes, rivers and reservoirs) in the prairies tend to be shallow and eutrophic. Water quality and quantity affect recreation directly. Climate variability is expected to alter lake levels and affect the salinity and flora and fauna composition of the lakes. Warmer temperatures and shallow depth will result in warmer water, which encourages algae and plant growth. Increased algae and plant growth take up large amounts of oxygen and, in the case of shallow bodies, may lead to the expiration of fish life due to a reduction in dissolved oxygen. Warmer temperatures could also mean a later freeze and an earlier melt of ice on lakes, rivers and reservoirs.

Decreased run-off and shorter run-off periods are also predicted by some climate change models.

Vegetation

The distribution of vegetation is closely related to climate. Thus, all vegetation types, be they grasses, wild flowers, fungi or large coniferous trees, will be affected by climate change. The prairies are characterized by grassland vegetation which is drought resistant and tolerant of temperature and precipitation extremes. The prairie ecozone spanning the three provinces is bordered by the boreal forest which is less suited to temperature extremes and drought. Various climate change scenarios suggest that the climate of the boreal forest will be replaced by that of the prairie ecozone because of warmer and drier conditions. Thus, it can be expected that the prairie ecozone with its grassland species will expand northward. Which species will migrate and which species will become extinct, however, are difficult to predict since species adaptation and migration depend on a number of factors. Soil types, how they reproduce, daylength preferences and the types of predators and competition all have a bearing on this. Also, adaptation tends to occur slowly rather than quickly. Current climate change scenarios based on a doubling of the concentration of carbon dioxide in the atmosphere do not predict how quickly a doubling will take place. They are also too sparse in their application to specify regional and local changes in the kind of detail that is necessary for predicting species adaptation, migration, and extinction.

Wildlife

Wildlife is directly dependent on vegetation for food and shelter. Changes in habitats and the decreased severity of winter will result in alterations of the distribution and numbers of major big game, waterfowl, and upland game bird species. As the prairie ecozone displaces the boreal forest, species that are adapted to the prairies and aspen parkland can be expected to increase in these areas. Milder winters may also mean higher winter survival rates of species not adapted to cold and snow.

Effect on Recreation Activities

Recreationists have a degree of flexibility in their response to these impacts. Travelling to alternative locations with favourable conditions, reducing participation when conditions are unfavourable or ceasing to participate in their usual activities at all, are all options that can be pursued. People can also undertake new activities or increase their involvement in other activities. The constraining factors will be free time and personal economic wellbeing (More, 1988). Putting these constraints aside, the effect of changing weather patterns and climate is looked at below.

Warmer temperatures will have a great effect on recreation and tourism. The magnitude of this effect is still to be determined, however. Warmer water and air temperatures are expected to increase swimming activity which will also stretch over a longer period of time. However, a decrease in the quantity of water and quality of the resource will reduce swimming activity.

The expected increase in algae and plant life will inhibit swimming. It will also have a negative effect on fishing. If fish populations decrease because of a lack of dissolved oxygen, fishing may be ruled out as a recreational activity at many spots where it now takes place. Increases in air temperature will likely result in a longer season in which water based and dry terrain activities can take place. Decreased lake area and depth due to rising temperatures could result in less opportunity for sailing, boating and water skiing, however. This is especially true if boat docks become stranded above the water line and new docks have to be built. Decreased run-off and shorter run-off periods in the spring and early summer will also influence the quality of white water rafting and kayaking. While the summer season may be extended and provide more opportunities for outdoor recreational activity, it is uncertain whether this extended season will be taken advantage of. People's recreational choices are not only influenced by the weather but also by the amount of leisure time that they have available to them. So, the bulk of recreational activity may continue to take place at the same peak times as it does now: around the school holidays.

An extended summer season does not bode well for activities such as skating, ice fishing, and lake snowmobiling, though. The season for these activities is expected to be shortened substantially since at least 15cm of ice is necessary to support the weight of an adult. Other winter activities such as cross-country and downhill skiing are also expected to be affected. A study in Quebec revealed that the downhill ski season can be expected to be shortened by 50 to 70 percent as a result of climate change. More (1988) and Wittrock et al., (1992) express the same concern for the prairie provinces, although they have not quantified by how much the season can be expected to be shortened. If snow storms come later in the Fall, there may be insufficient snow for both types of skiing during the Christmas holiday season.

Scenarios of vegetation change and resulting movement of wildlife indicate a higher survival rate for species that enjoy warmer winters. Many of the prairie species will move north. Wildlife enthusiasts and bird watchers can look forward to more sitings of winter survivors and they may travel north in order to view wildlife which they usually view in the south now. Hunting activities can be expected to shift north along with the wildlife population. This may have implications for out of province hunters who will have to travel longer distances in order to hunt. They may be unwilling to do so, especially if the costs become prohibitive. The species hunted are also likely to change as hunters adjust to new species in their habitual hunting grounds. As the demographics of the region alter hunting patterns will more than likely alter too. More rural people than urban people tend to hunt. If agriculture in the south becomes less viable because of climate change, there will be fewer farmers and hence fewer hunters.

Socio-Economic and Environmental Consequences of a Change in the Mix of Activities

Tourism and outdoor recreation benefit the economies of many communities. Now, with the loss of subsidies such as the crow rate, more and more communities are looking toward the recreation and tourism industry as a way of diversifying their economies. As the climate and the mix of recreational activities changes these economies can be expected to be affected. If communities do not have access to information on the relationship between recreation and the possible effects of climate change, they could be making decisions to diversify their economies in an unsustainable way.

Unfortunately, very little analysis has been done on how, and the degree to which, economies will be affected by the impacts of climate change on recreation and tourism. Speculation is that for those activities that cost recreation managers little in capital development or operating expenses, the economic impact of shifting recreation patterns will be negligible. Activities involving facilities that are costly to construct and maintain are expected to incur the greatest economic repercussions. Downhill and cross-country skiing are examples of such activities. A study in Alberta found that consumers will invest large amounts of time and money in these activities. However, they expect to have a satisfying experience. If conditions are sub-optimal and the activity becomes costly then they are likely to alter their recreation habits. Making snow is costly and resorts will have to recoup this cost through revenues. If attendance drops it is likely that many ski resort operators could go out of business. The indirect effects of this include loss of tourism revenues to local restaurants, hotels and other forms of amusement as well as the loss of jobs for people within the community.

Tourism and recreation activities do not take place in a vacuum and as such interact with many other sectors. The most obvious on the prairies being agriculture. As has already been mentioned, many of the outdoor recreation activities on the prairies are dependent on the availability of water in large quantities. As the prairie region gets drier and experiences more drought conditions recreational water users will be competing with farmers and industry for that water source. This holds the potential for conflicts among users for limited supplies of good quality water. Other resource conflicts that can arise are between recreationists and the forestry, mining and commercial fishing industries.

Environmentally speaking, the migration of recreational activities northward along with the ecozone could lead to pressure on vulnerable wilderness areas. Longer, warmer summers may lead to greater visitation to parks which could result in degradation, over development and over use. Fewer hunters in the south could also mean overpopulation of big game species which would require new management techniques.

Recommendations to Enhance Adaptation

In order for the tourism and recreation sector to adapt to climate change, more information is necessary on all aspects. Very little research has been done to date on what this sector can expect on the prairies. Current general circulation models are not fine enough to reflect possible changes at specific locations in the prairies. Scenarios still refer to general locations within the region. As scenarios become more specific to locales within the region changes in recreational activities can be anticipated and the necessary contingency plans made.

A deeper understanding of the economic costs is also required. So far very little has been done to determine what the costs will be of creating favourable conditions for swimming, golfing, winter skiing, etc. Since there is limited understanding of how consumers will respond to changing weather, conditions, and costs, it is difficult to know whether these costs can be justified. Hence, a study needs to be conducted on how consumers will adjust their recreational choices as well. No mention has been made of competing attractions outside the prairie provinces and how people will respond to these if the conditions necessary for recreation on the prairies change. This is because the author was unable to find written material relating to this topic. To gain a realistic view of what can be expected to happen in the tourism and recreation sector as a whole it will be necessary to look at competing attractions elsewhere and their capacity to draw recreationists from the prairie provinces and elsewhere.

It is thought that the ecozone will shift northward as a result of climate change. More research is needed on this so that shifts in demographics, vegetation and wildlife populations can be better anticipated. As various users-both people and wildlife-begin to compete for increasingly scarce resources (especially water) new management strategies will need to be developed that take this into account. Resource conflicts need to be anticipated and legislation or a process established for resolving these conflicts.

7

Popularisation of Sustainable Tourism

Introduction: Recent and Future Trends in World Tourism

Tourism can be considered one of the most remarkable socioeconomic phenomena of the twentieth century.

From an activity "enjoyed by only a small group of relatively well-off people" during the first half of the last century, it gradually became a mass phenomenon during the post-World War II period, particularly from the 1970s onwards. It now reaches an increasingly larger number of people throughout the world and can be considered a vital dimension of global integration.

Although domestic tourism currently accounts for approximately 80% of all tourist activity (UN, 1999a), many countries tend to give priority to international tourism because, while the former basically involves a regional redistribution of national income, the latter has now become the world's largest source of foreign exchange receipts. According to the latest figures compiled by the World Tourism Organization (WTO), foreign exchange earnings from international tourism reached a peak of US$ 476 billion in 2000, which was larger than the export value of petroleum products, motor vehicles, telecommunications equipment or any other single category of product or service (WTO, 2001a).

While tourism provides considerable economic benefits for many countries, regions and communities, its rapid expansion can also be responsible for adverse environmental, as well as socio-cultural, impact. Natural resource depletion and environmental degradation associated with tourism activities pose severe problems to many tourism-rich regions. The fact that most tourists chose to maintain their relatively high patterns of consumption (and waste generation) when they reach their destinations can be a particularly serious problem for developing countries and regions without the appropriate means for protecting their natural resources and local ecosystems from the pressures of mass tourism.

The two main areas of environmental impact of tourism are: pressure on natural resources and damage to ecosystems. Furthermore, it is now widely recognized not only that uncontrolled tourism expansion is likely to lead to environmental degradation, but also that environmental degradation, in turn, poses a serious threat to tourism activities.

Pressure on natural resources In addition to pressure on the availability and prices of resources consumed by local residents—such as energy, food and basic raw materials—the main natural resources at risk from tourism development are land, freshwater and marine resources. Without careful land-use planning, for instance, rapid tourism development can intensify competition for land resources with other uses and lead to rising land prices and increased pressure to build on agricultural land. Moreover, intensive tourism development can threaten natural landscapes, notably through deforestation, loss of wetlands and soil erosion. Tourism development in coastal areas—including hotel, airport and road construction—is often a matter for increasing concern worldwide as it can lead to sand mining, beach erosion and other forms of land degradation.

Freshwater availability for competing agricultural, industrial, household and other uses is rapidly becoming one of the most critical natural resource issues in many countries and regions. Rapid expansion of the tourism industry, which tends to be extremely water-intensive, can exacerbate this problem by placing considerable pressure on scarce water supply in many destinations.

Water scarcity can pose a serious limitation to future tourism development in many low-lying coastal areas and small islands that have limited supplies of surface water, and whose groundwater may be contaminated by saltwater intrusion. Over-consumption by many tourist facilities—notably large hotel resorts and golf courses— can limit current supplies available to farmers and local populations in water-scarce regions and thus lead to serious shortages and price rises. In addition, pollution of available freshwater sources, some of which may be associated with tourism-related activities, can exacerbate local shortages.

Rapid expansion of coastal and ocean tourism activities, such as snorkelling, scuba diving and sport fishing, can threaten fisheries and other marine resources. Disturbance to marine aquatic life can also be caused by the intensive use of thrill craft, such as jet skis, frequent boat tours and boat anchors. Anchor damage is now regarded as one of the most serious threats to coral reefs in the Caribbean Sea, in view of the growing number of both small boats and large cruise ships sailing in the region. Severe damage to coral reefs and other marine resources may, in turn, not only discourage further tourism and threaten the future of local tourist industries, but also damage local fisheries.

Damage to Ecosystems

Besides the consumption of large amounts of natural resources, the tourism industry also generates considerable waste and pollution. Disposal of liquid and solid waste generated by the tourism industry has become a particular problem for many developing countries and regions that lack the capacity to treat these waste materials.

Disposal of such untreated waste has, in turn, contributed to reducing the availability of natural resources, such as freshwater.

Apart from the contamination of freshwater from pollution by untreated sewage, tourist activities can also lead to land contamination from solid waste and the contamination of marine waters and coastal areas from pollution generated by hotels and marinas, as well as cruise ships. It is estimated that cruise ships in the Caribbean Sea alone produced more than 70,000 tonnes of liquid and solid waste a year during the mid-1990s (UN, 1999a). The fast growth of the cruise sector in this and other regions around the world has exacerbated this problem in recent years. In fact, it is sometimes argued that the rapid expansion of cruise tourism calls for "the enforcement of an environmental protection 'level playing field' across the world's oceans and between the world's maritime tourism destinations" (Johnson, 2002).

In addition, relatively high levels of energy consumption in hotels—including energy for air-conditioning, heating and cooking—as well as fuel used by tourism-related transportation can also contribute significantly to local air pollution in many host countries and regions. Local air and noise pollution, as well as urban congestion linked to intensive tourism development, can sometimes even discourage tourists from visiting some destinations.

Uncontrolled tourism activities can also cause severe disruption of wildlife habitats and increased pressure on endangered species. Disruption of wildlife behaviour is often caused, for example, by tourist vehicles in Africa's national parks that approach wild cats and thus distract them from hunting and breeding; tour boat operators in the Caribbean Sea that feed sharks to ensure that they remain in tourist areas; and whalewatching boat crews around the world that pursue whales and dolphins and even encourage petting, which tends to alter the animals' feeding and behaviour.

Similarly, tourism can lead to the indiscriminate clearance of native vegetation for the development of new facilities, increased demand for fuelwood and even forest fires. Ecologically fragile areas, such as rain forests, wetlands and mangroves, are also threatened by intensive or irresponsible tourist activity. Moreover, as will be discussed below, it is increasingly recognized that, the rapid expansion of nature tourism (or 'ecotourism') may also pose a threat to ecologically fragile areas, including many natural world heritage sites, if not properly managed and monitored.

The delicate ecosystems of most small islands, together with their increasing reliance on tourism as a main tool of socioeconomic development, means that this environmental impact can be particularly damaging since the success of the tourism sector in these islands often depends on the quality of their natural environment (UN, 1999b). In addition, pollution of coastal waters—in particular by sewage, solid waste, sediments and untreated chemicals—often leads to the deterioration of coastal ecosystems, notably coral reefs, and thus harms their value for tourism.

The equally fragile ecosystems of mountain regions are also threatened by increasing popular tourist activities such as skiing, snowboarding and trekking.

One of the most serious environmental problems in mountainous developing countries without appropriate energy supply is deforestation arising from increasing consumption of fuelwood by the tourism industry. This often results not only in the destruction of local habitats and ecosystems, but also in accelerating processes of erosion and landslides. Other major problems arising from tourist activities in mountain regions include disruption of animal migration by road and tourist facilities, sewage pollution of rivers, excessive water withdrawals from streams to supply resorts and the accumulation of solid waste on trails.

Environmental threats to Tourism

In many mountain regions, small islands, coastal areas and other ecologically fragile places visited by tourists, there is an increasing concern that the negative impact of tourism on the natural environment can ultimately hurt the tourism industry itself. In other words, the negative impact of intensive tourism activities on the environmental quality of beaches, mountains, rivers, forests and other ecosystems also compromise the viability of the tourism industry in these places.

There is now plenty of evidence of the 'life-cycle' of a tourist destination, that is, the evolution from its discovery, to development and eventual decline because of over-exploitation and subsequent deterioration its key attractions. In many developing and developed countries alike, tourism destinations are becoming overdeveloped up to the point where the damage caused by environmental degradation—and the eventual loss of revenues arising from a collapse in tourism arrivals—becomes irreversible.

Examples of such exploitation of 'non-renewable tourism resources' range from a small fishing village in India's Kerala state—which saw its tourist sector collapse after two decades of fast growth, because inadequate disposal of solid waste—to several places in the industrialized world, such as Italy's Adriatic coast and Germany's Black Forest. It can also be argued that environmental pollution and urban sprawl tend to undermine further tourist development in major urban destinations in developing countries, such as Bangkok, Cairo and Mexico City.

In addition, tourism in many destinations could be particularly threatened by external environmental shocks, notably the potential threat of global warming and sea-level rise. Significant rises in sea level could cause serious problems to tourism activities, particularly in low-lying coastal areas and small islands. Global warming is also expected to increase climate variability and to provoke changes in the frequency and intensity of extreme climate events—such as tropical windstorms and associated storm surges and coastal flooding—that may threaten tourism activities at certain destinations.

Sustainable Tourism Development

Countries and regions where the economy is driven by the tourism industry have become increasingly concerned with the environmental, as well as the socio-cultural problems associated with unsustainable tourism. As a result, there is now increasing agreement on the need to promote sustainable tourism development to minimize its environmental impact and to maximize socioeconomic overall benefits at tourist destinations. The concept of sustainable tourism, as developed by the World Tourism Organization (WTO) in the context of the United Nations sustainable development process, refers to tourist activities "leading to management of all resources in such a way that economic, social and aesthetic needs can be fulfilled while maintaining cultural integrity, essential ecological processes, biological diversity and life support systems".

It is increasingly realized that promoting greater community participation in tourism development not only provides stronger incentives to conserve natural capital, but can also lead to a more equitable sharing of benefits and thus greater opportunities for poverty alleviation.

But while ecotourism and PPT both aim to increase community participation in general, PPT also goes beyond this goal in that it includes specific mechanisms to enhance the participation of and opportunities for the poorer segments of society. Three key components of the PPT approach are:

(a) improved access to the economic benefits of tourism by expanding employment and business opportunities for the poor and providing adequate training to enable them to maximize these opportunities;

(b) measures to deal with the social and environmental impact of tourism development, particularly the above-mentioned forms of social exploitation, as well as excessive pressure on natural resources, pollution generation and damage to ecosystems; and

(c) policy reform, by enhancing participation of the poor in planning, development and management of tourism activities pertinent to them, removing some of the barriers for greater participation by the poor, and encouraging partnerships between government agencies or the private sector and poor people in developing new tourism goods and services.

Some of these PPT concepts are beginning to be implemented in several developing countries, such as Ecuador, Namibia, Nepal and Uganda. In Namibia, for example, the implementation of a PPT approach to the development and management of the country's community-based tourism segment appears to have made a significant contribution towards poverty reduction.

Several studies have shown that financial returns from community-based natural resource management and tourism ventures in Namibia usually exceed their investments and are thus a viable option for generating sustainable economic returns, while promoting environmental conservation and cultural traditions in rural areas. There is now evidence of a successful introduction of the PPT approach by the Namibia Community-based Tourism Association

(Nacobta), a non-profit organization that supports poor local communities—including small entrepreneurs with inadequate skills or access to financial resources—in their efforts to develop tourism enterprises in the country.

Nacobta supports its members at both micro and macro levels, mainly through the provision of grants, loans, training, capacity building in the areas of institutional development and marketing training, as well as in negotiations with relevant government agencies and the mainstream tourist industry. Nacobta is explicitly propoor not only because it represents the poorest segment of the country's tourism industry, but also because most of its members live on communal land areas, where themajority of the inhabitants have an average per capita income of less than US$1 a day and depend on subsistence agriculture. One of the main objectives of Nacobta is "to raise the income and employment levels of these areas through tourism, in order to improve the living standards of people in communal areas".

The pro-poor tourism approach of Nacobta is thus different from conventional tourism because members of local communities both own and manage the tourism enterprises, whose economic benefits flow directly into community funds or as formal sector wages, temporary remuneration to casual labourers and income to informal sector traders. There is also evidence that the financial returns from most community-based tourism enterprises supported by Nacobta "has changed their communities from being poor or very poor to being better off".

The Impact of Tourism on Tribals

Tourism can be a very destructive force. Over years it can lead to the development of certain coastal areas and other sites, to become dedicated almost entirely to the business of tourism. Once the tourist demand changes and heads elsewhere, all that is left is an area full of hotels, bars and over used parks, that are basically degraded and not attractive for more tourists. One good example of this is the East Coast of Spain, which became very popular with tourists during the 1970s, but during the 1980s Spain fell out of favour. Everyone considered that particular coastline to be very degraded and so the crowds headed to Turkey instead.

This pattern is not just confined to coastal areas. Tribal and minority peoples in developing countries are also targeted by tourism and that has complicated effects on how such people see themselves or how they are treated in the development process. Perhaps one good example of this is the Masai in Kenya who happen to live near the large safari parks believe that the influence of tourism on the Masai has not been positive or at least that the Masai have not benefited from tourism as much as they could have. Often they are presented to foreign tourists as part of the safari package and "model" Masai villages have great numbers of tourists visiting to observe their lifestyle. Anthropologists would use the term "staged authenticity" for the idea that because one has travelled long distance, it is important to go and see something that is different, exciting, exotic and remote. Many places such as Peru, Thailand and India practice this. It doesn't necessarily follow that the people who partake in these exercises are necessarily having a bad impact upon the tribal communities. However, sometimes it hinders the integration of these people within wider society and it can also increase barriers between minority and majority groups who live in the country as a whole.

In Thailand, most tribes-people are found in the north and migrated over 100 years ago from the southern part of China into Laos, Myanmar (Burma), Vietnam and Thailand. Many argue that they have preserved their way of life. The impact tourism has had on this is controversial. There are six major tribes, the Karen, Hmong, Yao or Mien, Lisu, Lahu, Lawa and Akha. They have maintained their distinctive cultures and tourists do visit these hilly areas to catch a glimpse of their way of life. There are several smaller tribes including the Paduang, or the "Long Necks."

The term 'long-neck' stems from the practice of women adorning their necks with brass coils. This tribe has proved to be a major tourist attraction ever since they began fleeing Burma, more than a decade ago. By tradition, girls begin to wear coils before puberty, and these are augmented until they weigh as much as 11 pounds. The coils force the chin upward while pressing down the collar bones and ribs, elongating the neck.

Some critics argue that the custom has become distorted and exploited by tourism as busloads are encouraged to come and view the women, with their elongated necks.

Has tourism led to any breaches of human rights or the displacement of local communities?

This is one of the great controversies of tourism. There are many examples of national parks being formed by removing people to parks elsewhere. For example, to create the Lake Rara national park in Nepal, they had to move some 400 villagers, the Chhetri people, somewhere else. This is a big debate simply because on the one hand ecologists would like to believe that the park should be left to the native animals and plants. On the other hand, anthropologists and sociologists would like to see the people and the landscape together—indeed the landscape wouldn't exist if the people were not there already. Clearly, the problem is how far tourism can be used as a way to put into practise policies for moving people, which wouldn't be allowed under normal circumstances.

There are many examples of national parks, which have people involved: the question is how many people and also what sort of people? The Tambopata reserve in Ecuador is famous for its integration of the indigenous people who inhabit the forests. Tourists come to look at the forest area and observe local practices. Sometimes, the problem is that once a national park is created, there are new incentives for people to move into the area, cut down the trees, cultivate agriculture and then claim special status for being there. One of the real problems in creating a national park is deciding who is going to be included and who is not.

The Impacts of Different Kinds of Tourism from Backpackers to Package Tourism

There are many types of tourism and we should differentiate between them. When tourism simply consists of backpackers moving into a place, living in local houses and then moving on, it doesn't generally have much of an environmental or social impact. However, the other extreme where large hotels and theme parks are developed obviously has huge impacts upon the local environment, employment opportunities and the very nature of development within the region. It is important to differentiate between the two. Although a lot of people believe that once you start having backpacker tourism, over time, gradually it will change and become more like mass tourism, especially once a market has been established.

Many villages in developing countries around the world receive great numbers of tourists visiting to observe their lifestyle. Anthropologists would use the term "staged authenticity" for the idea that because one has travelled a long distance, it is important to go and see something that is different, exciting, exotic and remote. Many places such as Peru, Thailand and India practice this. It doesn't necessarily follow that the people who partake in these exercises are necessarily having a bad impact upon the tribal communities. However, sometimes it hinders the integration of these people within wider society and it can also increase barriers between minority and majority groups who live in the country as a whole.

This tour notice board shows a "native" with a bone through the nose. It shows the mainstream view of hill tribes as primitive, using a colonial image of a black man with a bone.

It is up to the local authorities and governments to regulate these activities. Some may actively promote such cultural tourism. Others may wish to stringently police tourist behaviour in the presence of these communities.

Have governments and NGO's noted the negative impact mass tourism has had in some areas and what is being done about it?

Virtually all NGO's have noted the potential negative impact of tourism. The WWF is very keen to regulate the use of safari areas and concerned about the potential damage to wildlife resulting from tourism. Many governments, however, take a very different line. The government of Bhutan in the Himalayas, for example, is unusual because it has imposed a very high tourist tax upon tourists going into Bhutan—it can be something like $100-200 a day. This is a radical effort to try and reduce tourist numbers but also increase the revenue coming from tourism—a very successful strategy. Nepal on the other hand, just next door, doesn't take that strategy. It has gone for the "high numbers of tourists" approach. This might cause overloading of certain cities and trekking routes. Other countries such as Kenya and Peru are also very keen on increasing the number of tourists into the country.

How can sustainable tourism practices be made widely attractive and implemented? How much regulation of tourism is there already?

I think it is important to define sustainable tourism precisely. Many people talk about sustainable tourism, when they are actually thinking about ecotourism. Ecotourism is tourism which focuses upon remote ecological and attractive areas such as rainforests or reefs. It can also look at remote people such as the Masai. Many people believe that this can be an ecologically friendly form of tourism but there is a considerable body of research to suggest that this is not the case and that it can actually wreak a lot of damage on fragile eco-systems or increase the pressure upon remote people such as the Masai. It is much more important, I think, to talk about sustainable tourism which deals with all sorts of tourism from the mass tourism on the beaches of Spain, to the cultural tourism of Stratford upon Avon, as well as travelling to exotic rainforests and reefs. It is important to somehow try and increase awareness of the potential damages of tourism in particular localities. The trouble is that it is very difficult to achieve and one of the key problems in achieving sustainable tourism is that there is no such thing as "the" tourism industry. Tourism exists because of the juxtaposition of many different industries such as airlines, tour operators, hotels, tour guides and ice-cream sellers, all operating together at the same time. It is very difficult to come up with policy measures to try and integrate all these different people working in the same direction at the same time.

How do different countries respond to the need for sustainable tourism? Are developing countries more effective regulators than the developed world?

Generally speaking, developing countries have a harder time regulating tourism than the wealthier countries of Europe and

North America. This is basically because these countries are much more used to dealing with tourism. They have a much greater local capacity for implementing policy, making decisions and regulating laws whereas in many developing countries it is very difficult to do anything once you are outside the capital city.

That said, there are some interesting initiatives going on. Bhutan is a good example of one country that has decided not to encourage large amounts of tourism. Within other countries there are other measures for managing tourism. One approach, for example, is land use zoning, which basically means you might send one kind of tourist to an area where they might do drinking, beaches, theme parks, and another sort of tourist such as bird watchers or cultural tourists somewhere else, and never mix the two.

This can increase the great ability to profit from both sides of the market as long as what happens at each place is carefully controlled. It is interesting to note that many developing countries are trying to overcome the ability for tourists to pick and choose between places by trying to market each location as distinctively special. During the 1970s, countries would only market places on the basis of sun, sea and sand, which was great, but so many places in the world offer those things.

However, if you try and present an image of a country as having not only sun, sea and sand but also offering a specific type of wildlife or culture then this can increase a regular flow of tourists who really want to visit that particular country. For example, have you ever seen an advert for Malaysia which doesn't have a picture of an orangutan in it? This is just one technique with which Malaysia can say, "Look we're different, come here".

The World Tourism and Travel Council has set up a number of schemes to try and regulate international tourism. This is a body that has been set up by many large tourism companies to try and regulate tourism and increase communication between different parties and to try and improve the level of tourism throughout the world.

In many ways it does a very good job but many developing countries also criticise the WTTC for not doing enough. The WTTC set up an organisation called Green Globe, which was an attempt to try and increase the environmental performance of tourism companies. However, it has also given a lot of awards to hotels in different countries, which have been criticised widely by local NGO's and activists for overlooking the rights of local people. The actual rules by which environmental performance is governed is extremely controversial.

Advertising exactly what environmental performance is remains a major problem, not just in tourism but in all areas of environmental policy. It is difficult to demonstrate that many people make claims about environmental performance, which are highly controversial. It's a sad fact that many high value tourist resorts advertise themselves as environmentally efficient and friendly just because they might use things like low wattage light bulbs or recycle a lot of waste within the hotel, but in fact they may not want to employ local people to work in the place and there might be all sorts of implications for land prices and access to scarce water supplies or fuel supplies which may impact negatively on other people in the area. There has to be a much more holistic approach to integrating tourist development with local communities and local environments.

What can companies and the private sector do to help? Is there self-regulation?

There are a lot of examples of self-regulation and many of these are quite successful within their own areas. For example, the sustainable hotels initiative is a generally successful programme to try and increase the adoption of environmental practices within hotels. This is the case mainly in developed countries, England in particular and some of these practices might include not washing towels every day because it wastes electricity; or using low wattage electricity bulbs or recycling soap containers.

These of course are not to be dismissed—they are important measures. However, they are somewhat reductionist. They are very easy to see within a hotel but they do not get involved with any issues outside the hotel.

One particularly controversial example is that many NGOS would like hotels to advertise that their customers should not get involved with local prostitution. But the hotels claim this is not their concern and do not want to be seen preaching to customers. Both sides have very good reasons for stating their own position. Knowing where to draw the line between how far a hotel can act and what it really shouldn't be involved with is a very difficult decision.

Travel Ethic for Responsible Travel

As the new millennium unfolds, we are becoming increasingly aware of the finite, interconnected and precious nature of our planet home. Likewise, tourism is becoming an increasingly popular expression of this awareness. With advances in transportation and information technology, ever more remote areas of the earth are coming within reach of the traveller. In fact, tourism is now the world's largest industry, with nature tourism the fastest growing segment. In response to this increasing appreciation of nature experiences, a new travel ethic has arisen which is now called ecotourism. The Nature Conservancy has joined the World Conservation Union (IUCN) in adopting the following definition of ecotourism:

> *"Environmentally responsible travel to natural areas, in order to enjoy and appreciate nature (and accompanying cultural features, both past and present) that promote conservation, have a low visitor impact and provide for beneficially active socioeconomic involvement of local peoples."*

Travelarks is a strong proponent of responsible travel ethics and here are a few pointers that will go a long way in ensuring

- Consumption of alcoholic beverage and smoking is prohibited
- Participants should try and be one with the group and add value to the ambiance
- Try not to venture alone without informing the concerned authority
- Please be responsible and take care of your own belongings and also remind others if they fail to do so
- Please do not litter-Leave nothing behind other than your foot prints (boot prints should we say!)
- Please do not harm the ecological balance
- Do not contribute unwanted decibels to the environment
- Respect the local culture and tradition
- Travelarks would not fetter you with undue restrictions, but when required please abide by them
- Remember that you are special in your own way and add a lot of value to the group in a unique way-please bring the best of your spirits.

OECD Tourism Trends & Policies 2010

The tourism sector, a vital driver of job-creation and growth, is under pressure. Facing an increasingly competitive landscape, tourism in many OECD countries has started to lag, in both growth rate and productivity. This book defines the major trends and challenges facing tourism in the next decade – from globalization to environmental issues.

To address these challenges, the book then provides specific policy guidance and recommendations for making tourism more competitive and environmentally sustainable. Tourism data from 42 countries are presented and analysed including all OECD countries, and fast-growing tourism centres such as Brazil, Chile, China and India.

OECD countries continue to play a predominant role in international tourism, representing about 60% of the global tourism market. They also benefit from a domestic tourism which is in many economies more important that international tourism.

During the last 20 years, the growth rate of international tourism arrivals in OECD countries, whilst 1.6% below the worldwide rate, has averaged 2.8% per year, well ahead of the GDP growth rate of 2.4% for the zone, with OECD countries accounting for about 60% of the global tourism market. In the OECD area, tourism GDP accounts for up to 11% of GDP and even more in terms of employment.

Many of the 12 non-member economies (Brazil, Chile, China, Egypt, Estonia, India, Indonesia, Israel, Romania, the Russian Federation, Slovenia and South Africa) included in this report have a tourism economy representing significant shares of GDP and of total employment. They are also among the fastest growing countries as international tourism destinations.

2010 Commonwealth Games

The 2010 Commonwealth Games are the nineteenth edition of the Commonwealth Games, and the ninth to be held under that name. The Games are scheduled to be held in Delhi, India between 3 October and 14 October 2010. The games will be the largest multi-sport event conducted to date in Delhi and India generally, which has previously hosted the Asian Games in 1951 and 1982.

The opening ceremony is scheduled to take place at the Jawaharlal Nehru Stadium in Delhi. It will also be the first time the Commonwealth Games will be held in India and the second time the event has been held in Asia (after 1998 in Kuala Lumpur, Malaysia).

In addition to the Commonwealth Games, the city of Pune, Maharashtra hosted the 3rd Commonwealth Youth Games between October 12 and 18, 2008. The Youth Games offered nine sports: athletics, badminton, boxing, shooting, swimming, table tennis, tennis, weightlifting and wrestling.

Organisation

Organising Committee

The organisation was beset by delays: in January 2005, the Indian Olympic Association vice-chairman Raja Randhir Singh expressed concern that Delhi was not up to speed in forming and organising its games committee and, following a 2009 Indian Government report showing two thirds of venues were behind schedule, Commonwealth Games Federation president Mike Fennell stated that the slow progress of preparations represented a serious risk to the event. Singh called for a revamp of the games' organizing committees: Jarnail Singh, a former Secretary of the Government of India, was appointed as the Chief Executive Officer and Indian Olympic Association president Suresh Kalmadi was appointed as head of the committee. In spite of delays, commentators stated that they are confident that India will successfully host the games and do so on time.

Costs

The total budget estimated for hosting the Games is US$ 1.6 billion and this amount excludes non-sports-related infrastructure development in the city like airports, roads and other structures. This will likely make the 2010 Commonwealth Games the most expensive Commonwealth Games ever, being larger than the previous games in Melbourne 2006 (approx. US$ 1.1 billion).

Transport

In response to concerns over the large number of trains that pass by the Delhi metropolitan region daily, construction of road under-bridges and over-bridges along railway lines has been started. To expand road infrastructure, flyovers, cloverleaf flyovers, and bridges have been planned to improve links for the Games and city in general.

Road-widening projects have begun with an emphasis being placed on expanding national highways. To improve traffic flow on existing roads, plans are underway to make both the inner and outer Ring roads signal free.

To support its commitment to mass transport, nine corridors have been identified and are being constructed as High Capacity Bus Systems. Six of these corridors are expected to be operational in 2010.

Additionally, The Delhi Metro will be expanded to accommodate more people and boost the use of public transport during the 2010 games. At 420 km long, it will be one of the world's longest networks and it will extend to Gurgaon and the Noida area. For this exponential increase of the network, Delhi Metro will deploy 14 tunnel boring machines, an unprecedented number in an Asian country.

Indira Gandhi International Airport is being modernized, expanded, and upgraded. Costing nearly US$ 1.94 billion, Terminal 3 will improve airport passenger capacity to more than 37 million passengers a year by 2010. A new runway is being constructed, allowing for over 75 flights an hour and – at over 4400 metres long– it will be one of Asia's longest. The entire airport will be connected to the city via a six-lane highway and the Delhi Metro.

Venues

Existing and new stadia in Delhi will be used to house the sports during the Games:

- Jawaharlal Nehru Stadium, Delhi – Weightlifting
- Dhyan Chand National Stadium – Hockey
- Indira Gandhi Arena – Archery, cycling, gymnastics, wrestling
- Delhi University sports complex – Rugby sevens
- Thyagaraj Stadium – Netball
- Siri Fort Sports Complex – Badminton, Squash
- Dr. Karni Singh Shooting Range – Shooting

- Talkatora Stadium – Boxing
- SPM Swimming Pool Complex – Aquatics
- RK Khanna Tennis Complex – Tennis
- Yamuna Sports Complex – Table tennis.

The opening and closing ceremonies, athletics, lawn bowls, and weightlifting will take place at the Jawaharlal Nehru Stadium, Delhi, which will have a capacity of 75,000 spectators after renovation for the games.

Archery, cycling, gymnastics, and wrestling will take place at the Indira Gandhi Arena, the largest indoor sports arena in India and the second-largest in Asia, which seats 25,000 people. Located at the Indraprastha Estate in the eastern region of New Delhi, the arena will be connected to other venues via dedicated bus lanes and mass transportation. The arena will be renovated for the Games. There are 26 new stadiums which will be utilized for the Commonwealth Games. Some older ones will be upgraded and some new will be constructed.

Green Games

The organisers signed a Memorandum of Understanding (MoU) with the United Nations Environment Programme to show the intention to host a "sustainable games" and to take the environment into consideration when constructing and renovating venues. Thyagaraj Stadium is intended to be a key example of environmentally-considered construction.

In opposition to this intention, a number of environmental controversies arose and the adverse ecological impact of various aspects of the games have been protested by city residents. City residents filed a public interest petition to the Supreme Court of India against the felling of 'heritage' trees in the Siri Forest area to make way for Games facilities. The court appointed architect Charles Correa to assess the impact and he severely criticized the designs on ecological grounds. In spite of this, in April 2009 the Supreme Court allowed the construction on the grounds that "much time had been lost" and "the damage already caused to the environment could not be undone".

The Commonwealth Games village, located on the flood plains of the Yamuna, has also been the subject of controversies about the flouting of ecological norms. After a prolonged legal battle between city residents and the state, construction was permitted to continue on the basis of an order of the Supreme Court of India in July 2009, which held that the government had satisfied the requirements of "due process of the law" by issuing public notice of its intention to begin construction work in September 1999 (a date four years prior to the acceptance of Delhi's bid for the games).

Marketing

The games mascot is an anthropomorphic tiger called Shera; a name derived from the Hindi word Sher – meaning tiger.

Other Preparation

In preparation for an influx of English-speaking tourists for the Games, the Delhi government is implementing a program to teach English, and the necessary skills for serving tourists, to key workers – such as cab drivers, security workers, waiters, porters, and service staff. In the two years prior to the Games 2,000 drivers were taught English. The program aims to teach 1,000 people English per month in the hope of reaching all key workers by March 2010. In addition to Delhi, the Indian Government plans to expand the program to teach people in local tourist destinations in other parts of India.

To prepare for the energy-usage spike during the Games and to end chronic power cuts in Delhi, the government is undertaking a large power-production initiative to increase power production to 7,000 MW (from the current 4,500 MW). To achieve this goal, the government plans to streamline the power distribution process, direct additional energy to Delhi, and construct new power plants. In fact, the government has promised that by the end of 2010, Delhi will have a surplus of power.

In addition to physical preparation, India and Delhi will offer free accommodation for all athletes at the Games Village, as well as free transport and other benefits, such as a free trip to the famed Taj Mahal and a reserved lane for participants on selected highways. The Games Village will house over 8,000 athletes and officials for the Games. Indian states will train state police forces to handle tourist-related issues and deploy them prior to the Games.

A massive construction and "beautification" project has resulted in the demolition of hundreds of homes and the displacement of city dwellers – at least 100,000 of New Delhi's 160,000 homeless people have removed from shelters, some of which have been demolished. Bamboo screens have been erected around city slums to separate visitors from the sights of the slums, a practice which human rights campaigners have deemed dishonest and immoral.

The Delhi High Court is set to implement a series of "mobile courts" to be dispatched throughout Delhi to relocate migrant beggars from Delhi streets. The mobile courts would consider each beggar on a case-by-case basis to determine whether the beggar should be sent back to his/her state of residence, or be permitted to remain in government-shelters.

Queen's Baton Relay

The Queen's Baton relay began when the baton, which contains Queen Elizabeth II's message to the athletes, left Buckingham Palace on 29 October 2009. The baton will arrive at the 2010 Games opening ceremony on 3 October 2010, after visiting the other 70 nations of the Commonwealth and travelling throughout India, reaching millions of people to join in the celebrations for the Games.

The baton was designed by Michael Foley, a graduate of the National Institute of Design. It is a triangular section of aluminium twisted into a helix shape and then coated with coloured soils collected from all regions of India.

The coloured soils are a first for the styling of a Queen's Baton. A jewel-encrusted box was used to house the Queen's message, which was laser-engraved onto a miniature 18 carat gold leaf – representative of the ancient Indian 'patras. The Queen's baton is ergonomically contoured for ease of use. It is 664 millimetres high, 34 millimetres wide at the base, and 86 millimetres wide at the top and weighs 1,900 grams.

The Queen's baton has a number of technological features including:

- The ability to capture images and sound
- Global positioning system (GPS) technology so the baton's location can be tracked
- Embedded light emitting diodes (LEDs) which will change into the colours of a country's flag whilst in that country

- A text messaging capability so that people can send messages of congratulations and encouragement to the Baton bearers throughout relay.

Sports

The triathlon appears likely to be excluded from these games as there is no suitable location for the swimming stage. The organisers have also proposed removing basketball, but want to include archery, tennis, and billiards and snooker for men. Cricket, although in strong demand, may not make a come-back as the Board of Control for Cricket in India were not keen on a Twenty20 tournament, but the organisers did not want a one day tournament.

Participating Nations

There are currently 71 nations planning to field teams at the 2010 Commonwealth Games. As Fiji is suspended from the Commonwealth, it has been banned from participating in the Games. Rwanda may field a team for the games since becoming a Commonwealth member in 2009. Controversies

Labour Violations

Campaigners in India have accused the organisers of enormous and systematic violations of labour laws at construction sites. Although official numbers have not been released, it is estimated that over 415,000 contract daily wage workers are working on Games projects. Unskilled workers are paid 85 to 100 Indian rupees (INR) per day while skilled workers are paid 120 to 130 INR per day for eight hours of work. Workers also state that they are paid 134 to 150 INR for 12 hours of work (eight hours plus four hours of overtime). Both these wages contravene the stipulated Delhi state minimum wage of INR 152 (approx. US$3) for eight hours of work.

These represent violations of the Minimum Wages Act, 1948; Interstate Migrant Workmen (Regulation of Employment and Condition of Services) Act 1979, and the constitutionally enshrined fundamental rights per the 1982 Supreme Court of India judgement on Asiad workers. The public have been banned from the camps where workers live and work – a situation which human rights campaigners say prevents the garnering of information regarding labour conditions and number of workers.

There have been documented instances of the presence of young children at hazardous construction sites, due to a lack of child care facilities for women workers living and working in the labour camp style work sites. Furthermore, workers on the site of the main Commonwealth stadium have reportedly been issued with hard hats, yet most work in open-toed sandals and live in cramped tin tenements in which illnesses are rife. The High Court of Delhi is presently hearing a public interest petition relating to employers not paying employees for overtime and it has appointed a four-member committee to submit a report on the alleged violations of workers rights.

During the construction of the Games Village, there was controversy over financial mismanagement, profiteering by the Delhi Development Authority and private Real Estate Companies, and inhumane working conditions.

8

Infrastructure and Tourism Development

Case Study

General Information

Location: The Philippines is an archipelago consisting of about 7,100 islands. The country is divided into three major island groups: Luzon, Visayas and Mindanao. It is bounded on the north by the Bashi Channel, on the west by the South China Sea, on the South by the Sulu and Celebes Seas, and on the east by the Pacific Ocean.

Its northernmost islands, the Batanes, are approximately 240 kilometers south of Taiwan, while the southernmost islands, the Sulu group, lie approximately 24 kilometers from the Borneo coast. Situated between the Pacific and Indian Oceans, and between Australia and mainland Asia, the Philippines is at the crossroads of international travel routes.

Land Area. The total land area is approximately 300,000 square kilometers. The archipelago stretches out for about 1,800 kilometers from north to south, and for about 1,050 kilometers from east to west.

Topography. The Philippines has an irregular configuration of extensive coastline, vast extent of mountainous country lying close to the sea, narrow and interrupted coastal plains, and a generally north-south trend of inland water bodies.

Population. As of 1995, the population was estimated at 70 million with persons 15 years old and above considered the productive segment of the economy, comprising 63 per cent. The population density is about 234 persons per square kilometer of land.

Updates on the Philippine Economy

The economic turn around that began in 1992 continued to gain momentum in 1995 with the real growth in gross national product (GNP) accelerating at 5.7 per cent, an improvement on the previous year's 5.3 per cent. On the production side, industry and services expanded significantly, accounting for about 96 per cent of increase in aggregate domestic production during the year which offset the weak showing of agriculture which was hit by typhoons and other natural disasters. Meanwhile, strong exports and personal consumption expenditures accounted for growth in the demand side, the highest so far since 1992. Inflation was at single digit levels as of end 1995 and is expected to attain the same level by year end 1996.

The bright economic picture can be attributed to a number of factors, foremost of which were measures to maintain a stable macroeconomic environment and reforms to create a liberalized environment for business. Furthermore, the necessary conditions for growth such as political unity, peace and order, and infrastructure support were attended to by the government. The government recognized that physical infrastructure development must keep in step with economic growth. The huge cost to the economy of under-investment in infrastructure was witnessed in 1992-1993, at the height of the power crisis. Cognizant of the huge investment requirement in infrastructure and the insufficiency of public funds to bridge this investment gap, the government instituted policies that encouraged private sector participation. The decision to mobilize private sector involvement in power generation proved to be fruitful as the crisis was resolved in 1994.

The government has adopted reforms and initiatives towards easing the entry of foreign and local investors into industries. Industries whose growth were previously hampered by government regulations like telecommunications and inter-island shipping were deregulated. The efficiency gains are visible. In telecommunications, for example, waiting time for a telephone connection has been drastically reduced while charges for overseas calls declined. As a result, markets are getting integrated both domestically and internationally, and mutually beneficial transactions are being realized in the process. The liberalization of the shipping industry, on the other hand, opened up domestic routes to other firms.

The noteworthy performance of the economy over the period 1993-95 is no reason to be complacent. The development strategy that has been embraced has opened up the economy to global competition. This means that policies supportive of long-term growth must continue. Raising agricultural productivity, in particular, is a major challenge, given the inclusion of trade in agriculture in the World Trade Organization (WTO). To the extent that majority of poor families are dependent on traditional subsistence agriculture, success in raising agricultural productivity begets success in poverty alleviation.

The government recognizes that public policies based on privatization, liberalization, deregulation, and decentralization provide incentives for efficiency and growth. They expand the economic opportunities of people, enabling them to raise their standards of living. The Ramos Administration is committed to pursue, and to accelerate where possible, these structural policy reforms, all of which have contributed to the sound economic performance from 1993 to 1995 and have provided a foundation for meeting any economic and social challenges in the future.

Long-term Objectives for Infrastructure Development

As the backbone of development of any economy, the provision of infrastructure is a prerequisite towards attaining economic growth and improving the country's productive capacity. The anticipated growth of the economy is expected to exert more pressure on infrastructure support facilities.

There are two major objectives for the infrastructure sector in the long-term: (1) to provide adequate, convenient, fast and safe facilities and competitively priced services to meet the primary needs of the population and; (2) to provide support facilities for the productive sectors and act as catalyst of development in desired areas.

Strategies for Infrastructure Development to Support National Objectives

The government has to design the proper policies and corresponding strategies for infrastructure development to ensure that the appropriate infrastructures will be provided in the right places at the right time. The following are the general policies and strategies to be pursued in the next three years in support of the sector's development under the Medium-Term Philippine Development Plan. (MTPDP):

1. Further encourage increased and broad-based private sector investments in the provision, operation and maintenance of infrastructure facilities through but not limited to the Build-Operate-Transfer (BOT) scheme;
2. Improve coordination among national government agencies, local government units (LGUs), the private sector and affected communities in the formulation and implementation of infrastructure plans and projects;
3. Ensure provision of adequate funds for required capital investment and operations and maintenance (O & M) with priority on the latter;
4. Strictly implement and upgrade maintenance and rehabilitation programs and standards;
5. Enhance integration of environmental and socio-cultural concerns in the planning and implementation of infrastructure projects;
6. Strengthen infrastructure support to socially depressed areas and to growth centres and areas with the highest growth potentials;
7. Promote, where feasible, labour-based technology in infrastructure activities;
8. Promote research, development and use of innovative construction materials and environment-friendly technology for energy-efficient structures and costefficient construction design;
9. Adjust fees and charges to approximate real costs incurred in the provision of infrastructure services;
10. Adopt the integrated area development approach in the planning, programming and implementation of complementary support infrastructure for regional growth centres, tourism areas, and identified poverty areas;
11. Give priority to appropriate sanitation infrastructure facilities (e.g. toilets, water supply and sewerage) in Metro Manila and other urban centres, especially in depressed areas; and

12. Strengthen local technical and financial capacity for project implementation and service management through broad-based training programs and organizational and fiscal reforms.

Subsectoral Objectives, Policies Strategies and Priority Subsector Activities

Going down to the different subsector of infrastructure, the objectives and specific policies and strategies adopted for each and the corresponding priority activities are as follows:

Energy

The objectives of the energy subsector on ensuring the availability and security of market-based energy supply; promoting the judicious and efficient use of energy resources; and averting negative impacts of energy activities to health, safety and environmental quality in the design and operation of energy projects will be supported by the following policies and strategies.

To ensure energy availability and security:

1. Diversify sources and types of local and imported energy;
   - i. utilization of natural gas for power generation or other competitive uses;
   - ii. explore and develop oil and geothermal resource potential;
   - iii. mine-mouth coal power plant operations for low-grade coal deposits;
   - iv. large-scale utilization of new and renewable sources of energy including small-and mini-hydro resources, solar, wind and biomass-based resources;
   - v. promote the use of decentralized energy systems for areas outside electricity grids; and
   - vi. rationalize expansion of petroleum distribution networks.
2. Expand coverage of electrification for the energy needs of countryside development;
3. Secure existing and future sites of power and energy resource development projects;
4. Enhance private sector participation in energy projects; and

5. Promote competition and long-term efficiency in the energy industry.

To promote judicious and efficient use of energy:

1. Pursue least-cost options;
2. Restructure electricity tariffs to reflect cost of provision;
3. Strictly implement comprehensive O & M and rehabilitation programs;
4. Enforce standards of efficiency and reliability in power generation and distribution utilities;
5. Promote energy conservation, energy efficient technologies, and energy R & D;
6. Move towards the deregulation of downstream oil industry to promote efficiency, e.g. petroleum product pricing and distribution.

To avert negative impacts of energy activities to health, safety and environmental *quality*:

1. Promote adoption of clean technologies for utilization of coal and other hydrocarbons;
2. Integrate environmental and socio cultural concerns in the planning and implementation of energy programs and projects, e.g., environmental management and community relations activities in energy project sites.

Priority Subsector Activities

1. Maintenance, rehabilitation and construction of power plants, transmission lines and substations in the Luzon, Visayas and Mindanao grids;
2. Exploration and development of indigenous energy resources including downstream activities;
3. Expansion of electrification coverage and improvement in the efficiency of distribution through the construction, rehabilitation, upgrading and maintenance of facilities; and
4. Implementation of research and development, institutional strengthening and energy conservation programs.

Transportation

As the economy expands toward the countryside and aims at global markets, the transport objective on strengthening interregional and urban-rural linkages to ensure people's mobility and continuous flow of goods; ensuring the safety and efficiency of transport services to meet the needs of an increasing population and dynamic market demands; and developing international gateways to optimum standards to enhance the country's global competitiveness; will be supported by the following policies and strategies:

1. Identify and provide basic transport infrastructure to ensure access and allow the integration of depressed communities;
2. Maintain existing transportation facilities properly to prolong their use;
3. Continuously upgrade transport facilities and service standards to make sure that their quality and quantity are responsive to traffic growth;
4. Promote multimodal transport to facilitate trade;
5. Develop the arterial road network consisting of a north-south backbone, east-west laterals, and other strategic roads;
6. Provide the transport facility requirements of agriculture, fishing, and agrarian reform areas, regional industrial centres, and tourism areas;
7. Proceed with the development of feeder ports under the Nationwide Feeder Ports program in preparation for the devolution of their O & M to LGUs;
8. Establish specialized handling facilities for grains and bulk cargo in selected ports and construct additional fishing ports;
9. Implement urban transport management measures and develop alternative modes of transport in coordination with LGU's to alleviate traffic. Expand existing mass transit systems to provide affordable means of transport, and pursue new projects, including expressways and tollways;
10. Intensify transport safety programs to minimize accident risks and protect lives through the implementation of relevant recommendations of the Civil Aviation Master Plan, Maritime SafetyMaster Plan, and the Road Safety Program;

11. Strictly enforce environmental protection measures controlling vehicle emissions, water pollution, and noise pollution to safeguard the health of the population;
12. Strengthen institutional and inter-agency coordination of planning and project implementation to ensure effective and efficient intermodal linkage and reduce disruption of services;
13. Promote private sector participation in transport development, e.g., construction, maintenance, and operation of roads, expressways, mass transit systems, ports, railways, and terminals;
14. Enhance the capability of LGUs in administering, implementing and developing infrastructure facilities, i.e., local roads, municipal ports, as embodied in the Local Government Code;
15. Pursue efficiency-and competition-enhancing measures such as deregulation, decentralization, appropriate pricing mechanisms, and rationalization of user charges;
16. Adjust truck load limits along with road design standards to achieve a proper balance between trucking and infrastructure costs, and strictly enforce load limits;
17. Rehabilitate the PNR Mainline South, study the rehabilitation and possible extension of the northern line in Luzon and explore the feasibility of adopting rail as means of transportation in other areas of the country; and
18. Upgrade the NAIA and explore the use of the reverted baselands for its relocation or as a site for transport-related industrial complexes;

Priority Subsector Activities

1. Upgrading of national arterial and secondary roads to all-weather roads, and conversion of all bridges along these roads into permanent structures;
2. Construction and improvement of airport facilities including aircraft movement areas, terminal buildings, fire stations, etc.;
3. Upgrading and modernization of air navigation and communication facilities, and crash-fire-rescue vehicles;

4. Development and improvement of national ports and port facilities, feeder, fishing, and municipal ports, and river landings;
5. Acquisition and upgrading of aids to maritime navigation, search and rescue vehicles, hydrographic fire-fighting vessels, marine pollution control vessels, and other vessels;
6. Expansion and development of urban rail transit in Metro Manila, including the rehabilitation of LRT Line 1, the construction of new LRT lines, and the rehabilitation of PNR's Commuter Line South; and
7. Completion and the rehabilitation of PNR's Main Line South and study of viability of adopting rail transport in various areas of the country.

Communication

Increased globalization of production and finance requires that the Philippines keep pace with the latest advancements in the area of communications. In this connection, the sector will strive to interconnect all local telephone exchanges into the main backbone; strengthen the regulatory and management capability of government to enable the private sector to meet the growing demand for telephone and other value-added services, and to achieve and maintain a high quality of telecommunications service; and expand postal service to far-flung/unserved areas and improve delivery efficiency in those areas covered. To attain these objectives; the following policies and strategies will be pursued:

1. Privatize all government telecommunications assets by 1998 as mandated by Republic Act 7925; allow more open entry of private firms to promote greater competition and efficiency in telecommunications services;
2. Phase out unnecessary taxes and fees that divert resources away from rapid growth of the sector, wean government away from the ownership, provision and direct operation of telecommunication services and privatize the postal service;
3. Adopt clear and simpler rules for interconnecting all public networks; encourage toll revenue sharing schemes that will ensure the financial viability of the local exchanges; and establish rules and regulations for a more rationalized delivery of broad band and personal communication services;

4. Reorient the regulatory system, initially towards forward arbitration of the issues arising from interconnection, revenue-sharing, rates restructuring based on cost radio spectrum usage, and complex technical options under a multi-operator business environment;
5. Increase telephone density and widen coverage consistent with the developmental stage of the various localities and the needs of the business, by private entities in concert with government investing their respective resources to anticipate and build capacities accordingly;
6. Upgrade the quality of postal communication service to internationally accepted standards; establish postal circuits in barangays not effectively covered by existing post offices and postal stations;
7. Introduce value-added services and initiate advanced users on the business and professional opportunities arising from the convergence of computers and communications; and
8. Modify the legal framework to permit and promote more electronic-based transactions, aside from phasing in deregulation measures as the sector achieves maturity.

Priority Subsector Activities

1. Installation of telephone main stations and public calling office (PCOs) throughout the country;
2. Construction of postal offices buildings and improvement of mail distribution service;
3. Improvement of the quality of telecommunications service; and
4. Establishment of telecommunication facilities to improve weather forecasting, enhance safety and improve information exchange.

Water Resources

In support to the objectives of increasing the provision of irrigation, safe and adequate water supply, sanitation services and appropriate flood control and drainage mechanisms are the following policies and strategies:

1. Pursue a decentralized, coordinated and efficient management of water resources; adopt an integrated

planning and development strategy for an area-wide development schemes combining irrigation, power, flood control, and domestic and industrial water supply;

2. Determine investments in water resources and sanitation development would be based on demand and local initiative;
3. Encourage/facilitate participation of LGUs, NGOs, and private groups in sector development;
4. Integrate quality and quantity concerns in resource management and introduce appropriate environmental charges to protect public health and ensure environmental sustainability;
5. Implement cost-efficient water resources development projects for increased productivity and employment opportunities;
6. Integrate the provision of improved sewage and sanitation services in all water development programs and projects;
7. Determine the allocation of water among users where the primary bases shall be the socio-eocnomic consideration/ greater beneficial use.

Priority Subsector Activities

1. Construction, rehabilitation and maintenance of national and communal irrigation facilities nationwide;
2. Construction and upgrading of water supply and sewerage/sanitation facilities nationwide; and
3. Construction and implementation of flood control and drainage projects in the 12 major river systems in the country including Metro Manila.

Strategies for Supporting Regional Infrastructure Development

In support of programs for regional cooperation in infrastructure development, the following strategies shall be pursued in the sector:

1. Rapid expansion and integration of the network/facilities across urban and rural areas;
2. Active involvement of the private sector under the Local Government Code in local governance to ensure delivery of basic infrastructure facilities/services;

3. Integrate infrastructure planning with urban and regional planning, land use, environment, industry, agriculture, tourism and other sectors of the economy; and
4. In telecommunications, exploit the opportunities created by the overlaps of broadcasting and telecommunications through the production of cultural and entertainment programs geared for the Asia-Pacific market.

Scope and Priorities of Infrastructure Programs and Projects

Under the MTPDP, we have also identified specific programs and projects to implement such policies with corresponding key measurable targets. These targets will enable our government to monitor the implementation of programs and projects on infrastructure. They are the following:

Energy

1 More than 2,000 megawatts of new power-generating capacity to be put on stream up to the year 1998 to meet the projected 11.7 per cent yearly growth in power demand;
2. Integrate the three major island groups of the Philippines into a single grid in the next five years to strengthen system reliability and to allow the flexible shifting of power from areas with excess supply to deficient ones;
3. Dependence on imported energy to be reduced to 57 per cent of the total energy consumption of 258 million barrels of fuel oil equivalent by year 1998 from 67 per cent in 1995;
4. Expand rural electrification coverage to benefit an additional 1.1 million households under the government assisted electric cooperatives to 63 per cent by 1998 from 55 per cent in 1995;
5. Convert Clark Air Base into a freeport zone and investment haven just like Subic Bay Freeport Zone;
6. Rehabilitate and improve 100 per cent of national arterial roads and 95 per cent of national secondary roads into all-weather roads;
7. Improve major ports and airports and upgrade to international standards the Mactan, Davao and Zamboanga airports;
8. Construct new light rail transit lines in Metro Manila;

9. Install 4.2 million telephone lines to improve telephone density to 7.37 lines per 100 population from 2.01 in 1995;
10. Install public calling offices in all 1,565 municipalities;
11. Increase the proportion of the population served with potable water to 79 per cent from 72 per cent in 1995; and
12. Provide an additional 106,011 hectares with irrigation facilities.

Tourism Development

The overall objective for the development of the tourism sector hinges on the promotion of the Philippines as an attractive tourist destination not only for foreigners but also for Filipinos as well.

In support, the following policies and strategies will be aggressively pursued:

1. Promotion of destination clusters for major island groups, i.e., corresponding to the Luzon, Visayas and Mindanao island groups, where each cluster will be supported by at least one major international gateway and tourism estates/ zones connected to a variety of satellite destinations;
2. Promotion of history, culture and arts;
3. Promotion of a mix of destinations and products for various tourist segments;
4. Conduct policy review in response to changing trends;
5. Establish and strengthen linkages and networking to ensure the provision of adequate infrastructure facilities and services in tourism areas, as well as the development, enhancement and promotion of existing and potential tourist attractions.

Priority Subsector Activities

1. Formulation of tourism master plans for all regions and detailed physical plans for priority tourism areas or 'must-see' destinations identified in the regional development framework;
2. Preparation of a Cluster Development Plan for Luzon, Visayas and Mindanao including the development of an integrated tourism infrastructure plan along the lines of conserving the socio-cultural heritage and preserving the environment;

3. Conduct of market research programs to identify target segment, product offerings, pricing, etc.;
4. Promotion of investments by both local and foreign developers in tourism priority areas;
5. Establishment of regional tourism training centres including the formulation of training modules at crafts/ skills level and mobile training units in the regions;
6. Establishment of cultural and heritage centres in areas identified in the TMP and regional master plans including the restoration of national parks, historical sites and shrines, e.g., Rizal Park, Intramuros, Vigan, Taal and Nayong Pilipino.
7. Conceptualization and packaging of "freedom trail tours" in line with the Philippine Freedom Centennial Celebration;
8. Pursuit of aggressive marketing campaigns focusing on the thematic campaign "Islands Philippines" during the Plan period culminating in the holding of a "Philippine Visit Year" Campaign in 1998.

Administrative Structure for Policy-making and for the Implementation of Infrastructure Programs and Projects

In explaining the administrative structure for the approval and implementation of infrastructure projects in the Philippines, discussions will be limited to BOT projects for brevity. The main actors in the BOT approval/implementation process are as follows:

Infrastructure Committee (INFRACOM) of the NEDA Board

The INFRACOM is a policy-level committee of the NEDA Board composed of the Secretaries of NEDA, DPWH, DOTC, DBM, DOF, DOE, and the Executive Secretary from the Office of the President. NEDA acts as the Secretariat to the Committee. In addition to its regular functions, it is tasked to coordinate the discussion/resolution/reformation of policies an issues pertinent to the implementation of the Build-Operate-Transfer Schemes.
Investment Coordination Committee (ICC) of the NEDA Board
The Investment Coordination Committee (ICC) is another cabinet committee of the NEDA Board composed of the Secretaries of DOF, NEDA, DBM, DTI, DA, BASP, DOE, CCPAP and the Executive Secretary from the Office of the President. Its basic mandate is to

coordinate the utilization of fiscal resources for the public investment program, approve the implementation of major projects and monitor the same thereof.

With respect to BOT projects, ICC shall approve national projects costing up to 300 million and local projects costing more than 200 million pesos. ICC shall recommend the approval of national projects costing more than 300 million pesos to the National Economic Development Authority (NEDA) Board and all Build-Operate and Own projects to the President.

Implementing Agency

The implementing agencies for infrastructure development, such as the Department of Public Works and Highways, the Department of Transportation and Communications and the National Power Corporation, perform the following functions:

1. Identify and recommend particular projects for BOT;
2. Undertake at least the pre-feasibility studies for the projects;
3. Ensure that projects are part of its development program;
4. Secure ICC approval of the project before bidding;
5. Responsible for leading the project through bidding, negotiation and approval; and
6. In the absence of an appropriate regulatory body, issue a franchise to operate.

Local Government Unit (LGU)

The LGU identifies and recommends projects for BOT. It then secures project confirmation of the local development council or regional development council or the Metropolitan Manila Development Authority (for Metro Manila projects) prior to bidding. It is likewise responsible for leading the project though bidding, negotiation and approval. Finally, the LGU or appropriate regulatory body may issue a franchise to operate, as provided by existing laws.

Coordinating Council of the Philippine Assistance Program (CCPAP)

The Coordinating Council of the Philippine Assistance Program (CCPAP) has been tasked to handle the promotion of the BOT scheme and projects. It provides training/information to lead actors for BOT implementation, technical assistance for a prefeasibility study to assess if a project is suitable for BOT implementation, and support for tender document preparation, marketing and contract compliance.

Private Sponsors

The private sector agent is responsible for leading the project through packaging, negotiation and approval of the security package. It assembles the needed financial commitments for the project.

There are also other actors that have important roles to play in the BOT approval process. These are:

- o *Local Development Council*
  - Evaluates/approves/integrates the project into a larger development plan
- o *Local Sanggunian or Council*
  - Approves the project prior to call for bids
- o *Board of Investments (BOI)*
  - Decides if a project is eligible for investment incentives
- o *Department of Environment and Natural Resources (DENR)*
  - Reviews compliance with environmental laws
  - Issues the Environmental Compliance Certificate
- o *Regulatory Agencies*
  - Ensures that tolls and fees are just

Market Preparations for Private Sector Investment

As in any country in the world, the Philippines' economic growth cannot be sustained and further improved without continuously adopting measures to enhance the infrastructure system. To realize this, a broad policy framework has been adopted by the government to encourage private sector to participate in economic development, e.g. financing, operation and construction of vital infrastructure facilities.

Current Laws Affecting Infrastructure Development

In the formulation of policies and programs for infrastructure development and in the course of implementation of such projects, we are bound by certain laws, foremost among which are the Build-Operate-Transfer (BOT) Law, the Public Service Law and other regulations.

BOT Law

Although provision of infrastructure facilities and services is mainly the responsibility of government because of its "public goods" aspect, severe fiscal constraints in the case of the Philippines, has resulted in the decline of public investment in infrastructure development. In consonance with the new era of low public sector deficits which the government aims to impose to contain inflation within manageable levels and ensure sustainable long-term growth, we are constrained to restrict our expenditure program. This means putting a limit to public investments in infrastructure projects. On the other hand this forces our government to seek other sources of financing such as Official Development Assistance (ODA) and private investments, either domestic or foreign. This kind of scenario opens a great number of opportunities for the BOT scheme.

Republic Act (RA) No. 6957 enacted on July 9, 1990 institutionalized the BOT/BT concept in the Philippines and this served as an avenue for the Philippine Government to address the following national concerns:

1. To encourage private sector participation in the financing, construction, operation and maintenance of infrastructure and power projects, the lack of which is considered one of the overriding barriers to economic growth in the Philippines;
2. To reduce the fiscal burden on the part of the Government of the Philippines (GOP) by making the private sector an effective partner and/or participant in infrastructure building; and
3. To effectively encourage the inflow of foreign capital financing, technology and expertise, especially in the operation of major and capital-intensive infrastructure projects.

Recognizing the need to put in place an environment conducive to private sector's entrepreneurial initiatives RA 6957 was enacted. RA 6957 initially sought to provide the necessary policy framework and clear-cut implementation of BOT/BT projects. In the course of its implementation, it became evident that further changes in some provisions were necessary in order to further stimulate private sector participation. In line with the government's commitment to a liberal and facilitative socioeconomic environment, amendments to the Law were introduced through RA 7718 which was enacted on 05 May 1994. The amended BOT Law allows more types of infrastructure projects to be implemented by the private sector. In addition to traditional projects like power plants, highways, ports, airports and similar projects, new ones have been added. These are solid waste management, information technology networks and database infrastructure, education and health facilities, tourism projects, government buildings, and other projects that may be approved by the President of the Philippines.

The scope of the amended BOT Law has also been liberalized and widened. Nine variations of contractual arrangements that go beyond building, owning, operating and transferring are now allowed. These new features include leasing, contracting, adding, rehabilitating, developing adjacent areas, etc.

Unsolicited project proposals may be accepted on a negotiated basis subject to certain conditions. Furthermore, direct negotiation shall be resorted to when there is only one complying bidder. This was not allowed before.

The amended BOT Law likewise now allows government appropriation and/or access to ODA of up to 50 per cent of project cost for projects with difficulty in sourcing funds. The Implementing Rules and Regulations of the amended BOT Law also requires that the economic viability indicators of the project shall be evaluated against a hurdle rate of 15 per cent.

Rate setting will be deregulated for projects which are bid out. On the other hand, the appropriate regulatory agencies will approve the rates for negotiated contracts. In the case of negotiated contracts for public utility projects which are monopolies, the rate of return base will not exceed 12 per cent.

Investment incentives contained in the Omnibus Investment Code as well as direct cost-sharing and credit enhancements may be extended to projects as necessary. Considering the overwhelmingly favourable reactions to the new BOT law, we are very optimistic that more private investors will signify their interest to invest in infrastructure projects in our country.

Public Service Law of 1936

The Public Service Law defines "public utilities" as including:

1. Roads and thoroughfares
2. Railways and Urban Rail Mass Transit

3. Distribution (not production) of Electricity and Gas
4. Water Distribution and Sewerage Systems
5. Telephone Systems
6. Wireless Broadcast Stations
7. Any common carrier, either for freight or passenger.

Proposed amendments to the Public Service Law are now pending in Congress which seek to remove the following activities from being classified as "public utilities":

1. Domestic messenger and parcel delivery services
2. Shipyards, marine railways, marine repair shops, wharves or docks
3. Ice plants and ice-refrigeration plants
4. Irrigation systems
5. Warehouses
6. Airships within the Philippines;
   - The Foreign Investments Act of 1991;
   - The Omnibus Investments Code of 1987 and
   - The Investment Priorities Plan.

The Foreign Investments Act identifies the areas where foreign investors can enter while the Omnibus investments Code identifies the kind of fiscal incentives that may be availed of by investors under certain conditions. The Investment Priorities Plan identifies the areas in which these incentives can be availed of. It is drawn up annually.

There are pending proposals in Congress to amend the Foreign Investments Act and the Omnibus Investments Code to further liberalize the entry of foreign investments into the country, including national treatment of equity investments put in by multilateral financing agencies.

The General Banking Code

Sections 111 and 112 of the General Banking Code establishes a single-borrower's limit of 15 per cent for Philippine banking institutions. This means that a Philippine bank cannot lend out more than 15 per cent of its capital base to any single entity.

This could have the effect of restricting domestic term loans to large BOT infrastructure projects. However, these projects would have to be very large, as the single borrower limit for the top five commercial banks is between five hundred million and one billion pesos per bank.

Executive Order No. 215

Executive Order No. 215 is the legal basis for tapping private sector power generation prior to the more expansive BOT Law. It is noteworthy for two reasons:

1. It allowed the private sector to participate in the generation of power.
2. It gave the National Power Corporation the authority to develop the implementing rules and regulations. In particular, NPC was given the leeway to determine (a) process of bidding and awarding of projects, thus allowing them to avoid-to some degree-the lengthy approval process for BOT projects, and (b) credit enhancements it could give in order to make the project more attractive to the private sector.

Local Government Code

The Local Government Code encourages the participation of the private sector in local governance, particularly in the delivery of basic services, to ensure the viability of local autonomy as an alternative strategy for sustainable development.

Government Commitment, Support and Riskmanagement

The critical challenge facing the government is to constantly monitor, improve, and refine policy measures and general guidelines when and where required. This is necessary to motivate and enable interested parties to take a more competitive form under a global climate of rapid change.

To encourage further private sector participation, the government has maintained its open-mindedness and receptiveness to suggestions on how to improve the process, e.g. possible amendment of the IRR of the amended BOT law to remove sources of irritants and bottlenecks and to resolve conflicts with other laws. In this regard, there is an inter-agency goverment committee that can be convened anytime there is a need to review or revise the IRR.

The country has come a long way since the path of liberalization was taken in developing the infrastructure crucial to the country's industrialization. Having put in place institutional measures to open up the sector to competition, coupled with a market demand projected to increase in size in the future, the government has succeeded in stimulating significant investment in the sector.

Since the adoption of policies geared towards a more liberal business environment, many foreign and local industry observers agree that the Philippine market is increasingly competitive, e.g. in telecommunications, power, transportation. These are on top of what the country now offers, e.g. political stability, an investor-friendly legal framework, free market for foreign exchange and guaranteed repatriation rights.

Bidding Procedures/Process For Government Infrastructure Projects

In line with its effort to achieve economy and efficiency in the implementation of public infrastructure projects, the government formulated in 1978 and in 1987 a standard set of rules and regulations for civil works and consultancy contracts, respectively, with the aim of: a) minimizing project cost through the adoption of sound practices in contract management; b) promote a healthy partnership between the government and the private sector in furthering national development; and c) enhance the growth of the local construction and consulting industries.

The government's bidding procedure generally advocates for an open competitive selection process. However, it also allows negotiated contracts under exceptional circumstances such as in times of emergencies or where there is lack of qualified bidders.

Foreign contractors/consultants may participate in the bidding of projects provided that they comply with the documentary requirements stipulated in the rules and regulations. In cases of consultancy contracts, foreign consultants are required to associate themselves with Filipino consultants in the interest of bringing about the transfer and introduction of new technologies into the country.

The government's bidding process is similar to that of foreign lending institutions like the World Bank, ADB and OECF except for some extra features/provisions which are basically designed to address unique local conditions.

Following hereunder are the steps in the procurement of consulting services for government infrastructure projects. A flowchart of the process is presented in Annex 4.

1. Announcement of the project. The requirements for consulting services is announced for at least two (2) times within a period of not more than two (2) weeks in at least two (2) newspapers of general circulation. Copies of the announcement are also posted in any conspicuous place in the agency concerned.
2. Issuance of qualification statements to interested consultants. Only those consultants who express their desire to offer their services for the work contemplated are included in the long list and requested to submit prequalification statements.
3. Preparation of the short-list of consultants. The pre-qualification statements are evaluated by the agency concerned to determine the short list of consultants. The following are considered in drawing-up the short list of consultants: applicable experience of the consultant, qualification of personnel to be assign to the project, and current work load relative to capacity.
4. Issuance of invitations to the short-listed consultants to submit proposals. The invitation generally includes the Terms of Reference, information required to be submitted by the consultants such as its experience and capability/ current work assignments, criteria and system of rating the consultants, etc.
5. Evaluation of technical proposals. As a general rule, the two envelope-two stage procedure is adopted whereby the short-listed consultants are requested to submit their technical and financial proposals in two (2) separate sealed envelopes. The first stage involves the evaluation and ranking of the consultants' technical proposals vis-à-vis certain predetermined criteria. Once the rankings of the consultants' technical proposals have been established and approved by the appropriate authority, the first-ranked firm is then invited for negotiation and their financial proposal opened in their presence (second stage). The first-ranked firm's financial proposal shall be the basis upon which negotiations shall be conducted to arrive at a fair and reasonable contract amount. Should negotiations with the first-ranked consultant fail, the financial proposal of the second-ranked consultant shall then be opened and

negotiations conducted, and so on until an acceptable agreement with a consultant is reached.

6. Preparation of Agreement/Contract. The Agreement/ Contract is prepared after negotiations with the selected consultant had been finalized. The contract includes, among others, the scope and cost of services, method of payment, obligations of the consultant and agency concerned, and the list personnel to be involved in the project.
7. Approval of Agreement/Award of Contract. The Head of the agency shall approve the contract. In case of foreign-assisted projects, the agreement is submitted to the financial institution for concurrence.
8. Issuance of notice to proceed. After the contract had been approved, the agency concerned issue the notice to proceed to the selected consultant.

For civil works contracts, following hereunder are the procedures adopted by the government. A flowchart of the process is presented in Annex 5.

1. Announcement of the project. The project is advertised for at least three (3) times within a period of not less than two (2) weeks in at least two (2) newspapers of general circulation. Copies of the announcement are also posted at any conspicuous place in the agency concerned.
2. Issuance of qualification statements to prospective bidders. The agency concerned provides the prospective bidders with the notice to pre-qualification to guide them in evaluating their capabilities and decide whether or not to participate in the bidding.
3. Pre-qualification of contractors. In the evaluation of the qualification statements, both the technical capability and financial capacity of the contractor is considered. The technical capability of the contractor is gauged by the extent of his relevant experience, suitability of available construction equipment and adequacy of his proposed organization and personnel. The financial capacity of the contractor, on the other hand, is based on his ability to obtain a credit line statement from a reputable bank or financing institution licensed by the Central Bank of the Philippines.

4. Issuance of plans, specifications, proposal book forms and draft contract to pre-qualified bidders. The agency concerned issue the tender documents to the prospective bidders in accordance with the schedules stated in the rules and regulations. For projects costing less than P= 1.0 million, for example, the tender documents are issued to the bidders 15 days before the date of bidding. For projects costing more than P= 100.0 million, the tender documents are issued 90 days before the date of bidding.
5. Submission, opening and abstracting of bids. Bids are submitted in two (2) sealed envelopes. The first envelope contains, among others, the manpower schedule, construction schedule, equipment utilization schedule, and construction methods. The second envelope contains the bid prices, detailed estimates and cash flow by quarter.
6. Evaluation of bids. A bid which does not comply with the conditions of the bid documents is rejected by the agency. At the time of the opening of bids, there should be at least two (2) competing bidders. In case there is only one bidder, the agency can either consider the lone bid for award provided it does not exceed the approved agency estimate (AAE), or return the lone bid unopened and conduct a rebidding thru sealed canvass of at least five (5) qualified contractors.
7. Award/Approval of contract. No award of contract is made to a bidder whose bid price is higher than the allowable government estimate (AGE) or the AAE, whichever is higher, or lower than 70 per cent of the AGE. The AGE is equal to one half the sum of the AAE and the average of all responsive bids. Responsive bids pertain those bids not higher than 120 per cent of the AAE or lower than 60 per cent of the AAE. The head of the agency shall approve the contract.
8. Issuance of notice to proceed. Once the contract had been approved, the agency shall issue the notice to proceed to the successful bidder.

Index

□□□